The Lord has risen indeed.

Luke 24:34

*Why is it thought incredible by any of you
that God raises the dead?*

Acts 26:8

*The resurrection of the dead constitutes the
confidence of Christians. By believing it
we are what we claim to be.*

Tertullian

Risen Indeed

Making Sense
of the Resurrection

Stephen T. Davis

WILLIAM B. EERDMANS PUBLISHING COMPANY
GRAND RAPIDS, MICHIGAN

Library of Congress Cataloging-in-Publication Data

Davis, Stephen T., 1940-
Risen indeed: making sense of the resurrection/
Stephen T. Davis
p.   cm.
Includes bibliographical references and index.
ISBN 0-8028-0126-9
1. Resurrection.   2. Jesus Christ — Resurrection.   I. Title.
BT872.D38   1993
236'.8 — dc20   93-13847
                                                         CIP

Portions of this book appeared in somewhat different form in a variety of publications. The author and publisher wish to thank the editors of the publications listed on page 220 for permission to use this material in the form in which it appears in this book.

Unless otherwise noted, the Scripture quotations in this publication are from the Revised Standard Version of the Bible, copyrighted 1946, 1952 © 1971, 1973 by the Division of Christian Education of the National Council of Churches of Christ in the U.S.A., and used by permission.

Contents

Introduction

I have been thinking seriously about the resurrection of Jesus Christ ever since I was a teenager. It is a subject that interests me; it is hard for me to remember a time when I was not fascinated by arguments for and against it, by various interpretations of it, and by its implications.

For several years I have wanted to write a book about the notion of resurrection. Being a philosopher by profession, it is natural that at first I envisioned the book as entirely philosophical in nature. It was to deal with those aspects of resurrection — for example, the rationality of belief in miracles, the problem of personal identity in resurrections — that philosophers would professionally consider. But the more I thought and wrote, the more it became clear that I was going to have to delve into other areas as well.

Scholars who reject Christian resurrection claims do so not only for philosophical reasons — on the grounds that the very idea of a resurrection from the dead is absurd, for instance — but on the grounds that the New Testament resurrection texts are too conflicting, vague, apologetically motivated, and temporally distant from the events they describe to be credible. I soon saw that I was going to have to say something about these points (and others) if the overall argument of the book was to have any chance of being convincing. The result, as you will see, is a somewhat eccentric mixture of philosophy, Christian theology, New Testament scholarship, and perhaps even preaching.

I make no pretense of having covered in this book all the crucial aspects of resurrection; indeed, the only excuse I can offer for the somewhat scattered nature of the topics dealt with here is that these are just the items that are relevant to the Christian resurrection claim in which I have found myself professionally interested during the last several years. My own training as a philosopher will, I hope, be clear throughout; my status as merely an amateur theologian and biblical scholar will, I fear, be even more obvious.[1]

Each of the chapters of this book constitutes an independent argument — indeed, many of them appeared first as separate journal articles — but they fit together to form a connected, extended argument as well. The thesis of the book is that the two central Christian resurrection claims — namely, that Jesus was bodily raised from the dead and that we will be raised from the dead — are defensible claims. In a day and age when standard Christian views about resurrection are frequently attacked — even, oddly, by clergy and scholars within the Christian community — I will argue on behalf of a fairly traditional understanding of them.

Christians typically distinguish between the resurrection of Jesus Christ, on the one hand, and the general resurrection (i.e., the resurrection of human beings in the eschaton) on the other. In this book I will be concerned with both. The two are intimately connected in Christian thought in that the resurrection of Jesus has traditionally been taken to be both the guarantee and the model of our resurrection (see Rom. 8:11; 1 Cor. 15:20, 23; Phil. 3:20-21; 1 Thess. 4:14; 1 John 3:2). But it needs to be seen that the two are not exactly analogous. Jesus' resurrection occurred at a certain point in history, while our resurrection will occur at the eschaton; Jesus' resurrection preserved him from bodily decay, or at least from all but its initial stages, while our resurrection will occur after bodily decay; only Jesus' resurrection is the resurrection of the Son of God and thus exalts the Son to his rightful place (Acts 2:32-36; Rom. 1:3-4); and only Jesus' resurrection has universal redemptive significance (Rom. 4:24-25).[2]

"If Christ has not been raised, then our preaching is in vain and your faith is in vain. . . . If Christ has not been raised, your faith is futile and you are still in your sins" (1 Cor. 15:14, 17). These frequently quoted words of St. Paul underscore the importance for Christians of the topic

---

1. I have avoided extensive use of the Greek language in this book for two reasons. First, I want it to be accessible to laypersons and nonscholars. Second, although I can use New Testament Greek reasonably well, I make no pretense of being an expert in it.

2. See Gerald O'Collins, *Jesus Risen* (New York: Paulist Press, 1987), p. 180; and Murray Harris, *Raised Immortal* (Grand Rapids: William B. Eerdmans, 1983), pp. 109, 114.

of resurrection. There is, he says, no redemption or forgiveness of sins apart from the resurrection of Jesus. Moreover, it is probable that apart from the belief of Jesus' followers that he had been raised by God, there would exist today no Christian faith or Christian church. Possibly no one today would ever have heard of the man Jesus of Nazareth. Consider the vivid picture of the two Emmaus disciples in Luke 24: convinced that Jesus was dead, they were sad and spoke of him as one "who *was* a prophet" (past tense). "We *had hoped* that he was the one to redeem Israel," they said. Or, as we might put it, he was a godly man with some good ideas, but the hopes we had for him have been smashed.

Given the importance of resurrection in the Christian scheme of things, it is puzzling that many believers today either ignore or misconstrue Christian teachings about the subject. Anyone who has taught adult classes in churches on the topic, as I have, knows that many church-going people ignorantly hope for something after death more like the immortality of the soul or even reincarnation than bodily resurrection. Perhaps such folk have been influenced by the common use of the word *soul* in the Bible. Or perhaps they have been influenced by popular spiritualist or reincarnational or "New Age" teachings. Even those Christians who can affirm credal statements about bodily resurrection often find that the doctrine plays no foundational or ordering role in their understanding of themselves or of their faith. It does not speak to them as it should. Somebody needs to tell these people what the Christian tradition actually teaches about the subject of resurrection and what it ought to mean to Christians today. I hope to take some small step in that direction in this book.

In this connection, let me separate two questions about the resurrection of Jesus. The first is: *Did it really happen?* (or *What* really happened?). The second is: *What does it or should it mean to us?* A surprising number of Christian scholars believe that the second question is more important than the first. Some argue that the first question is a modern question, quite alien to the New Testament texts.[3] Hans Küng says, "All questions about the historicity of the empty tomb and the Easter experiences cease to count beside the question of the significance of the resurrection message."[4] After discussing what he takes to be the theo-

---

3. See, e.g., Norman Perrin, *The Resurrection according to Matthew, Mark and Luke* (Philadelphia: Fortress Press, 1977), p. 78; and Raymond Brown, *The Virginal Conception and Bodily Resurrection of Jesus* (New York: Paulist Press, 1973), p. 20n.

4. Küng, *On Being a Christian,* trans. Edward Quinn (New York: Pocket Books, 1976), p. 379.

logical significance of the resurrection of Jesus in the synoptic Gospels, Norman Perrin says, "These are the meanings of the resurrection so far as the evangelists are concerned, and as such they are more important than the question of 'What actually happened' in terms of appearance stories and empty tomb traditions."[5]

For myself, I would not know how to judge which of our two questions is more important. I am not even sure that such a judgment would mean anything that could be coherently expressed. But I am convinced that the resurrection means little unless it really happened. If the resurrection of Jesus turns out to have been a fraud or a pious myth or even somehow an honest mistake, then there is little reason to think about it or see meaning in it. Perhaps it would provide some lessons about courageously facing death, but that would be about all. Furthermore, it is not true that the first question is unbiblical. I agree that the New Testament authors were interested in proclaiming the resurrection faith and that their writings ought not primarily to be classified as examples of scientific history or philosophical theology. But I am quite sure that they were deeply interested in convincing people that Jesus really rose from the dead. And I am not sure how you go about convincing people that x rose from the dead without having to talk about "what really happened to x after x's death."[6]

Accordingly, within certain limits, I *am* going to talk about "what really happened." That is not the only topic I shall address, naturally. I am interested in the second question, too (as well as others). But there are a number of topics that are important in Christian theology or New Testament scholarship that I will not address. For example, I will not try to develop a Christian theology of death and dying.[7] Nor will I discuss the theological significance of the crucifixion of Jesus, though there are important links between resurrection and crucifixion. Nor do I offer a detailed exegetical or historical analysis of the New Testament accounts of the resurrection appearances of Jesus. Nor will I consider the relationships among the various pictures of resurrection in the New Testament, in such categories as resurrection versus exaltation (see Eph. 4:10;

5. Perrin, *The Resurrection according to Matthew, Mark and Luke*, p. 84.

6. Peter Carnley suggests that producing apologetic arguments in favor of the resurrection was part of the earliest Christian kerygma. See *The Structure of Resurrection Belief* (Oxford: Oxford University Press, 1987), p. 140.

7. As, e.g., Ray Anderson skillfully does in *Theology, Death, and Dying* (New York: Basil Blackwell, 1986).

Phil. 2:9; 1 Tim. 3:16).[8] Finally, I will not discuss in any systematic way the crucial matter of tradition versus redaction in the resurrection accounts in the Gospels.

In recent years some scholars have suggested, in effect, that proper historical research can be done only on the basis of methodological assumptions that many would judge to be inimical to and indeed inconsistent with Christian faith. One of these assumptions is the idea that history is a closed continuum of cause and effect that not even God can interrupt.[9] I will discuss the ramifications of this claim at various points in the book, but let me signal here that I reject it. I believe in God, in God's ability to act in human history, and in the resurrection of Jesus; I willingly admit that I approach any investigation of the resurrection with those beliefs intact. My aim in this book is not to demonstrate the reality of the resurrection so that I can then believe it. Nor do I hope to prove the resurrection to the satisfaction of all rational people (as I will explain in Chapter 1, I doubt that that can be done). My aim is to argue that the belief in the resurrection that I already have (and that millions of Christians have) is rational on historical, philosophical, and theological grounds.

In Chapter 2, I discuss the impact that one's worldview has or can have on one's opinions about the resurrection; I argue that belief in the resurrection as a divinely caused miracle can be rational for people who accept the worldview that I call supernaturalism. I proceed to take up two issues that are related to history — (1) Is the resurrection an event in history? and (2) Do the canons of historical research preclude any recognition of events like the resurrection? I will also discuss briefly in Chapter 2 what I call reductive theories of resurrection — theories that affirm that "Jesus is risen" but interpret these words in ways that do not involve the idea of the dead Jesus actually living again. In Chapter 3, I mention various interpretations of the resurrection of Jesus that are current among scholars and argue in favor of interpreting it as a bodily resurrection. Since the New Testament tradition of the empty tomb of Jesus has frequently been attacked by recent and contemporary scholars, in Chapter 4 I argue that there is good reason for Christians to continue to affirm the empty tomb.

8. Harris convincingly argues that resurrection and exaltation are complementary notions in the New Testament (*Raised Immortal*, pp. 57-58, 76-86).

9. See Van Harvey, *The Historian and the Believer* (Philadelphia: Westminster Press, 1966); and Barry W. Henaut, "Empty Tomb or Empty Argument: A Failure of Nerve in Recent Studies of Mark 16?" *Studies in Religion* 15 (1986): 177-90.

Moving to the general resurrection, in Chapter 5 I defend what I take to be the traditional Christian view, which is based on metaphysical dualism. This view says that after death our souls go to be with God, and in the eschaton our bodies will be raised from the ground, transformed, and reunited with our souls. While this is the theory of general resurrection I personally affirm, I am of the opinion that the Christian notion of resurrection is viable on physicalist assumptions as well — that is to say, even if human beings are essentially and entirely physical objects.[10] I argue in support of this view in Chapter 6. In Chapter 7, I consider a serious philosophical objection that has been raised against the concept of resurrection — the so-called "duplication" objection. If cogent, this argument imperils the versions of resurrection discussed in each of the previous two chapters.

In Chapter 8, I discuss the issue of judgment in the afterlife and argue against the doctrine known as universalism. In Chapter 9, I return to the resurrection of Jesus and argue that we have good historical reason to believe it. Finally, in Chapter 10, I ask what Christian resurrection claims mean for us today if they are true. If this chapter has a slightly different tone than the others — if it sounds more like a homily than a scholarly article — that is because it grew out of a series of three sermons I preached during the Easter season of 1983.

Several friends and colleagues have provided invaluable assistance to me by reading and commenting on various parts of this book (or earlier versions of those parts). Not all of these people would agree with what I say here, but on many occasions they pointed me in helpful

---

10. My own thought on what philosophers call the mind-body problem has evolved in recent years, and I need to be honest about that. At one time I would have described myself as a materialist or at least a functionalist; I was acutely aware of the difficulties these theories face, but I vaguely hoped they could be overcome. Recently I have come to feel that the difficulties are much more serious than I once thought, and I have chosen to commit myself to a version of dualism. (Richard Swinburne offers a clear discussion of most of the problems of physicalism in *The Evolution of the Soul* [Oxford: Clarendon Press, 1986], especially pp. 21-61; see also Lynne Rudder Baker, *Saving Belief* [Princeton: Princeton University Press, 1987].) I outline the version of resurrection that I now wish to defend in Chapter 5; I have added the material in Chapter 6 because I still feel that one can consistently be a resurrectionist and a physicalist (if any version of physicalism should turn out — contrary to present appearances — to be defensible). Furthermore, I have recently read John W. Cooper's excellent book *Body, Soul, and Life Everlasting* (Grand Rapids: William B. Eerdmans, 1989), and I am convinced by his argument that what he calls holistic dualism is most consistent with biblical anthropology.

directions and saved me from errors. I particularly want to thank Tom Morris and Eleonore Stump, who read and commented on the initial version of the entire manuscript, and Don Hagner, Carey Newman, and Alan Padgett, who read and commented on the penultimate version. Sincere thanks are also due to William Alston, W. S. Anglin, John Cobb, Adela Yarbro Collins, William L. Craig, Robert Gundry, James Hanink, John Hick, Jerry Irish, Kai Nielsen, Joseph Runzo, John Sanders, Alex Steuer, Jack Verheyden, Richard Warner, and Linda Zagzebski, who in various settings commented on various parts of the manuscript.

I also want to thank two of my graduate students, Alan Scholes, who made suggestions about much of the manuscript, and Darin Jewell, who prepared the bibliography and helped with the proofreading. Much of the research for the book, as well as the writing of the final draft, was completed while I was the recipient of two different summer research fellowships from Claremont McKenna College. I am grateful for that support and wish to thank those who supervised the awarding of the fellowships, especially one former dean of the college, Prof. Gaines Post. I would also like to thank Pat Padilla, one of the philosophy secretaries at Claremont McKenna College, for her diligence and accuracy in typing the manuscript.

1

Resurrection and Miracle

I

The resurrection of Jesus from the dead is by universal consent a crucial doctrine of the Christian faith. Thus it is understandable that Christian philosophers who believe the doctrine will ask what they can or ought to do to defend it. Naturally, their first impulse is to engage in some kind of rational apologetic. Though apologetics is an enterprise that is often maligned, I believe this is an understandable and quite acceptable impulse. I will argue in this chapter against a certain way of doing apologetics, but I believe all Christians engage in the enterprise.

Let me distinguish between two sorts of apologetic arguments in favor of the resurrection of Jesus. Let us call a "soft apologetic argument" one that attempts to demonstrate the rationality of belief in the resurrection of Jesus. And let us call a "hard apologetic argument" one that attempts to demonstrate the irrationality of unbelief in the resurrection of Jesus. One of my aims in this chapter is to show the limits of what philosophy can achieve on this issue. I am opposing what I consider to be overblown claims that are made on both sides of the issue — that is, by those who hold that rational argument can either verify or falsify the resurrection. I do not believe it can do either (at least not in strong senses of those terms), as I will try to show. As one who believes in the resurrection, I naturally hold and will argue that Christians are within their intellectual rights in believing that Jesus was raised from the dead.[1]

---

1. And indeed that he was *bodily* raised from the dead, as I argue in Chap. 3.

But I do not believe it can be shown that religious skeptics are not within their intellectual rights in rejecting the doctrine.

There is a paradox that faces any philosopher who writes about the possibility of the resurrection of Jesus. On the one hand, some of those who believe in the resurrection hold that the evidence in its favor is overwhelming. (I once knew a seminary professor who was known to say, "Any rational person who honestly looks at the evidence for the resurrection of Jesus must be convinced by it and become a Christian.") On the other hand, many of those who do not believe in the resurrection view the claim that Jesus was raised from the dead as perfectly absurd. (As an undergraduate I studied under a man who liked to debunk the biblical miracles; one day in class he dismissed the resurrection with the statement "I hope everybody here knows that dead people stay dead.")

What is the reason for this puzzling phenomenon? Why is it that people on both sides are so convinced they are obviously correct and others are obviously wrong? We do notice that both sides can offer explanations of the strange behavior of the other — believers can claim that nonbelievers are blinded by sin; nonbelievers can claim that believers are blinded by credulity and wishful thinking. But is there anything that Christian philosophers can helpfully say at this point? I will try. Let me begin with some remarks on the concept of miracle.

II

The resurrection of Jesus from the dead is typically classified as a miracle. The fountainhead of virtually all contemporary discussion of miracles among philosophers is David Hume's argument in Section X of *An Enquiry concerning Human Understanding.* Section X is a dense and compact chapter, full of fascinating arguments and asides, and has been interpreted in a variety of ways. I interpret Hume as arguing that it is never rational to believe that a miracle has occurred, if a miracle is understood (as Hume defines it) as "a transgression of a law of nature by a particular volition of the Deity, or by the interposition of an invisible agent."[2] Let me briefly summarize what I take to be the general thrust of Hume's argument.

Section X is divided into two parts. In the first part, Hume tries to show that the evidence against the occurrence of any purported

---

2. Hume, *An Enquiry concerning Human Understanding* (1758; reprint, La Salle, Ill.: Open Court Publishing, 1946), p. 121.

miracle is typically going to be so strong as to overwhelm the evidence in favor of it. In support of this conclusion, Hume suggests the epistemological principle that wise people proportion their belief to evidence. So in the case of two conflicting claims (e.g., the claim that a miracle occurred and the claim that it did not occur), wise people weigh the evidence for and against each claim and accept the stronger of the two.

Now the evidence in favor of a miracle is normally going to be in the form of testimony from people who claim to have observed the miracle. Notice, Hume says, that we are suspicious of testimony in favor of anything if the witnesses contradict each other, or if there are too few of them, or if they are of a doubtful character, or if they have something to gain by convincing us to accept what they say, or if they give their testimony either too hesitantly or too violently. But the most important reason of all to doubt what witnesses say is if we know that what they testify to is highly unlikely. The more unusual an alleged event, the heavier the evidence against it. If we know that in all other situations similar to the one in question miracles did not occur, this will constitute strong evidence that in this case no miracle occurred. Indeed, as transgressions of natural laws, miracles virtually by definition will have what Hume calls "the uniform experience" of human beings against them. Sensible people allow their expectations of what will happen to be guided by their experience of what has happened. Thus miracles are, as we might say, maximally unusual and must be considered highly unlikely.

Hume's epistemological principle of proportioning belief to evidence can be stated in another way: in the case of two conflicting claims, he says, always "reject the greater miracle." That is, always accept the more probable (the less miraculous) of the two. Thus, says Hume, no testimony can rationally establish a miracle unless the occurrence of the miracle itself would be a lesser miracle than the circumstance of all of the testifiers to the miracle being wrong. A simpler way of making Hume's point is to suggest that we ask which would be *more improbable* or *harder to believe* — that the miracle occurred, or that those who claim that it occurred are wrong. Then we simply reject the option that is more improbable or harder to believe. But since Hume has already established (1) that all sorts of things can easily make us suspicious of testimony in favor of something, and (2) that miracles are uniformly contradicted by past human experience, it follows that it would be very difficult indeed ever rationally to establish a miracle. Thus, Hume concludes, the evidence against a miracle claim will usually greatly outweigh the evidence in its favor, and so wise people will reject it.

In the second part of Section X, Hume presses his argument further and tries to show that when we examine specific miracle claims, the evidence in favor of them never comes close to outweighing the evidence against them. As he says, "there never was a miraculous event established." Hume's main complaint is that no purported miracle that he knows about has been supported by the testimony of a sufficient number of people of unquestioned good sense, education, learning, and integrity. Doubt is cast on all such miracle claims because (1) people love to gossip about marvelous and surprising events, (2) some religious people are quite prepared to tell lies if that will help spread their beliefs, (3) purported miracles apparently occur mainly in what Hume calls "ignorant and barbarous nations," and (4) purported miracles occur in incompatible religions, and members of one religion tend to discredit miracles that are alleged to have occurred in other religions.

Hume's conclusion is that no amount of evidence could ever render belief in a miracle rational. It will always be more sensible to hold that the testifiers to a miracle are wrong than it will be to believe that the miracle occurred. Thus Hume concludes that it is never rational to believe that a miracle has occurred: "No testimony for any kind of miracle has ever amounted to a probability, much less to a proof."[3]

Is Hume's argument convincing? Probably not as it stands. Indeed, I believe it is generally recognized among philosophers that Hume overstates his case. We cannot a priori rule out the possibility of miracles or of rational belief in miracles.[4] But Hume is not the sort of philosopher whom one can dismiss with a casual wave of the hand. Much of his argument is beyond reproach. He is mistaken when he asserts that our past experience of the normal course of events by itself settles the question of whether a miracle can ever occur, but he is surely correct that we base our rational expectation of what *will* happen on our best available knowledge of what *has* happened. He is mistaken when he asserts that it can never be what he calls the "greater miracle" for all the testifiers to a miracle to be wrong, but he is surely correct that rational people are inclined to accept the epistemological principle of always

3. Hume, *An Enquiry concerning Human Understanding,* pp. 133-34.
4. See, e.g., C. D. Broad, "Hume's Theory of the Credibility of Miracles," in *Human Understanding,* ed. A. Sesonske and N. Fleming (Belmont, Calif.: Wadsworth Publishing, 1965), pp. 86-98.

rejecting the greater miracle. He is mistaken when he asserts that it can never be rational to believe that a miracle has occurred, but he is surely correct that rational people will require strong evidence indeed before they will believe that a miracle has occurred.

Suppose a person, Jones, claims that some extraordinary event E occurred — say, that last night between 1:00 A.M. and 2:00 A.M. the Washington Monument levitated six feet above the ground. Naturally we would be extremely suspicious of such a claim — for the very Humean reason that E is contrary to all our previous experience of the behavior of objects like large monuments and thus is contrary to our expectations about how the Washington Monument will have behaved last night. And our bias in this case seems eminently reasonable. We would be quite right to be extremely suspicious of any evidence that Jones produced or testimony that Jones or others gave, even if we could not refute their evidence or explain the reason for their strange belief.

It is true that the twentieth-century revolution in physics has made most scientists far more open to the possibility of highly unusual events than religious skeptics or even some rationalistic theologians would have us believe. The physicists whom I know, at any rate, are seldom prepared to rule out miraculous events — what Hume would call transgressions of natural laws — on a priori grounds. They have learned from quantum mechanics that the current consensus of scientific opinion is not always an infallible guide to what is causally possible or impossible in nature. But, as noted above, it still seems a sound epistemological principle that rational expectation about what is likely to occur must be based on what we know *has* occurred. And since we know of no past cases in which large monuments have levitated, while we cannot rule out on a priori grounds the possibility that E occurred, we have strong reason to doubt that E occurred.

Accordingly, Hume is correct that we have and rightly should have a powerful bias against accepting claims that extraordinary events have occurred. We can imagine cases — and E is certainly one such — where it would be exceedingly difficult for this bias to be overcome. I confess that *I* could not easily be convinced that the Washington Monument levitated last night. But surely a point would come, if massive evidence in favor of E continued to pile up, where the rational thing would be to lay aside or amend our bias against events like E and accept the claim that E has occurred. At what point would such a change of mind rationally come about? Surely we can give no general rule. All we can say is that it would depend on the strength of our bias against events like E, the weight of evidence in favor of E, and the possibility and plausibility of alternative explanations. Critics of Hume are certainly correct in pointing out that there have been countless cases in which such biases and the expectations that they create have been rationally overcome. Rational people would once have scoffed at the idea of airplanes, vaccines, and trips to the moon.

However, Humean arguments are still being presented by philosophers. For example, Antony Flew offers three arguments, much in the spirit of Hume, against those who believe in miracles.[5]

1. People who offer historical or probabilistic arguments in favor of the occurrence of a given purported miracle, Flew says, themselves presuppose the very regularity of nature and reliability of nature's laws that they argue against. Their position is accordingly inconsistent.

2. Once violations of natural law are in principle allowed, what control have we over the explanations of events that are offered? For instance (these are my examples, not Flew's), why not say that in some physically inexplicable way Jesus' body simply disappeared after the tomb was closed? Or why not say that the Jewish leaders removed the body from the tomb but later were quite unable to produce it and thus falsify the disciples' claims because for some psychologically inexplicable reason they completely forgot that they had removed it?

3. Even if we grant a violation of a natural law, Flew says, how could we ever be sure it was *God* who was responsible for it? How could we know that it was a *miracle* and not just a surprising and unexplained anomaly that merely reveals the fallibility of current science? Since God is said to be an incorporeal being who cannot be seen or touched, the problem seems insurmountable. Notice also, Flew adds, that when theists talk about certain theological problems, notably the problem of evil, they stress our inability to comprehend God or fathom God's ways. How then could we ever have rational expectations about what God will do in given circumstances?

Much of what Flew says here is correct. As to his first point, theists do indeed presuppose regular workings of nature in order to argue that certain irregularities (i.e., miracles) occur. But this hardly shows that their position is inconsistent. Why cannot nature, so to speak, almost but not quite always act regularly and (if we knew enough) predictably? If it did, then those who wished to argue for certain irregularities would naturally do so on the basis of regularities seen elsewhere. If there did turn out

5. See Flew, *God and Philosophy* (New York: Delta Books, 1966), pp. 148-52.

to be unique events, not analogous to any others (and some scientists argue that there are such events — e.g., the "Big Bang"), we would have no choice but to try to argue for them on the basis of regular and repeatable events.

Michael Root offers an even stronger argument in the area of Flew's third point. In effect, he argues that belief in miracles based on the testimony of others or even based on personal observation is existentially self-refuting. "Unless I believe that nature is uniform," he says, "I have no basis on which to find any causal judgment plausible or implausible at all." He goes on to say, "If we believe that nature is uniform, then we have reason to believe that testimony is a reason for belief, but if we believe that nature is not uniform, we don't."[6] Presumably Root means something like this: if Jones believes that God occasionally performs miracles (i.e., acts that involve violations of natural laws), then *none* of Jones's beliefs based on testimony or personal experience is well founded. Even if Jones seems in a normal situation to see something in the backyard that he takes to be his wife, the belief that it *is* his wife is not justified. It may in fact be a replica of his wife miraculously placed in the backyard by God. That is, this may be one of those occasions where God has interrupted the uniformity of nature.

But this is hardly a convincing argument. Those who believe in miracles are naturalists most of the time (i.e., they are committed to giving naturalistic explanations of events wherever possible). They, too, have a bias against supernatural events; they are not prepared to proclaim a miracle at the drop of a hat. Those who believe in miracles will nonetheless be inclined to reject the proposed miracle of the replica of Jones's wife in the backyard — indeed, they will not even seriously consider it — unless there is overwhelming evidence in favor of it. So there is no inconsistency in a miracle-believer holding that miracles are rare, maintaining that nature normally behaves naturally, or basing belief on those normal and natural operations of nature. Theists certainly believe that nature is uniform in the sense that the future will in many ways resemble the past. This is sufficient to form part of the foundations of the causal judgments they make about testimony. What is not required as part of the foundation of those judgments is the very different claim that nature is uniform in the sense that it is a closed and deterministic causal nexus.

6. Root, "Miracles and the Uniformity of Nature," *American Philosophical Quarterly* 26 (October 1989): 339, 341.

As to Flew's second point, the only control we either have or need have over proposed explanations of events, once miracles are allowed, is the same control we have, quite apart from miracles, over proposed explanations in science and history in general. We simply accept the most plausible explanations that we can find and reject the others. Since I believe in the existence of an omnipotent God, I find it more plausible to hold that God raised Jesus from the dead than to say, for example, that his body inexplicably disappeared or that the Jewish leaders forgot that they had removed it. Defenders of Flew might want to claim that I am not allowed to include my belief in God in the body of total evidence to be used in determining the best explanation. But why not? I will not allow them to disallow me from doing so. (I discuss this point further in Chap. 2.)

As to Flew's third point, he is correct that it seems impossible ever to prove for sure that a given event was caused by God. But if a certain event is scientifically inexplicable, seems to some people to have moral and religious significance, and coheres with the views of God and God's aims that are held by those people, it may very well be rational for them to believe that the event was brought about by God. Indeed, it may be the best explanation, given their background beliefs. Suppose there is good reason ahead of time to believe that a miracle-working God exists who is likely in certain circumstances — say after prayers or as aspects of epiphanies or incarnations — to cause events like this one. Then it seems reasonable to hold, even in the absence of strict proof, that this event was caused by God.[7] (Of course even if such a God exists, each miracle that God brings about will still be from our viewpoint uncontrollable and unpredictable — otherwise it won't be a miracle.)

It might be objected that this criterion of coherence is useless because any purported miracle, however bizarre, might with some imagination be understood as fitting or cohering with some particular view of God. And it is true that given any purported miracle — say, the scientifically inexplicable event of all the redheaded people in the world being suddenly afflicted with an incurable head cold — some new religion could be imagined with which it would cohere, and even for already existing religions some explanation could at least be imagined as to "why God did it." But the point is that for Christians (and indeed for adherents

---

7. I am assuming here two points that I will not try to argue at this point: (1) that the notion of agent causation is coherent and (2) that incorporeal beings can be agents.

of many other religions as well), a sophisticated and highly developed theological tradition exists. Naturally there is disagreement among Christian thinkers concerning beliefs that are marginal to the tradition, and even in some instances about beliefs that are at its core. But few Christian thinkers would accept some such explanation as "God has decided to hate all redheads but not so much as to kill them" as a theologically sensible or acceptable thesis. Accordingly, few Christians could accept the above purported miracle as cohering with the Christian view of God.

III

It looks, then, as if Hume's argument against rational belief in miracles, even as expanded by Flew, fails.[8] So in theory at least, perhaps our strong commitment to such generalizations as "dead people stay dead" could be overcome. Just as we came rationally to believe in airplanes, vaccines, and trips to the moon, and just as we could come rationally to believe that the Washington Monument levitated, so in theory at least we could come rationally to believe in the miracle of Jesus' resurrection from the dead.

But in practice could such ever be the case? One difficulty that needs to be cleared up concerns the term *miracle*. For quite understandable reasons, the word is usually defined in terms of transgressions or violations of natural laws. Critics have been quick to point out a complication, however. Since laws of nature are human inventions (i.e., descriptions of observed regularities), if we really became aware of a violation of (what we understood to be) a law of nature, they say, we should not proclaim a miracle but rather simply amend our understanding of the law of nature in question — or even reject it altogether, if necessary. The issue here is complex, and I do not wish to explore it in detail here. Fortunately we need not do so, even in a book on the resurrection of Jesus, an event often considered *the* paradigmatic miracle. Christians won't greatly mind if it turns out, through some sound process of reasoning, that the biblical miracles don't violate any true natural laws

8. See also David Basinger and Randall Basinger, *Philosophy and Miracle: The Contemporary Debate* (Lewiston, N.Y.: Edwin Mellen Press, 1986), pp. 31-51; and Robert A. H. Larmer, *Water into Wine? An Investigation of the Concept of Miracle* (Kingston: McGill-Queen's University Press, 1988), pp. 31-42.

but merely establish that some purported laws are inadequate. As long as it is still true, for example, that due to the power of God Jesus was born of a virgin, healed people, turned water into wine, was raised from the dead, and the like, it will be a matter of profound indifference to Christians whether natural laws are ever violated. On the other hand, to accept such an understanding of the resurrection would necessitate important changes in the standard Christian way of conceptualizing it, and so in this book I am going to stick to the idea that the resurrection cannot be explained naturalistically, that it involves violations of natural laws.

It must at least be admitted that with the resurrection we are talking not just about a highly unusual event but about an event that, given our best knowledge of the workings of the world, seems causally impossible. Almost any event can be described in such a way as to have been or at least rationally seemed to have been highly improbable before it occurred. One hundred years ago or even five years ago, what would have been the odds that in 1993 a Claremont philosopher who coaches soccer and whose father was a Nebraska cattle rancher would write a book chapter entitled "Resurrection and Miracle" that you would read? The odds would have been low indeed, but the point is that there is nothing in this description — as there is in a description of the resurrection — that seems causally impossible given our best knowledge. The resurrection is not just a unique and improbable event but an intellectual scandal. It is the sort of event that conflicts so radically with so many well-established scientific laws that any attempt to revise them in such a way as to allow for resurrection would vitiate them. They would be left with little descriptive or predictive power.

Accordingly, an event should probably be considered a miracle only if no purported explanation of it that crucially omits God is a good explanation. It just might be possible to offer a good explanation of my writing and your reading this chapter in entirely naturalistic terms — that is, without mentioning God. Thus, our doing so, however improbable it might be, would not involve us in a resort to miracle. But the resurrection of Jesus, if it occurred, in all probability could not be explained without God, and so (if it occurred) it was probably a miracle.

Let me then define the term *miracle* as follows: a miracle is an event E that (1) is brought about by God and (2) is contrary to the prediction of a law of nature that we have compelling reason to believe is true. That is, the law predicts that, given the circumstances preceding E, some event other than E will occur; E occurs because God causes E to occur;

and no other law of nature or set of laws of nature could have helped us to have predicted, given the circumstances, that E would have occurred.[9] Now it is important to note that the occurrence of an event like E, irregular and unpredictable as it is, does not vitiate natural laws. Science is not overturned, because natural laws describe and predict not whatever happens but whatever happens in a regular and predictable way.

It is sometimes said that every miracle is ambiguous in that it can be interpreted either as an act of God or as a surprising and perhaps inexplicable natural event. But surely this can be said not just about miracles but about almost any event, as John Hick has often argued.[10] Name virtually any event, and the religious believer and the religious skeptic can disagree on how to interpret it. The one may well see it as an act of God, and the other will not. They differ, so to speak, not on the facts (both experience the event and acknowledge that it has occurred) but on how to interpret or account for the facts.

However, there is a difference between miracles and natural events in this regard. With natural events (e.g., someone's recovering from a serious illness), the believer and the skeptic do not differ on the question of whether the event occurred; both will agree that it did. Their disagreement concerns the cause and meaning of the event. With miracles, however (or at least with certain of them, such as the resurrection of Jesus), the believer and the skeptic will typically differ on the fundamental question of what precisely occurred. They differ here on the facts.

Accordingly, influenced by our earlier distinction between hard and soft apologetics, let us make a distinction between hard and soft miracles. A *soft miracle,* let us say, is a miraculous event that religious skeptics can consistently agree has occurred; it is just that they will disagree with religious believers on its cause and meaning. That is to say, they can affirm that the event occurred but deny that it is a miracle (as defined above). If after having been diagnosed to be suffering from a terminal and untreatable cancer, Jones is found to be well and free of cancer after

9. This definition is similar to those used by Richard Swinburne in several of his works. See, e.g., *Faith and Reason* (Oxford: Oxford University Press, 1981), p. 186: "I understand by a miracle a violation of the laws of nature, that is, a non-repeatable exception to the operation of those laws, brought about by God." See also *The Existence of God* (Oxford: Oxford University Press, 1979), pp. 225-43; and *The Concept of Miracle* (London: Macmillan, 1970).

10. See Hick, *Faith and Knowledge* (Ithaca, N.Y.: Cornell University Press, 1957), pp. 182-91.

having prayed and fasted, this may well constitute a soft miracle. Skeptics can consistently agree that Jones was gravely ill but now is well; they will simply deny that Jones's recovery was due to God or that it violated any natural laws. A *hard miracle,* on the other hand, is one that is very difficult for religious skeptics to explain naturalistically,[11] and so skeptics will not want to allow that it has occurred at all. The resurrection of Jesus appears to be a hard miracle: it does not seem likely that skeptics would be able to affirm that it occurred (at least not in the manner in which it is described in the Gospels) without abandoning their religious skepticism. The strategy of consistent skeptics must accordingly be to argue that the event did not in fact occur.

The distinction between the two sorts of miracles is epistemological rather than ontological. Both soft miracles and hard miracles are miracles (i.e., acts of God that involve violations of natural laws). A soft miracle is a highly improbable event that neither I nor the experts (the doctors, in my above example) can explain; but I can at least *imagine* a possible naturalistic explanation, or can rationally imagine that there is one. If what appears to be a soft miracle is in fact a miracle, however, the true explanation of the event must be that it was caused by God (as in the case of the hard miracle). A hard miracle, on the other hand, is an event that is so highly improbable that I cannot even imagine a plausible naturalistic explanation of it.

Hard miracles are obviously going to be appealing to rational apologists for religious faith. It is tempting to think of them as good devices for evangelism, as evidence that can be useful in converting people from religious skepticism to religious faith. But have any hard miracles occurred? Religious believers hold that the answer is Yes, and religious skeptics will say No. As a Christian, I believe that certain hard miracles have occurred and that the resurrection of Jesus is one of them. But have any events occurred that can be *shown* to be hard miracles? Here I am doubtful. It certainly seems possible for an event to occur about which it would be irrational for anyone to deny that it is a hard miracle. But to my knowledge no such events have occurred — not even the resurrection. Soft miracles, then, are religiously ambiguous because they can be interpreted as natural events; hard miracles are religiously

11. But perhaps not impossible. A skeptic who is present at the resurrection of a person dead for several days may well try to offer a naturalistic explanation of it ("spontaneous remission of death"?), but the point is that, based on our present knowledge, such an explanation would be so highly improbable as to be absurd.

ambiguous because the ones that have purportedly occurred can apparently be rationally denied. I will shortly turn to a consideration of how the resurrection can rationally be denied.

James A. Keller objects to the distinction between hard and soft miracles. "If one does not have a good reason to think that a naturalistic explanation could not be given (as one typically does not, in regard to soft miracles), why should one resort to a nonnaturalistic explanation?" he asks. "The very fact that an unbeliever could accept the fact that Jones had recovered while not accepting the resurrection would suggest that Jones' recovery is no strong indication that a miraculous event has occurred."[12]

As noted earlier, I agree that naturalistic explanations of phenomena ought to be preferred by rational people in the vast majority of cases. When Keller alleges that one *typically* has a good reason to think that naturalistic explanations can be given for soft miracles, he is right. But this is not always true. The question of whether the event ought rationally to be called a miracle (of either sort) depends in part on how plausible the available naturalistic explanations are. One reason to suspect that a soft miracle is a miracle is precisely the fact that most people (including the experts) are puzzled as to what has occurred, and the available naturalistic explanations look unconvincing or even foolish. So, contrary to what Keller says, a soft miracle (e.g., someone's suddenly recovering from what looked like a hopeless case of cancer) might constitute rational grounds for belief in a miracle. The naturalists might be wrong.

Keller also criticizes my larger argument about the possibility of rational belief in miracles. He argues that my thesis holds only if we observe an established pattern of divine miraculous activity in the world; since we observe no such thing, my thesis fails. Even if the biblical evidence were much stronger than it is, he says, we need "evidence that *God has in the past acted in nonnatural events for similar ends.*"[13] Now there is a point in the neighborhood here that is surely correct. Attributing an apparent nonnatural event to the activity of God is probably rational only for people who rationally believe (1) that God exists; (2) that God occasionally acts miraculously in the world; and (3) that God acts miraculously in the world on occasions like the one in question. But

---

12. Keller, "Contemporary Christian Doubts about the Resurrection," *Faith and Philosophy* 5 (January 1988): 42-43.

13. Keller, "Contemporary Christian Doubts about the Resurrection," p. 51; italics Keller's.

the problem is that Keller pushes this acceptable point to the absurd extreme of claiming that belief in a given divinely caused miracle is rational only if we already possess *proof* that God has acted similarly in the past.[14] He insists that these prior nonnatural events that form the believed-in pattern of divine activity must be proven or "clear" miracles. In order to assess the rationality of belief in one purported miracle, he says, we have to assess the rationality of belief in the purported miracles that are said to form its pattern. "If no clearly nonnatural events can be cited in biblical events or in our own lives, how can it be rational to believe that they *actually* occur?"[15]

This requirement is far too strong; note that it rules out rational belief in miracles *a priori* (something Keller says he does not want to do). I can rationally believe in miracle M1 only if M1 fits a pattern of clear or proven miracles M2 and M3; but I can rationally believe in miracles M2 and M3 only if they fit a pattern of clear or proven miracles M4-M7, and so on. We are in a kind of infinite regress in which rational belief in a miracle can never (for logical reasons) get started. This is enough to show that Keller's requirements are too stringent. It is my claim that in order rationally to believe that a given purported nonnatural event was caused by God, I need only rationally believe that God has acted non-naturally and similarly in the past. The rationality of this belief certainly could be established (in part) through proof of past miracles, but it need not be established in this way, and in fact need not be established at all, at least not to the satisfaction of those who do not share the belief. If I have the relevant rational belief, and if the purported nonnatural event does occur, it can be rational for me to attribute it to God.

Keller makes much of the fact that no hard miracles clearly occur today.[16] If by "clearly" he means "in a manner universally recognized" or "in a manner obvious to everyone (even naturalists)," I agree. As noted earlier, John Hick has taught us that all events are religiously ambiguous in the sense that they can be interpreted either religiously or irreligiously. The most natural and common event (e.g., the sun rising in the morning) can be treated by the religious person as evidence of God's presence, and the most startling of religious events (e.g., the Exodus) can be dismissed or

14. Keller, "Contemporary Christian Doubts about the Resurrection," p. 46.
15. Keller, "Contemporary Christian Doubts about the Resurrection," p. 54; italics Keller's. See also pp. 53, 54, 60n.31.
16. Keller, "Contemporary Christian Doubts about the Resurrection," pp. 53, 60.

interpreted innocuously by skeptics. So perhaps there can be no such miracle (a clear — i.e., universally recognized — hard miracle) as Keller asks for. In my own view, there are events both in biblical and in present times that are best explained as miraculous acts of God.[17]

IV

In order to make the problem we face more concrete, let us briefly look at the way those who believe and those who do not believe in the resurrection of Jesus can most persuasively present their respective cases. (We will take up these considerations much more extensively later in the book.)

Those who believe in the resurrection first stress the unity of the New Testament witness to the event. Despite differences in some details, say believers, the biblical writers, who give us our earliest testimony to the events after the crucifixion, unanimously agree that Jesus rose from the dead.

Second, those who believe in the resurrection point out that there are certain facts surrounding the resurrection that have virtually been demonstrated by historical scholarship and that are not denied by any competent biblical, theological, or historical scholar. They are, preeminently, that Jesus died on a cross, that certain people later came to believe that God had raised him from the dead, that a firm belief in the resurrection was at the heart of the message that these people proclaimed, and that they confessed that it was the reality of the resurrection that accounted for the radical change in their lives. Disheartened, confused, and fearful immediately after the crucifixion, they quickly became determined, bold, and courageous. The most plausible explanation of these facts, say those who believe in the resurrection, is that Jesus did indeed rise from the dead and show himself to the disciples. It does not seem sensible to claim that the Christian church, a spiritual movement with the vitality to change the world, was started by charlatans or dupes. If

---

17. In 1974 my own mother-in-law, after much prayer by many people, and after attending a healing service, was healed of or experienced remission from what had been diagnosed by several doctors and after several tests as a brain tumor. She is alive and well today as I write these words. Her story is told by H. Richard Casdorph, M.D., Ph.D., in *The Miracles: A Medical Doctor Says Yes to Miracles* (Plainfield, N.J.: Logos International, 1976), pp. 121-32.

the disciples knew that Jesus was not really risen, they were charlatans. If they believed he was risen when in fact he was not, they were dupes.

Third, believers point to something of an embarrassment in the position of those who do not believe in the resurrection: their inability to offer an acceptable alternative explanation of the known facts surrounding the resurrection of Jesus. The old nineteenth-century rationalistic explanations (hallucination, swoon theory, stolen body, wrong tomb, etc.) all seem to collapse of their own weight once spelled out, and no strong new theory has emerged as the consensus of scholars who deny that the resurrection occurred.[18] The plain fact is that most contemporary Christian theologians who do not believe that Jesus was dead for three days and then actually lived again offer no explanation. Many resort to vague poetic metaphors, speaking of such things as the "Easter vision of the disciples" or "dramatic imagery seen through the eyes of faith." Some hint that parapsychological phenomena were at work. But those who believe in the resurrection have to wonder whether such vague talk really means anything. Isn't it just theological jargon amounting to this: "I can't bring myself to believe that a real resurrection happened, but *something* (I don't know what) must have happened to account for the disciples' faith"? And surely all this is odd, the believer continues: if the resurrection did not occur, it is at least prima facie puzzling that no consensus alternative explanation of the known facts has emerged. All in all, believers will say, the most rational position is to believe that Jesus really did, as claimed, rise from the dead.

But those who do not believe in the resurrection can make an impressive case too. They will first argue that the biblical testimony is unreliable. It was written years after the event by unsophisticated, myth-prone people who were more interested in formulating statements of faith and in furthering Christian ends than in writing accurate history. Furthermore, the evidence they present is contradictory: How many women visited the tomb? Had the sun risen, or was it still dark? Was there one angel (or young man) or two? Were they inside the tomb or outside? Did the women keep silent or run to tell the disciples? Were

18. For an extended critique of rationalistic explanations of the resurrection event, see George Eldon Ladd, *I Believe in the Resurrection of Jesus* (Grand Rapids: William B. Eerdmans, 1975), pp. 132-42. One more full-blooded attempt to offer such an explanation is Hugh Schonfield's *The Passover Plot* (New York: Bantam Books, 1966), a bold and entertaining book. But with its highly fanciful hypotheses and selective use of evidence, it has drawn much criticism and precious little support from scholars.

the disciples told to stay in Jerusalem or to go to Galilee? Was the resurrected Jesus in physical or spiritual form? Did the ascension occur immediately after the resurrection, or forty days later?

But the nonbelievers' strongest argument will run as follows: "Granted we have no plausible alternative explanation of the known facts; and granted that just on the basis of the known facts and available possible explanations of them (i.e., without bringing in miracles and worldviews), the probability that the resurrection really happened is (let's be as generous as possible) something like 99 percent; still we must ask the following fatal question: *What are the chances that a man dead for parts of three days would live again?*"

In short, nonbelievers will claim that even if the believers' arguments are strong, and even if nonbelievers can't say for sure what *did* happen, by far the most sensible position is to deny that the resurrection occurred. For the probability that we should assign to the statement "People dead for parts of three days stay dead" is very, very high. Thus the position of the nonbelievers amounts to this: "We don't know exactly what happened after the crucifixion — it was, after all, nearly two thousand years ago, and by now it is very hard to tell — but whatever happened, it certainly wasn't a resurrection."

V

But we would be passing over a vital factor in the debate if we stopped here. We must consider the very different metaphysical worldviews typically held by those who believe and those who do not believe in the resurrection. The nonbelievers are probably convinced of their position not primarily because of evidence or arguments in its favor but because it is entailed by the worldview that they accept. Let's call that worldview *naturalism* and define it in terms of the following four statements:

1. Nature alone exists. The word *nature* is difficult to define precisely, but let us say that it is the sum total of what could in principle be observed by human beings or be studied by methods analogous to those used in the natural sciences. ("Nature" could also perhaps be defined as a sum total of that which consists of matter/energy — i.e., as the physical realm. For our purposes it will not matter which definition we choose.) Accordingly, naturalism excludes God, or at least the theistic God.

2. Nature is eternal.[19] Nature is an uncreated thing; there is no moment in time when it does not exist; nature is not contingent.
3. Nature is uniform. There are no nonnatural events (e.g., miracles); rather, nature is regular, continuous.
4. Every event is explicable. In principle at least, any event can be explained in terms of nature or natural processes (i.e., by explanatory methods similar to those used in the natural sciences).

Similarly, believers probably find their position convincing not primarily because of evidence or arguments in its favor but because it dovetails with the worldview they accept. Let's call that worldview *supernaturalism*. (I am not arguing that one must consciously be a supernaturalist or must consciously convert to supernaturalism *before* one can accept that the resurrection of Jesus occurred.) We can define supernaturalism in terms of an affirmation of the following four statements:

1. Something besides nature exists — namely, God.
2. Nature depends for its existence on God.
3. The regularity of nature can be and occasionally is interrupted by miraculous acts of God.
4. Such divine acts are humanly quite unpredictable and inexplicable.[20]

All people interpret their experience within a certain philosophical framework. The philosophical assumptions of many people preclude a belief in the existence of God and the possibility of miracles. Such people presumably reject the resurrection not because the evidence for it, considered neutrally, is weak. It would seem closer to the truth to say that their commitment to naturalism gives them a perspective on

19. This is not to deny that there were points in the past — e.g., before, during, or immediately after the Big Bang — when nature as we know it (through the natural laws with which we are familiar) was different than it now is.

20. There is an additional point that distinguishes most of those who believe in the resurrection from those who do not that is crucial to their different attitudes toward it: believers accept the view that the Bible is in some sense revelatory and reliable, and nonbelievers do not. E.g., Flew writes, "We must never forget that it is only if we take for granted that these events were part of a unique divine revelation that we have any reason to be sure that the available evidence must be sufficient" (*God and Philosophy*, p. 158). For my own views on this topic, see *The Debate about the Bible* (Philadelphia: Westminster Press, 1977).

the resurrection such that the evidence for it *must* be weak. Surely if the resurrection were not essentially miraculous (if it were, say, more like the event of the crucifixion), few rational persons would doubt it. Naturalists reject the resurrection primarily because it does not fit with their worldview. The essentially miraculous nature of the resurrection impels them to discount the evidence for it despite their inability to explain what *did* happen or how the disciples came to believe in the resurrection.

Well, then, it is natural to ask at this point whether the resurrection of Jesus did in fact occur. Which is more likely — that the resurrection occurred or that it did not? To put it in Hume's terms, which is the lesser miracle? My own view will come as no surprise. As a supernaturalist and as a Christian, I find the evidence in favor of the resurrection to be exceedingly strong. Perhaps it can even be said to be compelling for those who admit the possibility of miracles and who are Christians.[21] But the problem is that for those who don't and aren't, the available evidence is not likely to be compelling.

As we have seen, the odd thing is that most people adopt their belief about the resurrection on the basis of something other than the relevant historical evidence, pro or con. (Is this why miracles seem to bring so few people to faith, why Jesus was reluctant to perform spectacular public miracles?) Those who believe in Christ believe in the resurrection; those who are naturalists do not.

There is a curious circularity here. As I noted earlier, I believe philosophers have shown that Humean arguments against rational belief in miracles fail, that miracles (so far as we know) *can* occur; the real question is whether any *have* occurred. But when we turn to historical evidence for a purported miracle (e.g., the resurrection), it turns out that a decision as to whether or not it occurred normally turns on whether or not one believes that miracles can occur. Perhaps this circularity

---

21. More specifically, evidence for the resurrection will tend to be more compelling for those who accept the basic reliability of the New Testament. On this point, it should be added that there are, of course, many supernaturalists who allow for miracles but not the miracle of the resurrection of Jesus Christ. Typically, adherents of theistic religions other than Christianity would take such a position. It is not part of my purpose to argue that belief in the resurrection of Jesus is compelling for all supernaturalists but rather that belief in the resurrection of Jesus is rational from the perspective of supernaturalism. It may indeed be compelling for those supernaturalists (Christian supernaturalists, of course) who hold that the New Testament is revelatory and reliable, but that is not my main claim.

explains the puzzle with which we began — specifically, why Christians find the evidence for the resurrection so utterly compelling while non-believers think it sheer foolishness to believe in the resurrection. From the perspective of naturalism, the resurrection does seem like a prescientific myth. From the perspective of supernaturalism, or at least Christian supernaturalism, the resurrection seems by far the best explanation of the evidence.

VI

The upshot of what I have been arguing is that both belief and disbelief in the resurrection of Jesus can be rational. It is a mistake to argue either (1) that it is *never* rational to believe in the resurrection of Jesus or (2) that belief in the resurrection of Jesus is the *only* rational position. Both arguments have been presented by contemporary Christian scholars.

Some Christian theologians in recent years have argued against belief in a real resurrection of Jesus from what amounts to a perspective very near naturalism. Rather than rejecting talk of the resurrection entirely, as a religious skeptic might do, they typically offer what might be called reductive theories of the resurrection. "What 'Jesus rose from the dead' really means," they say, "is ————," where the blank is filled in with a way of understanding the resurrection that does not actually involve a dead man coming back to life. I will discuss such views, and the naturalism they presuppose, in Chapter 2.

Other Christian thinkers, especially theologically conservative ones, try to show that belief in the resurrection of Jesus is the *only* rational position.[22] But one lesson that I believe Christian philosophers and apologists should learn is that if God's existence and the possibility of miracles are not first allowed — that is to say, if naturalism is not first abandoned — it is difficult for evidence or arguments for the resurrection to produce a conversion. The seminary professor who argued that any rational person who honestly considers the evidence must convert was wrong. A naturalist can say — and unless we can refute naturalism, such a position seems to me rational — "Yes, the evidence for the resurrection

22. This seems to be the aim of some books of conservative apologetics, such as Josh McDowell's *The Resurrection Factor* (San Bernardino: Here's Life Publishers, 1981) and Gary Habermas's *The Resurrection of Jesus* (Grand Rapids: Baker Book House, 1980).

of Jesus is strong; I can't produce a good alternative explanation of what happened, but a resurrection just couldn't have happened."[23]

Apologists for the resurrection are quick to criticize this position, and if we insist on looking at it only from a certain rather acute angle, it does look weak. "True," the apologist says, "secular historians will not accept the resurrection because they insist on a priori grounds that it could not have happened. But why insist that? Why not be open-minded rather than dogmatic about what we might find in history or in our experience? Let history speak for itself; don't interpret it only from the perspective of preconceived assumptions."

Although I am ultimately in sympathy with this criticism of naturalism, I believe it is often presented in far too facile a manner. It ignores the rationality of our bias against extraordinary events. I ask how you would respond if somebody in all apparent sincerity told you that the Washington Monument levitated for an hour last night? Or how you would respond if someone in all apparent sincerity told you that John Lennon came back to life three days after his death?

What follows from this, I believe, is that the strategy of Christian philosophers who want to defend the resurrection should not be hard apologetics. Unless naturalism can first be refuted, it is pointless to try to produce rational arguments that will coerce conversions by their logical power, so to speak. Disbelief in the resurrection does seem to be a rational position. A better strategy for Christian philosophers who seek to defend the resurrection is soft apologetics. They should try to defend belief in the resurrection against the objections of critics, demonstrate the rationality of supernaturalism, and show that, given supernaturalist assumptions, belief in the resurrection makes good sense.

23. I interpret the rational naturalist not as saying "No matter how strong the evidence for the resurrection might be, it will always be outweighed by the principle that 'the dead stay dead'" but rather "Given the actual strength of the evidence for the resurrection of Jesus — even if one looks at it as sympathetically as possible — that evidence is outweighed by the principle that 'the dead stay dead.'"

2

Resurrection and History

I

Was the resurrection of Jesus an event in history? This question has been asked by many twentieth-century theologians and biblical scholars. Some of the things that have been written on the topic seem to me sensible and helpful; others seem confused and poorly argued. The main aim of the first section of this chapter is to expose what I take to be some of the errors made by certain people who discuss this question; I also want to formulate my own approach. In the second section I will discuss the views of some who hold that the proper practice of the academic discipline of history precludes belief in divine interventions in history. Finally, in the third section, I will discuss and criticize certain reductive or "historicist" theories of the resurrection of Jesus.

I want to begin by working backward, so to speak. After briefly clarifying the question of whether Jesus' resurrection is an event in history, I will state the position I wish to defend. Only then will I try to expose the deficiencies of other approaches by treating them as objections to my own position.

Let me first, then, strive to clarify the question itself. Now I am sure that historians and ordinary folk alike consider, say, Caesar's crossing the Rubicon or Napoleon's defeat at Waterloo to be events that occurred in history. This is primarily and perhaps entirely because historians and ordinary folk (those, at least, who have some knowledge of European history) believe that these events really occurred. That is, they think that Julius Caesar really did cross the Rubicon and that Napoleon Bonaparte really was defeated at Waterloo. The question at hand is whether the resurrection of Jesus is an event in history like these. And the difficulty in this case is that the answer one decides to give will not be entirely a function of whether one believes that Jesus really was raised from the dead. Naturally, people who doubt or deny that it occurred will also doubt or deny that it was an event in history. But the complication here is that there are scholars who apparently hold that the resurrection of Jesus occurred (in some sense or other) but deny that it was an event in history. Their denial might have something to do with their views about the nature of the resurrection of Jesus; it might have something to do with testimony in the resurrection accounts to the direct activity of God and the presence of angels; it might have something to do with their views about the verifiability (or lack of it) or more specifically the observability (or lack of it) of the claim that Jesus was raised; or it might have something to do with their views about the meaning or significance of Jesus' resurrection.

My own view (which I present in Chap. 3) is that the New Testament texts witness to a *bodily* resurrection of Jesus. That is, they claim that Jesus was actually dead for parts of three days, was miraculously raised by God, and was raised as a corporeal being (i.e., a being who could be seen, touched, weighed, located, measured, etc.). Jesus' raised life was a new manner of life, in many ways different from ordinary life, and mysterious to us. This is to say that the resurrection was not a mere resuscitation, a restoration of Jesus to his old earthly manner and mode of life. Nevertheless, the resurrection was a bodily resurrection as opposed to a "spiritual resurrection" (i.e., a restoration of Jesus' incorporeal soul or spirit or person to life quite apart from his body).

Does this imply that the disciples' "seeing" of Jesus in his resurrection appearances was like their seeing him before the crucifixion or like my seeing a colleague walking down the hall? In one sense, of course, the answer is No, and it is easy to appreciate the views of those theologians who insist that the two sorts of "seeings" are qualitatively different. The difference consists in the fact that the resurrected Jesus possessed a new, transcendent mode of life fit for the kingdom of God. But in another sense, the answer is Yes. The disciples' "seeings" of the risen Jesus were not hallucinations, visions, or even (whatever this curious term might mean) "objective visions." The disciples "saw" Jesus with their eyes in the normal sense in which anyone "sees" anyone else; they could if questioned have confirmed his presence in the same ways in which I might do so if for some reason I doubted that I was really seeing my colleague. Could a nonbeliever have seen the risen Jesus? I find it odd that so many scholars think the answer is No. For the texts imply that certain nonbelievers *did* see the risen Jesus — Thomas (John 20:26-29) and the apostle Paul (Acts 9:1-9; 1 Cor. 15:8) among them. The suggestion that only the eyes of faith could "see" the risen Jesus seems a twentieth-century import, quite foreign to New Testament tradition. Could a photograph of a resurrection appearance have been taken, had a camera been present? I see no reason to think not.

Now suppose I am right that this is indeed what the New Testament suggests. And suppose further that this is in part what the Christian church means or ought to mean when it affirms that "Jesus was raised from the dead." Was the resurrection of Jesus from the dead, understood in the above way, an event in history?

What exactly is "history"? There are several opinions on this question among contemporary historians and philosophers of history. Let me mention the two most important. *Historical realists* say that history is what historians discover. The aim of historians is to find out, relate, and explain what actually occurred in the real past. Historical realists believe that it is possible to achieve this end. *Historical constructionists* say that history is what historians create. The real past is completely inaccessible to us; what we call history is whatever the evidence discovered by historians forces us to believe about the real past; the historical past (as opposed to the real past) is constituted or constructed by historical research.[1] Now my inquiry in this book could proceed equally well on the basis of either view, but since it is the simpler of the two (as well as the more consistent with standard Christian views of history), I will presuppose in this chapter the realist view.

My first impulse, then, is to argue as before: those who hold that the resurrection of Jesus really occurred (in a bodily sense) believe that it was an event in history. It seems clear — indeed, axiomatic — that if the resurrection of Jesus actually occurred, then it is a fact about the past that it occurred. And if the word *history* is understood as *the events that occurred in the real past and that historians attempt to discover,*[2] then it follows

1. See Michael Krausz, "History and Its Objects," *The Monist* 74 (April 1991): 217-29, as well as other articles in this issue of *The Monist,* devoted to "The Ontology of History."

2. "History is what occurs, and which forms the content of the writings about it," says Tom Rockmore ("Subjectivity and the Ontology of History," *The Monist* 74 [April 1991]: 190).

that the resurrection of Jesus was an event in history.[3] (Of course, quite different results might emerge if we define the word *history* in some other way — e.g., as *the events that can be proved to have occurred in the past* or *the events that can be proved to have occurred in the past by methods acceptable to historians who do not believe in God,* or *events that occurred in the past quite apart from any divine intervention,* or the like.)

None of this should be taken as suggesting that the resurrection of Jesus was an *ordinary* event in history. It was certainly not that. The resurrection was an eschatological act of God, a unique and decisive act of divine intervention in history. Jesus' body was not resuscitated but transformed. Jesus was not just saved from death but glorified. Thus the resurrection of Jesus is disanalogous to all ordinary historical events because it was brought about by God as an eschatological act; it is *the* crucial act in the cosmic drama wherein God will eventually transform, redeem, and renew all of creation.[4]

Like every other historical event, it occurred in space and time, but it was unlike most of them in the manner in which God caused it to occur. Thus, again unlike most events in history, the resurrection of Jesus cannot be entirely explained or understood in terms of its social and cultural setting. No explanation of it that crucially omits God can be adequate. The resurrection of Jesus Christ is the decisive disproof of all forms of deism that exclude divine activity from the created universe: it shows that God *can* act in history, and has.

It is frequently pointed out that there were no witnesses in the tomb at the crucial moment and that therefore the resurrection itself was not observed. This is surely correct. Some go on to argue, however, that the resurrection was accordingly "unobservable," that in principle it *could not be* observed by human beings, and that this is what rules out the possibility of Jesus' resurrection being an event in history. Now I have no idea what if anything a hypothetical witness in the tomb at the moment of Jesus' resurrection would have seen. (There were certainly witnesses to other acts of God and miracles of Jesus recorded in the

3. Thus Wolfhart Pannenberg: "Whether or not Jesus was raised from the dead is a historical question insofar as it is an enquiry into what did or did not happen at a certain time" ("The Revelation of God in Jesus of Nazareth," in *New Frontiers in Theology,* vol. 3, ed. James M. Robinson and John B. Cobb, Jr. [New York: Harper & Row, 1967], p. 128).

4. See Pheme Perkins, *Resurrection* (Garden City, N.Y.: Doubleday, 1984), pp. 28-29. This point is also stressed by Peter Carnley in *The Structure of Resurrection Belief* (Oxford: Oxford University Press, 1987), pp. 25, 40, 94, 131.

Bible.) I only wish to point out two logical fallacies that are sometimes committed here: (1) the inference from the fact that the moment of resurrection inside the tomb *was not* humanly observed to the conclusion that it *could not have been* humanly observed;[5] and (2) the inference from the claim that the resurrection could not have been observed (if this be granted) to the conclusion that it is therefore not history. This last conclusion may or may not be true, but it does not follow from the premise alone. The death of the last dinosaur could not have been observed by any human, but it was still an event in (natural) history.

If the resurrection of Jesus is an event in history, could it appear in a historical record of the times (as, say, Caesar's crossing the Rubicon and Napoleon's defeat at Waterloo could appear in historical records of their times)? Certainly the fact that certain people believed in the resurrection could so appear. But I would argue that the event itself could as well. If the event really occurred, then it is a fact that Jesus was raised from the dead. And if this is a fact, then it is an "objective fact" (I am unsure what a "subjective fact" might be), fully datable and testable by historians. Now, any important event that did actually occur, and could appear in a historical record, *should* appear in a historical record. I am arguing that this is true of the resurrection of Jesus. The event *ought to* appear in histories of the times.

But then could the resurrection of Jesus from the dead appear in a record of the times written by a secular historian, by one who does not believe in (or at least doubts) the existence of God or divine interventions in history or violations of natural laws? And the answer here is probably No — at least not if the claim we are talking about is the proposition "*God* raised Jesus from the dead."[6] Such a historian, after studying the matter, could conceivably be so overwhelmed by the evidence in favor of the resurrection as to become a theist, but this seems unlikely. It does seem possible, however, for a secular historian to become convinced, purely on the basis of publicly verifiable evidence, both that Jesus genuinely died and that he later lived again, although such a historian would presumably be unable to provide a satisfactory explana-

5. "Strictly speaking," writes Carnley, the claim that the resurrection of Jesus is an event in history like, say, the death of Jesus "does not preserve the distinction that whilst the death and burial could have been observed by anyone in the vicinity at the time, the resurrection inside of the tomb was not available to observation by anyone" (*The Structure of Resurrection Belief*, p. 40).

6. According to Carnley, "the historian cannot say that the raised Jesus was seen in a vision without himself becoming a man of faith" (*The Structure of Resurrection Belief*, p. 89; see also p. 131).

tion of these events. But the most likely scenario is probably this: a secular historian who studies the evidence and is unable to disprove the resurrection is more likely simply to be agnostic about what actually occurred.

At this point an objection can be raised by those like me who believe that the resurrection is an event in history. If the question we want to answer is the one formulated at the beginning of this chapter, then why must our answer depend on what secular historians will say about it? Why should that count as the relevant criterion? Since I believe in God and hold that there have been divine interventions in history, I claim that secular historians who do not have such beliefs are simply mistaken. In the case of those events in human history that were caused or influenced by divine intervention, the explanations of those events offered by secular historians will be incomplete and inadequate, if not actually misleading. Thus it seems quite unpromising for any who believe in the biblical accounts of the resurrection of Jesus to allow secular historians to decide whether or not these accounts depict something that happened in history.

But it might be asked how we could ever show that an event in history had a divine cause. That would be an excellent and difficult question. In an exchange with C. F. D. Moule, Don Cupitt put it this way: "How can an historian, applying historical method, ever be justified in postulating a transcendent cause of certain historical events? As historian the furthest he can go is agnosticism: he must say, I can't explain it." Furthermore, "As for the historian, I think he (like the scientist) is committed as a matter of method to seek natural explanations and, where they fail, *not* to invoke supernatural explanations but to admit that he doesn't know, usually because he lacks evidence."[7]

We might formulate the question in this way: Could a historian *as a historian* affirm that Jesus was raised from the dead? Or (a different question), Could a historian *as a historian* affirm that *God* raised Jesus from the dead? If the phrase "as a historian" entails the methods and assumptions of historical research currently accepted by the guild of historians, and if those methods and assumptions presuppose a commitment to some version of naturalism or deism, then the answer to the second question at least is No. But why make such a commitment? I believe the answer to both questions ought to be Yes. An analogy might help. It might similarly be claimed that while individual physicians might believe in divine healings, no physician *as a physician* can explain a given

7. Cupitt, in "The Resurrection: A Disagreement," *Theology* 75 (April 1972): 514, 519.

cure in terms of divine healing. Again, there is truth in the neighborhood here, but the main claim is false. What is true is that for excellent and understandable reasons, historians and medical doctors alike normally presuppose a kind of methodological naturalism; they expect and look for natural explanations of the events they seek to explain. But what needs to be insisted on here is that if the truth were known (sadly, it is not widely known), divine healings would be listed as cures in medical texts, and divine interventions would be listed as causes in history texts.

As I argued in Chapter 1, if an event occurs that cannot sensibly be explained naturalistically, and if it fits a given religious context well (i.e., is the sort of thing that God — understood in that context — might be expected to do), then it is rational for people who belong in that religious context to take it as an act of God. Although C. F. D. Moule does not explicitly mention the second point, he replies to Cupitt's argument well: "I still (at present) find myself saying that if a historical event occurs for which there is no discernible explanation within the historian's ambit, it is not unreasonable to give weight to a well-supported claim that the explanation lies in some other realm. If the historian is confronted with a kind of 'surd' in his story, he has no right to say that because it is abnormal and unamenable to historical procedures, he will ignore it. It lies outside his territory, but it has left a dent in his territory which might be a signal that something outside is impinging on it in an exceptional way."[8]

II

In recent years, some theologians have argued that one can properly engage in the academic discipline of history only by assuming that history is "closed" — that is to say, by assuming that history is an unbroken continuum of cause and effect that is never interrupted from the outside. The most noted of these theologians is Rudolf Bultmann. In *Jesus Christ and Mythology*, he says, "The modern study of history . . . does not take account of any intervention by God . . . in the course of history. Instead, the course of history is considered to be an unbroken whole, complete in itself."[9] Bultmann's idea is that there are no unique events in history, that every

8. Moule, in "The Resurrection: A Disagreement," p. 516.
9. Bultmann, *Jesus Christ and Mythology* (New York: Scribner's, 1958), pp. 15-16. See also Bultmann's *Existence and Faith,* ed. Schubert Ogden (New York: Meridian Books, 1960), pp. 291-92.

event or purported event must be looked at by analogy with all other events, that all events are caused and accordingly explained by other events within history, and that the idea of a historical event being caused from outside the closed chain of cause and effect that we call history is unacceptable. Interpreting Bultmann, Norman Perrin says, "If the historian is faced with, for example, the resurrection of Jesus from the dead as a unique event within human history, then he can only say either that it is not unique or that it is not an event within the human history with which he deals. This is an important point which all practicing historians recognize."[10] In other words, the modern study of history requires a methodological commitment to atheism or at least some version of deism.

In Van Harvey's *The Historian and the Believer* we find a forceful and articulate defense of deism as a necessary presupposition of historical study. This book concerns past events that are of interest to both believers and historians — the resurrection of Jesus, for example. Harvey asks how a historian ought to approach such questions as "What really happened in the days just after the crucifixion?"

Harvey claims that historians cannot rationally attribute past events to divine intervention. Nor can they make decisions about what happened on the basis of faith or prior religious beliefs. To do either would be to corrupt historical inquiry and sacrifice intellectual integrity. The discipline of history, he says, is and must be based on accepted canons, warrants, and methodological procedures. These are what allow historians rationally to judge what did or did not happen — not the hopes, fears, wishes, or faith of individual historians. And it is essential to the discipline of history that historical investigation be based on our present knowledge: the explanation of events that historians offer must be consistent with "our present critically informed beliefs about the world."[11] Moreover, "faith has no function in the justification of historical arguments respecting fact," says Harvey. "When faith is used as a justification for believing historical claims that otherwise could not be justified by our normal warrants and backings, the machinery of rational assessment comes to a shuddering halt."[12]

10. Perrin, *The Promise of Bultmann* (Philadelphia: Westminster Press, 1969), p. 39.

11. Harvey, *The Historian and the Believer* (Philadelphia: Westminster Press, 1966), p. 90. See also pp. 71, 74, 77, 87, 114-17, 122.

12. Harvey, *The Historian and the Believer*, p. 112. See also pp. 17-18, 118, 123-24.

In short, historians must be prepared to give reasons for their results. They must be intellectually honest, avoiding wishful thinking, question begging, and special pleading.[13] This allows their colleagues in the intellectual community to assess their conclusions and rationally accept or reject them. Orthodox religious belief "corrodes the delicate machinery of sound historical judgment," says Harvey. "The accusation is not that the traditionalist lacks learning or does not possess the tools of scholarship but that he lacks a certain quality of mind. The failure to criticize his sources rigorously, the ambivalent relationship to present knowledge and rational assessment: these . . . are but manifestations of a deeper failure."[14] He goes on to say that "in history the development of an explanation necessarily presupposes some agreement as to what counts for and what counts against a conclusion or assertion. But it is just this that traditional belief makes difficult if not impossible."[15]

Following Troeltsch and others, Harvey suggests several principles that historians ought to follow.[16] The first is called *the principle of authority.* Historians, he says, must do their work free of all authority. Reason alone ought to be their guide. They do not practice proper historical inquiry when they allow themselves to reach conclusions merely because of the unassessed teaching of some authority, religious or otherwise. They must be able to give reasons for their assertions. Harvey calls the second principle *the principle of criticism.* It simply says that no historical judgments are absolutely certain; all of them are merely more or less probable and are always subject to revision. The third principle is *the principle of analogy.* It says that we are able to make historical judgments only if we assume an analogy or basic similarity between our own experience and the experience of persons in the past. The fourth principle is *the principle of correlation.* It says that the events of history are so causally interconnected that a radical change at one point in a nexus will cause changes in everything that surrounds it. There are no isolated historical events; all of them must be understood in terms of their antecedents and consequences. The fifth principle can be called *the principle of uniformity.* It says that all events are alike, that the causal nexus is closed, and that explanations of events in terms of categories such as the miraculous or the utterly unique are unacceptable to historians.

13. See Harvey, *The Historian and the Believer,* pp. 19, 210.
14. Harvey, *The Historian and the Believer,* p. 119.
15. Harvey, *The Historian and the Believer,* p. 122.
16. See Harvey, *The Historian and the Believer,* pp. 5, 14, 15-16, 40-43, 70-71.

Much of what Harvey says in *The Historian and the Believer* is beyond reproach. I accept the assertion that most of his principles are essential to the proper practice of the discipline of history. I agree with him that it will not do to argue for certain historical events "on faith." The only rational way to show that a given event occurred is by historical evidence; only historical research — not faith — can establish historical events as certain or even probable.

The principle of analogy also seems perfectly acceptable to me, because I believe that analogy with past experience can lead someone properly to judge that a given event is different from other events. As Gerald O'Collins argues, analogy can lead to the unfamiliar and the unique as well as to the typical and the usual.[17] The resurrection of Jesus *is* analogous, in countless ways, to all other historical events, but (as I have argued) it is strikingly unique in some ways too. The principle of analogy cannot sensibly be interpreted as insisting that there are no unique events in history; indeed, every event is unique in certain ways, and many events are unique in significant ways. But if the principle is taken as ruling out events that are unique in the sense that they were caused by God, then naturally I will have to reject the principle. (I will return to this point later in a discussion of the principle of uniformity.)

The principle of authority is puzzling, especially if we are meant to interpret it as insisting that we never accept historical claims "on authority" — that is, because someone told us so. Obviously, much of what we believe about the past is based on the testimony of somebody whom we take to be in a position to know. It is difficult for me to believe that any historian in practice accepts the principle of authority as stated by Harvey. Don't historians ever learn by reading journal articles or by consulting critical editions?

Much "belief on authority" is fully rational and indeed constitutes knowledge. No one alive today was there when Caesar crossed the Rubicon or Napoleon was defeated at Waterloo, and yet our belief that these events occurred are generally considered to constitute knowledge. The proper question in this case is not *why I believe* a given claim but *whether my belief can be justified*. This is simply to say that our authorities must be tested and evaluated before they can be considered authoritative. Perhaps this is what the principle should properly be taken as recommending: Never accept a historical claim on the basis of *untested* authority.

17. O'Collins, *Jesus Risen* (New York: Paulist Press, 1987), p. 94.

But then there is no reason why the same sort of criterion cannot be applied to religious beliefs. It may be the case that the efficient cause (if I may speak that way) of my belief in the resurrection of Jesus is that my parents told me that Jesus was raised from the dead. But the nature of the origin of my belief about this particular past event does not render that belief irrational or inimical to the proper practice of history. The question is whether my belief can be justified. In a sense, this book is an argument to the effect that it can be.

My main quarrel with Harvey concerns the sort of deism that is apparently required by his principle of uniformity (the same sort of deism affirmed by Bultmann). I do not see why the proper practice of history requires a methodological commitment to the idea that God never intervenes in history. While I concede that all rational people, including historians, are committed to giving naturalistic explanations of events whenever possible, I do not believe that that commitment rules out the possibility that God can and does occasionally intervene in history (i.e., that God is the efficient cause of certain events). Those who say that history is "closed" have already decided, by metaphysical fiat, the issue discussed in this book: no God (or at least no intervening God), no miracles, no resurrection from the dead. It would be odd indeed if metaphysical questions (such as the question of whether there are any divinely caused events) could be settled by methodological principles, and even odder if Christians were to accept such principles. I surely do not. If there is an inevitable conflict between Christian faith and the morality of historical knowledge (and I do not agree that there is), then I say it is too bad for the morality of historical knowledge, at least as it is defined by deists.

When Harvey insists that historical investigation must be based on "our present critically informed beliefs about the world," I have to wonder who constitutes the community referred to by the pronoun "our." If the intended community is, as I suspect, the set of historians who do not believe in an interventionist God, then Harvey's argument will be dismissed by those of us who do believe in such a God; the argument simply begs the question concerning belief in divine interventions in history. Unless Harvey can produce an argument to the effect that theism is irrational, how can he rationally rule out theism as a starting point for historical investigation? It begs the question egregiously simply to stipulate that Christians or theists are not part of the community of those whose "critically informed beliefs" must form such a starting point. Beliefs about the existence of God and about God's activities in history do form part of the basis of the "critically informed beliefs" of the community of which I am a member, and in this book I will have no compunctions about making reference to them.

Harvey seems to offer two main arguments in favor of the principle of uniformity (with its implicit deism) and hence *against* the idea of miracles in history. First, he says, attributing an event to divine causation or miraculous intervention rules out the possibility of seeing, explaining, or interpreting it in its historical context, as the principle of correlation says we must be able to do.[18] Second, he says, miracle claims are impossible to assess historically. How can we decide whether a given purported miracle is probable or improbable? Or of two purported miracle claims, how do we decide which is the *more* probable? There are no relevant standards of likeliness or unlikeliness here; there is no agreement among rational investigators on what might count for or against such explanations. Thus, "in the realm of the supernatural any discussion of possibility and probability flounders."[19]

There is surely some truth to Harvey's first point. If a historian decides to attribute an event to divine intervention in human history, the event cannot be explained in the normal way (i.e., in terms of its causation by antecedent historical events). The efficient cause of the event will not be prior historical events but rather the will and act of God. Now, Christians believe we can know at least some things about God's nature, will, and actions, and so explanation of the event in terms of God's motivation in producing it might still be possible. But it is certainly true that God is not subject to investigation by historians in the way normal events and causes are, and so the event will not be explicable in the normal way. But who says all events must be explicable in the normal way? Christians will treat any claim that all events must be naturally explicable as a piece of deist or naturalist imperialism. Furthermore, in all other aspects (i.e., besides divine causation), miraculous events *can* be seen and understood in their historical contexts. The resurrection of Jesus, for example, can be discussed in terms of the attitudes and motives of those responsible for the crucifixion, those who saw the risen Jesus, those who were changed by their belief in the resurrection, and so on. It is perfectly proper for a historian to ask whether the event really occurred and, if it did, whether it is best

18. Harvey, *The Historian and the Believer*, pp. 29-30.
19. Harvey, *The Historian and the Believer*, p. 15; cf. pp. 122, 229.

explained on the basis of divine intervention. A historical event caused
directly by God is still a historical event: it really occurred, and it really
occurred at a given time and place.

As to the second point, it is possible to sympathize with Harvey
in the difficulty he sees here. One can surely understand how a naturalist
or a deist might find it impossible to make judgments about the probability or likelihood of purported miracles. But from the perspective of
a supernaturalist, the problem is not nearly so daunting. Ordinary historical methods (interpreting artifacts, interviewing witnesses, reading
accounts, etc.) can be used to determine as best one can whether the
event in fact occurred. Current scientific knowledge — fallible though
it is — can be used to see whether the event seems so extraordinary as
to count as a miracle. One's community's views about God can be
explored to see whether this is the sort of event that can be responsibly
attributed to God. As I argued in Chapter 1, I see no reason why believers
cannot assemble arguments along these lines. Relevant and helpful judgments can be made.

III

Was Jesus really raised from the dead or not? Naturally, there are two
and only two answers that can be given to this question, Yes and No.
But anybody who is at all familiar with the work of recent Christian
theologians on this question knows that the matter is not so simple.
There are shades and nuances and subtleties that bear significantly on
this seemingly simple question.

Let me propose the following distinctions. Those who believe that
the answer is Yes, that Jesus *was* raised from the dead, divide into two
groups. The first group consists of those who hold that the resurrection
is a "bodily" resurrection. Let us define this position (which I take up
in greater detail in Chap. 3) as holding that Jesus' resurrection from the
dead entails that after the resurrection the tomb was empty because the
body was no longer there, and that the resurrected Jesus appeared in
corporeal form. The second group (also discussed in Chap. 3) consists
of those who hold that the resurrection was real but "spiritual." Let us
define this position as holding that Jesus' resurrection from the dead does
not necessarily entail that the tomb was empty, that what was raised was
not Jesus' body but rather his soul or spirit or person (whatever these
terms mean), and that the resurrection appearances of Jesus were visions

or incorporeal apparitions of some sort. People in both groups, we will say, hold that there was a *real* resurrection.[20]

Those who deny that Jesus was raised from the dead also divide into two groups. The first group consists of those skeptics and nonbelievers who deny outright that the resurrection occurred, dismissing it as a pious legend, a prescientific myth, or the like. The second group seems to consist largely of Christian thinkers and theologians of a radical stripe who offer reductive or "historicist" theories of the resurrection. Jesus' resurrection, they might say, means that his influence lives on in the lives of those who believe in him or consists of the church's powerful proclamation of the redemptive message of the cross, or something of the sort. (One imagines that such people might indignantly object to my imputing to them the position that Jesus was not really raised from the dead, but I think it is clear that this is in fact what they do hold.)

Influenced perhaps by views about the nature of history such as those that I have been criticizing, people who offer reductive theories of the resurrection typically affirm the statement "Jesus is risen" (and perhaps even stress that the statement is an essential part of Christian proclamation) but interpret it as not necessarily entailing the dead Jesus genuinely living again. Thus they do not altogether jettison talk of the resurrection of Jesus as a skeptic or nonbeliever might do; indeed, reductive theorists often make much of the theological significance of the resurrection, emphasizing its importance for Christians today. As I suggested in Chapter 1, what "Jesus is risen" really means, they say, is "———," where the blank is filled in with some statement that does not necessarily entail that a man dead for parts of three days lived again.

Thus Rudolf Bultmann says, *"Faith in the resurrection is really the same as faith in the saving efficacy of the cross."*[21] And Willi Marxsen says, "Talk of the resurrection of Jesus is an interpretation designed to express the fact that my faith has a source and that source is Jesus. . . . Jesus is risen in that His offer meets us today and in that, if we accept it, He

20. It is possible for there to be confusion here. Some scholars use the term "spiritual resurrection" simply to signal the idea that Jesus' raised body was transformed rather than resuscitated, that it took on new properties unlike an ordinary body. Given certain caveats to be discussed in Chap. 3 — e.g., that Jesus' raised body was indeed a body and was continuous with his premortem body — I fully endorse this theory. In this book, however, I will reserve the term "spiritual resurrection" for the much less orthodox and far more vague theory just described.

21. Bultmann, "The New Testament and Mythology," in *Kerygma and Myth,* ed. Hans Werner Bartsch (New York: Harper & Row, 1961), p. 41; italics in original.

gives us this new life."[22] Norman Perrin says that if he were asked "what actually happened" in the days after the crucifixion, he would say of the witnesses to the resurrection appearances of Jesus, "in some way they were granted a vision of Jesus which convinced them that God had vindicated Jesus out of His death and that therefore the death of Jesus was by no means the end of the impact of Jesus upon their lives and upon the world in which they lived."[23] When summarizing what he thinks "actually happened" according to Mark's Gospel, Perrin makes a statement in which even those familiar with the jargon of existential theology might have trouble finding coherent meaning: "What actually happened on that first Easter morning . . . is that it became possible to know Jesus as ultimacy in the historicity of the everyday."[24] Similarly, Robert F. Scuka says, "When the liturgy says 'The Lord is risen! The Lord is risen indeed,' this is not to be understood as a claim about the personal destiny of Jesus. Rather, it is a way of acknowledging the participant's own experience of the life-giving power of the Spirit that is understood to derive from Jesus, an experience of being liberated from the bondage . . . of self-preoccupation, and of being freed to live in joyful acceptance of the gift that is life."[25] Speaking of 1 Corinthians 15:3-8, Thomas Sheehan maintains that "the Kerygma says merely that Jesus 'was raised' — that is, was taken up (in whatever fashion) into God's eschatological future."[26]

22. Marxsen, *The Resurrection of Jesus of Nazareth,* trans. Margaret Kohl (Philadelphia: Fortress Press, 1970), pp. 143, 184.

23. Perrin, *The Resurrection according to Matthew, Mark and Luke* (Philadelphia: Fortress Press, 1977), p. 83.

24. Perrin, *The Resurrection according to Matthew, Mark and Luke,* p. 78.

25. Scuka, "Resurrection: Critical Reflections on a Doctrine in Search of a Meaning," *Modern Theology* 6 (October 1989): 79-80.

26. Sheehan, *The First Coming* (New York: Vintage Books, 1986), p. 111. Sheehan is perhaps the most radical of contemporary reductive theorists. He maintains that Simon Peter came to believe that "Jesus was now living in God's future" (p. 113). But does this manner of speaking make any sense at all? What does it mean to be living "now" "in the future"? Sheehan interprets the resurrection in terms of God's vindicating, rescuing, or appointing Jesus, but aside from clarity on the point that this has nothing to do with Jesus coming back to life after his death, the expressions are left vague. Furthermore, would this manner of speaking have made any sense to Peter and the other early proclaimers of the resurrection? Sheehan seems to envision a Peter who was theologically highly sophisticated at some points (see p. 117), and yet he claims at another point that "Simon was not theologically equipped to devise an elaborate theology of what had happened to Jesus" (p. 118).

In other words, reductive theorists say that "Jesus is risen" means, first, something like "Jesus still has influence on us today" or "We have a vivid sense that 'he is still with us' in our memory of him" or "Jesus' life and teachings still guide and influence our lives today" or "Our lives have been transformed and liberated by Jesus." Second, the words "Jesus is risen" constitute — so they say — an invitation to others to live life in a Christ-like or Christian way. That is the meaning of the Christian proclamation of the resurrection.

Bultmann does not try to hide the fact that his understanding of the resurrection of Jesus presupposes a basically naturalist position. (I say *basically* naturalist, because he does believe in God.) Modern people can no longer believe in mythological stories, he says. The idea of dead people rising is utterly inconceivable and incredible to us. In a famous passage, Bultmann says,

> It is impossible to use the electric light and the wireless and to avail ourselves of modern medical and surgical discoveries, and at the same time to believe in the New Testament world of spirits and miracles. We may think we can manage it in our own lives, but to expect others to do so is to make the Christian faith unintelligible and unacceptable to the modern world.[27]

Although there is much that I could say in response to this point of view, I will limit myself here to two comments. First, the rather condescending air that theologians such as Bultmann and Marxsen typically take toward premodern people, including those of New Testament times, seems to me altogether unwarranted. "Such people could believe in myths, spirits, and miracles," they say, "but we moderns cannot." The implication is that these poor benighted souls just didn't have the benefit of our modern scientific knowledge and reasoning power, and that is why they believed such silly things. But surely this is grossly exaggerated. If belief in miracles and resurrections was so commonplace in ignorant times such as the first century, why was the resurrection of Jesus taken to be so significant? The record of Thomas's reaction to talk of the resurrection in John 20 and the record of the Stoic and Epicurean philosophers' reaction in Acts 17 would seem to suggest that the idea of a dead man living again was no less intellectually scandalous to first-century people than it is to us. On the whole,

27. Bultmann, "The New Testament and Mythology," p. 5; cf. p. 39.

I believe first-century people were no more superstitious, credulous, or just plain stupid than we are.[28]

I do not claim that the concept of miracles held by first-century Jews and Christians is the same as that held by twentieth-century analytic philosophers. Roughly speaking, they seemed to view miracles not as violations of natural laws but as revelatory and awe-inspiring acts of God. Even so, I do not think these people tended to explain the common run of events any less naturalistically than we do today. Hence I would deny the claim often made by critics of the biblical miracles (e.g., Bultmann and Marxsen) that people in those days were much more gullible than we are toward miracle claims, that they were prepared to believe in miracles almost at the drop of a hat.

Second, naturalism is not the only rational position that a person can take. Bultmann's statement about the wireless is picturesque and pointed, but I see no reason to believe it. He does not say precisely why (or in what sense) it is impossible for a person who uses the wireless and the electric light to believe that miracles occur. Indeed, the evidence seems clearly weighted against his assertion, since there are many apparently quite rational contemporary people who both use the wireless and believe in miracles.

Interpreting Bultmann's remark, Van Harvey says,

> he meant that the act of turning a switch, speaking over a microphone, visiting a doctor or a psychiatrist is a practical commitment to a host of beliefs foreign to those of the New Testament. It is to say that the world of modern theory — be it electrical, atomic, biological, even psychological — is a part of the furniture of our minds and that we assume this in our reading of the newspapers, in our debates over foreign policy, in our law courts, and, it needs to be added, in our writing of history. In other words, our daily intercourse reveals that we, in fact, do not believe in a three-story universe or in the possession of the mind by either angelic or demonic beings.[29]

I do not wish to comment here on demon possession or on the famed three-story universe Bultmann and others find in the New Testament.

---

28. Carnley argues that doubt and incredulity were present even in the earliest Christians, let alone their enemies, and that this fact is reflected in the "doubt" and "slowness to believe" motifs of the appearance stories in the New Testament (*The Structure of Resurrection Belief*, pp. 30-31).

29. Harvey, *The Historian and the Believer*, pp. 114-15.

The real question is whether our modern beliefs and practices somehow commit us to naturalism or near naturalism. Again, I am unable to see why they should do so. It is quite true that we are committed to giving naturalistic explanations (i.e., explanations that do not involve appeals to miracles) for the vast majority of the events we see occurring. But so were first-century people. I fail to see any good reason, from either Bultmann or Harvey, why a contemporary person cannot consistently be a supernaturalist.

We have been discussing reductive theories of the resurrection. Let me now make a distinction between two sorts of reductive theorists. The first group consists primarily of people with a kind of intellectual honesty that one can only respect. In effect, they say, "There is much in Christianity that seems to me true and even authoritative. I want to remain a member of the Christian community, but I cannot bring myself to believe the New Testament claim that a dead man lived again. That idea I simply have to reject. The best sense I can make of the Easter affirmation that 'Jesus is risen' is '————,'" where, again, what fills in the blank makes no reference to a dead man living again. I disagree with these people. Against them I want to argue that it can be rational to believe in a real resurrection. But I respect their honesty nevertheless.

I have a much harder time with people in the second group. When they find that they are unable to believe in a real resurrection, they turn to hermeneutical arguments that allow them to interpret the New Testament writers as proposing or at least tacitly suggesting a reductive theory of the resurrection. They say, "When the New Testament writers say 'Jesus is risen,' *what they really mean* is '————,'" and here they fill in the blank with a reductive theory of the resurrection. In other words, these reductive theorists claim that their own theories, or something very like them, constitute what the New Testament writers were *trying* to say or really had in mind. Or they claim that their own theory is entailed by the deep structure or symbolic sense or demythologized meaning of what the New Testament writers said. Or they claim that their own theory is found in the earliest layers of New Testament witness. This, they say, is how the resurrection texts ought to be interpreted.

Willi Marxsen is one such interpreter. He affirms the crucial Christian statement "Jesus is risen" but claims that it really means "The activity of Jesus goes on" or "The source of my faith is Jesus." "All the evangelists want to show that the activity of Jesus goes on," says Marxsen. "The authors start from a reality. They came to believe in Jesus after Good

Friday. They express this in pictorial terms. But what they mean to say is simply: 'We have come to believe.' "[30]

I reject both sorts of reductive theories. My argument against the first sort of theory (which, in effect, is the argument of the entire book) is that Jesus really was raised from the dead. My argument against the second sort of reductive theory — those that claim to express what the New Testament *really* means — is that such theories fail for exegetical reasons. I want to be clear that I am not accusing reductive theorists of the second sort of intellectual dishonesty; I am sure they truly believe that they are interpreting the texts correctly. I am accusing them of failing to interpret the texts correctly, of doing exegesis under the influence of an ideology that prevents reading them correctly. Indeed, the whole venture seems ill-conceived and desperate. In general it is never easy to prove that when people say one thing, they really (for some arcane reason) mean something else. In the case of the New Testament, can it really be true that contemporary reductive theorists know what the writers were trying to say better than they themselves did? It seems an exercise in exegetical legerdemain to claim that the New Testament writers did not really mean what they plainly said — namely, that Jesus lived again after his death *in the sense that* he again walked and talked and acted on earth. It seems about as clear as any hermeneutical point can ever be that the New Testament writers should be interpreted as saying that the resurrection is essentially and primarily something that happened to Jesus and not to the disciples. These writers portrayed the resurrection of Jesus as a surprising act of divine grace that actually occurred and not just as a mysterious or symbolic or mythological way of revealing some sort of message.

As Gerald O'Collins points out, reductive resurrection theories that appeal to the New Testament for support either make its writers remarkably obtuse communicators who were quite unable to express their intended meaning or else remarkably deceptive communicators who intentionally hid their intended meaning behind the words they used.[31] Neither option seems plausible. What people ought to do is let the biblical texts say what those texts want to say. If some find it difficult to accept what the texts say, that is in my view unfortunate, but it is intellectually dishonest to try to make the texts say something that they

---

30. Marxsen, *The Resurrection of Jesus of Nazareth,* pp. 77, 156. See also Scuka, "Resurrection," pp. 79-80.

31. O'Collins, *Jesus Risen,* p. 106.

do not in fact say merely because one desperately wants to find something believable in them.

Furthermore, reductive theories of the resurrection that are combined with the sorts of hermeneutical claims that I have mentioned seem unable to explain the transformation of the lives of the earliest Christians and the existence of the Christian church. That is, they seem helpless to explain the historical power of the resurrection faith of the early church. Would the early believers have risked their lives merely for the belief that Jesus continued to influence their lives? Would the Christian church, an institution whose growth and dynamism soon transformed the entire Roman world, have come into existence because its earliest members felt personally liberated by Jesus' teachings? It seems obvious to me that the answer to these questions is No. I take it that this is why the vast majority of scholars — both those who believe in the resurrection of Jesus and those who do not — are quite prepared to grant that the earliest believers and New Testament writers sincerely believed that Jesus had been genuinely raised from the dead.

Finally (as in effect I will argue in Chap. 8), one must wonder whether it would be Christianity that would remain if a reductive theory of the resurrection were accepted. As we have seen, Willi Marxsen (for one) contends that the meaning of Jesus' resurrection consists in the fact that his activity goes on, that he is still able to call us to believe, that he gives us new life, and so on. But of course it is not necessary for Jesus to have undergone a genuine resurrection to effect these results. Socrates and Nostradamus and Mary Baker Eddy can still today "call people to believe" after a fashion, but to my knowledge no one wants to claim that these people were raised from the dead. Reductive theorists are of course entitled to believe in a nonreal resurrection if they want to do so, but those who believe in a real resurrection are entitled to point out that a Jesus who was raised from the dead merely in the sense that he still calls us to believe is not the Jesus of the Bible or of the Christian tradition.

An interesting psychological or sociological question can also be raised: Will adoption of a reductive theory of the resurrection be sufficient to sustain the commitment of Christians to the Christ-like life-style that reductive theorists typically recommend? Christianity does indeed proclaim a given message, and part of that message enjoins Christians to strive to live in a certain way and not in another. But most folks who choose to adopt that style of life do so because they accept as true certain metaphysical and historical claims — for example, that God exists, that

God commands us to live in the Christian way, that God graciously empowers us to do so, *and* that God miraculously raised Jesus from the dead (in an actual, nonreductive sense of the phrase "raised from the dead"). Could Christian commitment — indeed, could the Christian church — survive reductive theories of the resurrection if they were to be broadly adopted? I doubt it. I suspect that these theories will remain precisely what they are now — the domain of a relatively small theological elite.

These last remarks do not, of course, refute reductive theories or the deism that they typically presuppose. Theological and historical questions should be decided on the basis of their truth or falsity (as best we can determine it), not their effects if accepted. I am in effect arguing in this book that all reductive theories are false because Jesus really was raised from the dead.

3

Resurrection and Bodily Resurrection

I

Was Jesus' resurrection from the dead a *bodily* resurrection? The claim that it was seems firmly embedded in Christian tradition. For example, the Creed of Epiphanius (ca. A.D. 374) says, "The same Christ also suffered in his flesh; and he arose and ascended into heaven in that very body." The Second Council of Lyon (1274) declares, "The third day he rose from the dead by a true resurrection of the body. With the body of his resurrection and with his soul, he ascended into heaven on the fortieth day after the resurrection." The Second Helvetic Confession (1561) says, "We believe and teach that the same Jesus Christ our Lord, in his true flesh in which he was crucified and died, rose again from the dead, and that not another flesh was raised other than the one buried, or that a spirit was taken up instead of the flesh, but that he retained his true body." Finally, the Westminster Confession of Faith (1646) states, "On the third day he rose from the dead, with the same body in which he suffered; with which also he ascended into heaven, and there sitteth on the right hand of his Father."

But we live in an age when many theologians, biblical scholars, and clergy are expressing doubts about the notion that Jesus was bodily raised. Such doubts usually revolve around apparent inconsistencies in the New Testament accounts of Jesus' resurrection, around views about the dating of those accounts, or around claims that the concept of bodily resurrection is outmoded, old-fashioned, incredible, or the like. Some denials of bodily resurrection seem motivated by a desire to lessen or at least deemphasize the miraculous aspect of the Easter story

43

or by a desire to render it immune to the acids of historical-critical
scholarship. In this chapter, I will explore such claims. I will not ask
here — as I do elsewhere in the book — whether it is rational to
believe that Jesus rose from the dead (in some form or other); I will
simply assume that Jesus rose from the dead and ask whether it is
rational to believe that he rose *bodily*. I will argue that it is rational to
believe that Jesus bodily rose and that Christians ought to continue
to affirm it.

But first a clarification: let me explain briefly what I take to be the
various possible views that are or might be held by contemporary
Christians on the question of Jesus' resurrection. All four of the following
theories have their contemporary defenders among Christians (although
the first, to my knowledge, is not advocated by any scholar or theologically sophisticated Christian).

1. *Bodily Resuscitation.* This theory affirms that Jesus was indeed
genuinely dead and later genuinely alive, that the tomb of Jesus was
empty, that Jesus' physiologically identical body was restored in the
resurrection to the same sort or condition of life that it experienced
before the crucifixion, and that Jesus' resurrection body had the same
properties as it did before his death. The resurrection, in effect, prolonged
his once-interrupted life.

2. *Bodily Transformation.* This theory also affirms that Jesus was
genuinely dead and later genuinely alive and that the tomb was empty,
but it denies that Jesus was restored to the kind of life he experienced
earlier. In the resurrection, his earthly body was transformed into a
new "glorified body" that was indeed physical but possessed strange
new properties. There was continuity between the old body and the
new body, but the new body was no longer as bound by certain of
the laws of nature as was the old. (This notion of "continuity" can be
fleshed out in a variety of ways, many of which we will explore at
later points in this book. In the rest of the book, whenever I use the
term "bodily theories of the resurrection," I am referring to theories
1 and 2.)

3. *Spiritual Resurrection.* This theory also affirms that Jesus was
genuinely dead and later genuinely alive, but it does not necessarily affirm
that the tomb was empty. The idea is that what was raised was Jesus'
spirit or soul or self, quite apart from his body. His bones might still be
decomposing in Palestine, but nevertheless he lives. Now, there are many
ways in which the concept of spiritual resurrection can be interpreted;
perhaps the most natural is to view it in terms of a sort of Platonic

body/soul dualism.[1] I will explore this point further subsequently, but here I would just note that there are several theories that fall between bodily transformation and spiritual resurrection. One theory says that the tomb was empty and had to be so, that no corpse of Jesus was to be found there or elsewhere, that what was raised was Jesus' *person* but not his body. Another theory (which I discuss further in Chaps. 5 and 6) says that the tomb was empty and that Jesus' resurrection body was physical but that this body had no physical continuity with Jesus' pre-mortem body.

(4) *Reductive Resurrection Theories.* As noted in earlier chapters, these theories in effect deny that Jesus was genuinely dead and later genuinely alive; accordingly, no claim need be made about the tomb being empty. The resurrection appearances of Jesus are explained psychologically, in terms of the disciples' inner states of mind. The appearances are called visions, subjective visions, or even hallucinations. What "Jesus is risen" really means, advocates of such theories say, is something like, "The cross of Jesus has saving efficacy today" or "Jesus' work goes on" or "The source of my faith is Jesus." I call such views *reductive* because they deny or at least do not necessarily involve the claim that a dead man lived again.

Having discussed reductive theories of the resurrection in Chapter 2, I will largely ignore them here except for a few concluding comments. What I want to do is argue that the second theory, bodily transformation, is the one that ought to be accepted by those Christians who affirm a genuine resurrection. That is, I will argue against bodily resuscitation and spiritual resurrection in favor of bodily transformation.

II

The thing I find most interesting about the bodily resuscitation theory is that it is so frequently and vehemently attacked. It is not easy to understand exactly who is being criticized; perhaps some unlettered believers accept it, but as noted earlier, I am aware of no scholar who defends it (for reasons that I will mention momentarily). Perhaps the

---

1. As William L. Craig says, "With all the best will in the world, it is extremely difficult to see what is the difference between an immaterial, unextended, spiritual 'body' and the immortality of the soul" ("The Bodily Resurrection of Jesus," in *Gospel Perspectives,* vol. 1, ed. R. T. France and D. Wenham [Sheffield: JSOT Press, 1980], p. 64).

reason for the frequent attacks on this theory is that some advocates of spiritual resurrection and some advocates of reductive theories believe they have refuted *both* bodily theories of the resurrection once they have refuted bodily resuscitation (and of course many educated Christians do hold to bodily transformation).

At any rate, bodily resuscitation is an unacceptable theory of the resurrection because (as I will argue) the New Testament does not support it. The proper biblical inference is not that Jesus was restored to his old mode or condition of life (as the Gospels indicate that Lazarus, the daughter of Jairus, and the son of the widow of Nain were), only to die a second time at some later point. Rather, the New Testament suggests that Jesus was raised to a new and exalted condition of life, never to die again. He defeated death once and for all; he was transformed to a glorified condition of life.

Since I have now rejected the first and fourth theories of the resurrection, the main issue of the chapter is to argue on behalf of bodily transformation over spiritual resurrection. So it must be asked at this point exactly what the concept of spiritual resurrection amounts to. This is not an easy question to answer. It might be argued that theology has many vague areas, but this is an area where vagueness and imprecision seem commonplace. Theologians who affirm that Jesus was raised but deny that he was raised bodily almost never explain exactly what they mean.

As I suggested earlier, the most natural way to interpret spiritual resurrection is in terms of Platonic dualism. The survival-of-death doctrine associated with this theory is usually called immortality of the soul. The basic ideas of this form of dualism are:

1. Human beings consist of material bodies and immaterial souls.
2. The soul is the essence of the person (i.e., the locus of thought, feeling, personality, etc.).
3. During ordinary life the soul is incarnate in, or, to use the Platonic metaphor, imprisoned in the body.
4. At death the body permanently decays, but the soul escapes to live on because souls are immortal.

It can be doubted that this notion is what Christian advocates of spiritual resurrection have in mind. There are two reasons for this. First, it can easily be shown that biblical notions of human nature are quite unlike Plato's (despite the Bible's frequent use of the word "soul"). The

Bible seems rather to envision human beings as normally in a state of psychosomatic unity; souls are perhaps seen as separable from bodies in some sense (see Matt. 10:28; 2 Cor. 5:6-9; Rev. 6:9; 20:4), but certainly not in the sense postulated by Platonic dualism. The "soul" in the Bible is the principle of life; an ensouled person is a whole, living person, existing bodily (Mark 8:35; Luke 12:19-20). Second, the Bible makes it clear that resurrection is a surprising and unexpected gift of God, not a natural event we should all expect on the grounds that our souls are essentially immortal. Christians affirm that life is a gift from God, as is human nature itself, so it is un-Christian to affirm that once life has been granted by God, one naturally (i.e., without further divine intervention) survives death. This is to say that Platonic dualism is not the Bible's view. But if this doctrine is not what advocates of spiritual resurrection have in mind, it is not usually clear what notion of human nature they are suggesting.

To pick one theologian as an example, Hans Küng argues in *On Being a Christian* that the identical *person* rises from the dead but denies that there is any physiological continuity:

> *Corporeal resurrection?* Yes and no, if I may recall a personal conversation with Rudolf Bultmann. No, if "body" simply means the physiologically identical body. Yes, if "body" means in the sense of the New Testament *soma* the identical personal reality, the *same self* with its whole history. In other words, no continuity of the body: questions of natural science, like that of the persistence of molecules, do not arise. But an identity of the person: the question does arise of the lasting significance of the person's whole life and fate.[2]

What is obviously needed here is a precise explanation of what a "self" or "person" is quite apart from a "body": we need some proposals on the problems that philosophers call the mind-body problem and the problem of personal identity. And that, I say, is the sort of thing that advocates of spiritual resurrection almost never provide.

Such people are usually quite clear, however, in their rejection of bodily theories of the resurrection. It is often suggested that such theories were plausible in the first century but not today. The suggested or implied reason for this (to put it more bluntly than it would usually be put) is

---

2. Küng, *On Being a Christian*, trans. Edward Quinn (New York: Pocket Books, 1976), p. 351.

that the people who lived in those days were more credulous, superstitious, or just plain primitive than we are. The idea apparently is that
"modern people" will find some notion of spiritual resurrection far more
epistemically palatable than bodily resurrection.

Having discussed this point briefly in Chapter 2, let me simply ask
four questions:

1. If bodily resurrections were so commonly accepted in ignorant
   times like the first century, why was Jesus' purported bodily resurrection taken to be so significant?
2. If bodily resurrections were so commonly accepted, why is it that
   such ancient folk as the apostle Thomas, the Stoic and Epicurean
   philosophers whom St. Paul encountered in Athens, and others
   such as Celsus, Porphyry, and Valentius reacted so negatively to the
   claim that Jesus was bodily raised?
3. Why is it that there are so many otherwise quite rational "modern
   people" who have no difficulty in affirming that Jesus bodily rose
   — people such as Karl Barth, C. S. Lewis, and A. M. Ramsey?
   Aren't they representative of "modern people"?
4. Does the term "modern people" then just mean contemporary
   naturalists or deists — people who don't believe in an interventionist God or accept theistic assumptions about reality?

If the answer to the fourth question is Yes, then the claim that "modern
people" can't believe in bodily resurrections is true but not significant.
It is true only because of the way the term "modern people" is defined
— a way that I simply do not accept. But perhaps what the claim amounts
to is something like this: some people accept theistic or supernaturalist
assumptions (e.g., God exists, God occasionally intervenes in human
affairs, etc.) while others do not, and out of the total population, the
percentage of people who do not is higher in the twentieth century
than it was in the first century. Thus *most* modern people, or at least *more
people today than in premodern times,* find it impossible to believe in bodily
resurrection. Is this claim true? I do not know. It *may* be. But surely
what must be said here is that Christian theologians ought not to base
their formulations on the beliefs of those who reject Christian assumptions. Raymond Brown well reminds us that

> the fact that credal terminology involving bodily resurrection has been
> found satisfactory for a long time should make us very cautious about

change, but even long usage does not render terminology irreplaceable. On the other hand, if a critical modern investigation shows that as far back as we can trace the NT evidence, resurrection from the dead was an intrinsic part of Jesus' victory over death, then the observation that modern man does not find bodily resurrection appealing or meaningful cannot be determinative. Nor . . . can we allow Christian theology to be shaped by contemporary distrust of the miraculous.[3]

But perhaps critics can raise a more plausible argument than the one I have been considering about what is palatable to modern people. Perhaps critics of bodily resurrection can more sensibly be construed as trying to explain early Christian talk of Jesus' bodily resurrection in some such way as this: "The Jews of Jesus' day were expecting a bodily resurrection in the last days; enter Jesus, proclaiming the eschaton; put these two together and you naturally get a strong expectation on the part of Jesus' followers that he had bodily risen." But it need only be said in response to this (1) that the resurrection accounts in the New Testament make it quite clear that Jesus' disciples were *not* expecting him to be raised and (2) that the Jewish expectation of a *general* resurrection in the eschaton is quite different from the resurrection of just one person before the eschaton. This last was not part of Jewish eschatological expectation.

Quite apart from the justifications some theologians give it, my own view of spiritual resurrection theories is this: it might be possible to arrive at a theory of spiritual resurrection that avoids the theological problems associated with traditional dualism — that is, a theory that (1) is based on a solidly biblical view of human nature and (2) entails resurrection as a gift of God rather than a natural event. Moreover, I believe that the philosophical objections that have been raised against immortality in recent years (e.g., by Antony Flew and Terence Penelhum)[4] do not in fact refute it (see Chap. 5). Some form of spiritual resurrection (assuming it is clearly spelled out and not just vaguely suggested) seems to me a *possible* view of the resurrection. But I nevertheless have biblical reasons for denying that it is the proper Christian interpretation of Jesus' resurrection, to which I will turn shortly.

3. Brown, *The Virginal Conception and Bodily Resurrection of Jesus* (New York: Paulist Press, 1973), p. 72.
4. See Flew, "Can a Man Witness His Own Funeral?" *Hibbert Journal* 54 (1956): 242-50; and Penelhum, *Survival and Disembodied Existence* (New York: Humanities Press, 1970).

III

Let us now look in more detail at bodily transformation. One aspect of this theory is that it must emphasize both continuity and change between Jesus' pre-resurrection and post-resurrection bodies. It must emphasize *continuity*, naturally enough, to ensure that it was Jesus who was resurrected and not someone else (i.e., that the person who rose was the same person as the person who died). It must emphasize *change* to distinguish itself from bodily resuscitation theories.

Continuity is provided for by two aspects of the theory. The first is that the person remains the same. Jesus identified himself as Jesus ("It is I myself" — Luke 24:39); he was recognized by the disciples (albeit at times with difficulty); his memory, character, and personality remained the same, as did many of his bodily characteristics (e.g., the pre-resurrection wounds). The second is that there is material continuity between the two bodies: the one changes *into* the other (see Rom. 8:11; 1 Cor. 15:53; Phil. 3:20-21). Paul's simile is that of a seed growing into a plant: "You foolish man! What you sow does not come to life unless it dies. And what you sow is not the body which is to be, but a bare kernel, perhaps of wheat or of some other grain. But God gives it a body as he has chosen, and to each kind of seed its own body" (1 Cor. 15:36-38). In other words, the relationship of material continuity that obtains between Jesus' earthly body and his resurrection body is like the relationship that obtains between a grain of wheat and the plant that grows from it. Thus Paul's view, both here and elsewhere in his writings, is not, as is sometimes suggested, the *exchange* of one sort of body for another; it is that the one body *becomes* or is transformed into the other.[5]

In one way, of course, this is an imperfect analogy: presumably the seed does not in the proper sense of the word *die* (though it does cease existing *as a seed*). If it died, the plant would not emerge. The point, then, is that the seed has within it, so to speak, the power to be radically changed into a new plant-like rather than seed-like mode of existence. Still, I take it that the main point of the simile holds — that continuity is preserved because the one changes, through materially contiguous stages, into the other.

But change must be emphasized too. Just as the seed of wheat looks, and is, radically different from the plant it becomes, so the ordinary

---

5. See, e.g., Gerald F. Hawthorne, *Philippians* (Waco, Tex.: Word Books, 1983), pp. 172-73.

earthly body is radically different from the resurrection body. Again following Paul's argument in 1 Corinthians 15, the old body is subject to decay and death while the new body is immune to decay and death; the old body is dishonorable while the new body is honorable; the old body is weak while the new body is powerful; the old body is natural while the new body is spiritual (1 Cor. 15:42-44).

The apostle goes on to say that "flesh and blood cannot inherit the kingdom of God, nor does the perishable inherit the imperishable" (1 Cor. 15:50). This statement is frequently cited by defenders of spiritual or reductive theories of the resurrection against the bodily theories, but I believe they misuse it in doing so. Advocates of bodily transformation can quite sensibly interpret Paul's statement as implying simply that what inherits the kingdom of God is not the old natural body (with its frailty and corruptibility) but rather the transformed resurrection body. Understood this way, Paul's statement is quite consistent with, and indeed tends to confirm, the bodily transformation theory. Furthermore, this interpretation seems entailed by the synonymous parallelism that Paul is clearly using here. The "cannot inherit" clause is defined by the "nor does the" clause, which is to say that Paul is not denying that resurrection bodies are physical but rather that they are perishable. Indeed, Paul insists that what is raised is a body *(soma)*, even if it is a "new" or "spiritual" body. And the claim that what is perishable (i.e., the old natural body) does not inherit the kingdom is consistent with the bodily transformation theory. Thus, what Paul speaks of here is not a movement from bodily existence to incorporeal existence but rather a transformation of one sort of body (a frail, corruptible one) into another, superior sort of body.

IV

But at this point we encounter a serious difficulty, one that critics of the two bodily theories often use as an argument against them — the apparently quite different and perhaps even inconsistent understandings of the resurrection found in the New Testament. It is often claimed, for example, that Paul, the earliest (and therefore according to many scholars most reliable) of the New Testament writers who deal with the resurrection, presupposes some sort of spiritual theory of the resurrection, whereas the evangelists, and especially Luke and John, presuppose some crudely physicalist theory of the resurrection, invented later for apologetic purposes. It is further claimed that the two sorts of accounts are quite inconsistent.

For example, Gerald O'Collins says,

> Paul's notion of transformation through resurrection challenges and criticizes the picture of physical reanimation that the third and fourth Gospels seem to offer. In a debate with some Sadducees Jesus likewise denies that resurrection means a return to the existence and activities of this world (Mk. 12:24-27). He indicates that risen life will be a glorified, "angelic" state (Mt. 13:43). By insisting on the strict accuracy of the physical details in the Gospel narratives of Luke and John, we will flatly contradict the understanding of resurrection proposed by Jesus and Paul.[6]

Raymond E. Brown says,

> Paul does not conceive of the risen "body" in a merely physical way. His comments make us wonder whether he would be in agreement with Luke (who was not an eyewitness of the risen Jesus) about the properties of the risen body. Certainly, from Paul's description one would never suspect that a risen body could eat, as Luke reports. Moreover, Paul distinguishes between the risen body that can enter heaven and "flesh and blood" that cannot enter heaven — a distinction that does not agree with the emphasis in Luke 24:39 on the "flesh and bones" of the risen Jesus.[7]

Reginald Fuller speaks pointedly about Luke's story of the encounter of the risen Jesus in Luke 24:36-49. This account, he says,

> has received a highly apologetic coloring not merely absent from I Cor. 15:5, but quite contrary to it. The motif of doubt . . . has been redirected to provide the occasion for a massively physical demonstration. The Risen One invites his disciples to touch him so that they can see for themselves that he is not a "spirit" or "ghost" but a figure of flesh and blood. This new interpretation of the mode of the resurrection (resuscitation of the earthly body) is quite contrary to the apocalyptic framework of the earliest kerygma of I Corinthians 15:5,

6. O'Collins, *What Are They Saying about the Resurrection?* (New York: Paulist Press, 1978), p. 49.

7. Brown, *The Virginal Conception and Bodily Resurrection of Jesus,* p. 87.

to Paul's concept of the *pneumatikon soma* (see esp. I Cor. 15:35ff) and to the presentation in Mark 16:1-8 and in Matthew 28:16-20.[8]

And Willi Marxsen goes so far as to suggest that the inconsistencies in New Testament accounts of the resurrection show that the early Christians just were not interested in the facts about Jesus' resurrection body:

> All this forces one ultimately to ask whether the question which interests us today (the resurrection body of Jesus) was simply of no interest at the time? For this is what the picture's lack of unity would suggest. . . . When the evangelists were writing their Gospels, there was no longer a unified view in the primitive church about the mode of the Easter happening. This does not seem to have played the decisive part then which is often ascribed to it today. For if people had been really interested in the mode of the resurrection, this would surely have been depicted in uniform terms.[9]

Do we then have here evidence of two contradictory traditions about the resurrection of Jesus, an earlier spiritual tradition and a later corporeal and heavily apologetic tradition? I do not believe so. Let me say first that there are some apparent inconsistencies in the accounts of Jesus' resurrection appearances that seem difficult if not impossible to harmonize sensibly. But I believe critics are far too hasty to claim that we have such a case here. Let's take a look at the various accounts of the discovery of the empty tomb and of encounters with the risen Jesus, categorize them as "physical" or "spiritual," and see what we can say about the problem at hand.

I will call any resurrection appearance "physical" that either presupposes the empty tomb or implies in some way that Jesus' resurrection body was corporeal (e.g., he walked, he ate, the disciples were encouraged to touch his body, the same wounds were there). And I will call any resurrection appearance "spiritual" that implies that Jesus' resurrection body had strange new abilities that natural bodies do not have. (We must remember, of course, that the evangelists report Jesus as having some such properties — e.g., the ability to heal diseases — during his earthly ministry.)

8. Fuller, *The Formation of the Resurrection Narratives* (Philadelphia: Fortress Press, 1980), p. 115.

9. Marxsen, *The Resurrection of Jesus of Nazareth,* trans. Margaret Kohl (Philadelphia: Fortress Press, 1970), pp. 68, 75-76.

If we set out to classify the accounts on this basis, the following texts must clearly count as "physical," because they claim that the tomb was empty: Matthew 28:1-8; Mark 16:1-8; Luke 24:1-10; and John 20:1-10. Equally, the following texts must be classified as "physical": Matthew 28:9-10, because the disciples "took hold of his feet"; Luke 24:13-35, because the two disciples walked with Jesus on the road to Emmaus, and Jesus broke bread and gave it to them; Luke 24:36-43, because Jesus encouraged the disciples to see and handle him, and he ate a piece of boiled fish; John 20:11-18, because Jesus' words to Mary Magdalene — "Do not hold me" — seem to imply she could have held him; John 20:19-25, because Jesus showed the disciples (minus Thomas) his hands and side; John 20:26-29, because Jesus encouraged Thomas to feel his wounds; and John 21:1-25, because Jesus gave the disciples bread and fish.

The following texts may be classified as "spiritual": Luke 24:13-35 (the road-to-Emmaus story again), because of the strange way Jesus is said to have "vanished out of their sight"; John 20:19-25 and 26-29 (again), because of the emphasis on Jesus appearing in the room despite "the doors being shut"; and Acts 1:6-11 (one of Luke's two apparent accounts of the ascension), because of the curious way Jesus is said to have been lifted up into a cloud. Though not an account of an appearance per se, 1 Corinthians 15:35-37 might be taken to belong in the "spiritual" camp, because of Paul's already-noted emphasis on the differences between earthly bodies and glorified bodies.

There are also three resurrection texts that seem neutral or unclassifiable on the "physical"/"spiritual" scheme: Matthew 28:16-20 (an appearance to the eleven in Galilee); Luke 24:50-53 (Luke's other apparent account of the ascension, which might be classified as "spiritual" if we interpret it in terms of the apparently parallel Acts 1:6-11); and 1 Corinthians 15:3-11, Paul's list of the resurrection appearances of Jesus.

One of the things that we notice immediately is that "physical" and "spiritual" motifs are combined in the third and fourth Gospels, even in the same stories. The two Gospels that are most often criticized by defenders of spiritual resurrection for their "gross physicalism" are the very Gospels in which "spiritual" motifs are found.[10] This at least constitutes

---

10. Thus Peter Carnley is wide of the mark when he claims that "in Luke and John the raised Christ, who is said to have been not only seen but handled, seems hardly different from the historical Jesus of the days before the crucifixion" (*The Structure of Resurrection Belief* [Oxford: Oxford University Press, 1987], p. 235). In this regard, see Luke 24:31 and John 20:19, 26.

prima facie evidence that there is no inconsistency here. One could, of course, claim that "physical" and "spiritual" motifs come from quite different pre-Gospel traditions and were rather clumsily combined by the third and fourth evangelists. But this seems entirely improbable. Authors don't often offer as true explicitly inconsistent accounts of events. Unless Luke and John were rather dense people, it seems plausible to suppose that they had in mind an understanding of Jesus' resurrection body that unifies what we are calling the "physical" and "spiritual" motifs. (I am not here rejecting redaction criticism or the notion that there are layers of tradition or that there was editing; what I am rejecting is the claim that a purely "redactional" explanation is adequate in this case.)

My point, then, is that some critics argue that the earliest understanding was that Jesus experienced a nonbodily resurrection, something usually called glorification or exaltation, and that physical views of the resurrection (e.g., those reflected in the third and fourth Gospels) came later. But since Luke and John quite obviously consider the two theories (if they are two separate theories) quite compatible, we can ask (1) whether we have any good reason to believe that one is more primitive than the other, and (2) whether it is possible to arrive at an understanding of Jesus' resurrection body that unifies the "physical" and "spiritual" motifs that are present in the texts.

Let me propose a possibility. I suggest we admit that the Gospels are puzzling and attempt to interpret what they say about Jesus' resurrection body in terms of what Paul says in 1 Corinthians 15, which, despite being earlier, does more explicit theologizing about the meaning of the resurrection than do the Gospels. It is well known that Paul's first epistle to the Corinthians was written in response to quite specific problems that the church in Corinth faced. When Paul turned to the resurrection in chapter 15, he was probably speaking to those Corinthian Christians who were influenced by some sort of proto-gnostic tradition and who thought that their resurrection had already taken place at their baptism and who therefore concluded that there was no need for a general, eschatological resurrection.[11] (See 2 Tim. 2:17-18: "Among them are Hymenaeus and Philetus, who have swerved from the truth by holding that the resurrection is past already.")

Paul's understanding of the resurrection, which we have already partially discussed, avoids the extremes of both bodily resuscitation and dualistic spiritualism. The resuscitation theory — that resurrected persons

---

11. See Fuller, *The Formation of the Resurrection Narratives,* p. 19.

are restored to their former condition of life — was present in contemporary Jewish thinking. (See 2 Baruch 50:2: "For the earth shall then assuredly restore the dead. . . . It shall make no change in their form, but as it has received them, so it shall restore them.") Spiritualistic theories were also in the air at Paul's time — Platonic and proto-gnostic body/soul dualisms that held that the soul is imprisoned in the body and at death escapes to live on eternally.

In opposition to both extremes, Paul argues for what I am calling bodily transformation, whereby the natural body is changed into a new "spiritual body" in such a way that material continuity and personality are preserved. Though Paul nowhere speaks of the resurrection of the *flesh* (he usually used the term *sarx* to indicate something inherently perishable, weak, and even sinful), it is interesting that Luke seems to do so (see Luke 24:39: "See my hands and feet, that it is I myself; handle me, and see; for a spirit has not flesh and bones as you see that I have"). James Moffatt argues that Paul's theory constituted

> a startling challenge to those who saw no alternative to the 'flesh and blood' resurrection of popular Judaism (which meant the reunion of body and soul), except in some adaptation of the purely immaterial Greek idea. At the heart of Paul's thought is the affirmation that the life of Christians after death must continue to possess the capacities for action and affection, insight and understanding (xiii.12) which in the present body have a real though limited range. The spiritual, in other words, is not the immaterial.[12]

Thus we should not be misled by Paul's use of the term "spiritual body." He is not using this term to signify a body "formed out of spirit" or made of "spiritual matter," whatever that might mean, but rather a body that has been glorified or transformed by God and is now fully dominated by the power of the Holy Spirit.[13] The word *soma* itself carries heavy

12. Moffatt, *The First Epistle of Paul to the Corinthians,* Moffatt New Testament Commentary (New York: Harper, 1938), p. 260.

13. On this point, see Gerald O'Collins, *The Resurrection of Jesus Christ* (Valley Forge, Pa.: Judson Press, 1973), p. 113; A. M. Ramsey, *The Resurrection of Christ* (London: Fontana Books, 1961), pp. 108-9; and Ladd, *I Believe in the Resurrection of Jesus* (Grand Rapids: William B. Eerdmans, 1975), p. 116. Craig argues that the terms Paul uses here ought to be rendered in English not as "physical body" and "spiritual body" but as "natural body" and "supernatural body" ("The Bodily Resurrection of Jesus," p. 59).

connotations of physicality in Paul, but, more importantly, the word *pneu-matikon* does not mean "nonbodily." A "spiritual body" is a person taught, led, and animated by the Holy Spirit (see 1 Cor. 2:15; 14:37; Gal. 6:1).

It is clear to me that Paul's view of the resurrection is a physical view. And the crucial conclusion that can then be drawn is that physical understandings of resurrection are not (as is often charged) late additions to New Testament tradition. The physicalism of Luke and John cannot seriously be dismissed as late, legendary, or apologetic. New Testament resurrection traditions were bodily traditions *at least* as early as Paul.

V

We are now in a position to see that the New Testament accounts of Jesus' resurrection can best be understood on a bodily transformation model. The following points are crucial: (1) Jesus' resurrection was a bodily resurrection: the tomb was empty; the resurrection body could be touched; it was a genuine physical thing — not an apparition or a figment of the disciples' imagination (see Luke 24:37). (2) Jesus was one and the same person before and after the resurrection: he claimed to be Jesus; he recalled events that had happened before the crucifixion; he was recognized as Jesus by the disciples (albeit at times with difficulty); his wounds were still there. (3) There were also differences in the form that Jesus took after the resurrection: his body was transformed, not merely resuscitated. (Not even the third and fourth Gospels in their most corporeal passages suggest that Jesus' body was merely resuscitated.) Jesus lived in a new mode of existence, liberated from many of the limitations of ordinary life. This accounts for the strange new properties the evangelists report him as having — an apparent change in his physical appearance (Mark 16:12 [from the Markan appendix]: "He appeared in another form") that rendered him somewhat more difficult to recognize (Luke 24:31; John 20:14-15; 21:4-5), a luminous aspect in some of his post-ascension appearances (Acts 9:3; 22:6ff.; 26:12ff.; Rev. 1:16), and an apparent ability to "come and go" at will (Luke 24:31, 36; Acts 1:21) even despite closed doors (John 20:19, 26).

Thus we see that there is no necessary inconsistency between Paul and the evangelists or, more precisely, between "spiritual" and "physical" motifs in the relevant New Testament texts. The evangelists themselves, I believe, could well concur with Paul's statement that "flesh and blood cannot inherit the kingdom of God" (1 Cor. 15:50), for they nowhere imply that Jesus' earthly body was raised in the sense of restoring it to its old condition of life.[14] They too suggest that it was transformed to a new condition of life. Furthermore, the corporeal motifs of Luke and John (Jesus eating, being touched, etc.) do not deny bodily transformation but were clearly designed to convince the incredulous disciples that it was really Jesus who was raised, that it was not a ghost or a figment of their imagination. Nor do the unusual properties of the risen Jesus in some of the appearance accounts (e.g., the ability to appear or disappear, luminosity) entail incorporeality. Only a physical object can be located somewhere, can travel from point A to point B, or can glow luminously.

Surely there are some difficult questions we are entitled to ask here. For example, was the resurrected Jesus genuinely hungry, or was he just accommodating himself to the disciples' level of understanding? Was this the only way for him to prove that he was not an apparition? Can "spiritual bodies" get hungry and eat? Isn't eating an aspect of earthly decay? Can ordinary food be digested by glorified bodies? For that matter, how were the atoms and molecules of Jesus' earthly body related to the atoms and molecules of his glorified body? These are good questions, to which I have no complete answer, although I do make some suggestions in Chapters 5 and 6.

Indeed, it must be emphasized that there is a great deal of mystery involved in the resurrection of Jesus. As to the nature of Jesus' resurrection body, I believe that this much can be affirmed and confidently taught within the Christian community: it was numerically identical with his pre-resurrection body (i.e., it was one and the same body) but not qualitatively identical with it (some of the old properties were still there, but it possessed several new ones as well). As I have emphasized, Jesus was not resuscitated but resurrected; his body was transformed. Much more than this is mystery; the opinions of scholars about the exact nature of Jesus' body during the forty days that marked the span from the first to the last of his resurrection appearances is little more than educated hypothesizing or guesswork.

Notice, for example, the following three theories of the nature of Jesus' resurrection body (which I do not mean to suggest are at all exhaustive of the possibilities): (1) Jesus' resurrection body had one essential nature that did not change for the forty days. It was physical (i.e., it took up space, could be located, could be seen under the right

14. Craig argues convincingly that the Gospels steer the same middle course as Paul does between immortality on the one hand and resuscitation on the other. See "The Bodily Resurrection of Jesus," p. 68.

conditions, etc.) but also in some sense supernatural (which accounts for the "spiritual" motifs in Paul and some of the appearance stories in the Gospels). (2) Jesus' resurrection body was primarily and normally physical in the same sense in which his pre-resurrection body was physical, but miraculous acts of God occasionally gave it strange "spiritual" properties, such as invisibility and "agility" (a word used by medieval theologians to denote the ability to come and go unimpeded). (3) Jesus' resurrection body was primarily and normally spiritual and thus invisible, but miraculous acts of God occasionally gave it physicality so that it could be seen, touched, located, and the like.

It should be clear by now that I am inclined toward the first theory and would be prepared if pressed to argue against the other two. The first is in my opinion the simplest way to handle the complexity of the biblical texts. But I regard all three as acceptable theories in that they violate nothing found in either Scripture or essential Christian teachings. In plain fact, Scripture does not clearly answer the question of which of these three theories is best. Neither the second nor the third theory constitutes a denial of the classical Christian claim that Jesus was bodily raised from the dead.[15]

VI

Two final matters before concluding. First, a word about the empty tomb. My own view is that the New Testament tradition of the empty tomb is one of the strongest reasons for holding that Jesus was bodily raised. The empty tomb is not only compatible with the bodily transformation theory that I have been arguing for but is required by it. (Naturally, you

15. It is difficult to understand, then, let alone credit Norman L. Geisler's attack on Murray J. Harris, who defends a theory that seems to fit somewhere between what I am calling bodily transformation and spiritual resurrection. See Geisler's *The Battle for the Resurrection* (Nashville: Thomas Nelson, 1989). Geisler principally criticizes Harris's *Raised Immortal: Resurrection and Immortality in the New Testament* (Grand Rapids: William B. Eerdmans, 1983). For Harris's reply, see *From Grave to Glory: Resurrection in the New Testament* (Grand Rapids: Zondervan, 1990). It is most doubtful that Norman Geisler would ever accept me as an authoritative arbiter of what constitutes Christian orthodoxy. Although my own opinions on the topic of this curious controversy are closer to Geisler's than to Harris's, it nevertheless seems to me clear that Harris's views are orthodox and that the Christian community would more greatly benefit if Geisler would direct his energies toward criticizing liberal or non-Christian views of the resurrection of Jesus.

could have an empty tomb and a spiritual resurrection, but spiritual resurrection theories do not *require* an empty tomb, and defenders of spiritual theories in fact often argue against the empty tomb.)

Second, a word about how resurrection was viewed in the first century. The point is often made that first-century Jews envisioned a bodily resurrection. Conservative scholars use this claim in support of interpreting the New Testament texts in terms of bodily resurrection. If the New Testament writers affirmed bodily resurrection, they say, so should we. But critics of bodily resurrection can grant that the New Testament writers had bodily resurrection in mind and still insist that the theory is wrong. They might argue that the New Testament writers were not able or at least not inclined to comprehend or entertain other more plausible conceptions of life after death, that they simply misinterpreted the limited facts at their disposal and characterized a purely spiritual resurrection as the sort of physical resurrection they were expecting.

But it is interesting, as I noted in Chapter 2, that even the most radical Christian interpreters of the resurrection texts are fond of arguing that their own theories are what the New Testament writers were trying to say or really had in mind, that the proper interpretation of the texts is along the lines of their own theory. This sort of exegetical legerdemain has always struck me as the most grotesque aspect of reductive theories of the resurrection.

For example, theologian Gordon Kaufman holds that the resurrection of Jesus means something like "God's act begun in Jesus still continues." He explicitly points out that "the question whether Jesus was alive again or not does not bear directly on this issue."[16] He goes on to comment on the New Testament resurrection texts as follows:

> Although the earliest Christians certainly thought the man Jesus, who had died on the cross, had again come alive, a historical reconstruction of the evidence in the Bible hardly supports that interpretation. . . . The extraordinary hypothesis accepted by the early church . . . is not intrinsically connected with the central claim the church wished to make in proclaiming Jesus' resurrection, namely, that the God who had been acting through Jesus' ministry and especially in his death was still actively at work in the community of believers.[17]

16. Kaufman, *Systematic Theory: A Historicist Perspective* (New York: Scribner's, 1968), p. 430.
17. Kaufman, *Systematic Theory,* pp. 467-68.

Despite the reductive theories of such individuals as Kaufman (and others I noted in Chap. 2) who interpret the New Testament along these lines, I maintain that there is still significance to the argument that, in concert with contemporary Jewish thinking, the New Testament writers most probably had bodily resurrection in mind. A problem arises from the fact that this argument is sometimes oversimplified. For example, it is occasionally suggested that the Jewish mind simply had no other way of understanding the concept of life after death than bodily resurrection, that the New Testament writers wouldn't have comprehended, for example, what a spiritual resurrection was, and that therefore bodily resurrection was a well-intentioned but wrongheaded interpretation of the meaning of Jesus' resurrection. This is not a very convincing argument, however. Dualistic theories seem to have been very much alive in the first century, and even the Old Testament contains stories of entry into everlasting life (e.g., Elijah being taken into heaven) that are not strictly speaking bodily resurrection stories.[18]

It does seem sensible, however, to say that the disciples could not have believed, or convinced others to believe, that Jesus was alive without an empty tomb and appearances interpreted as bodily appearances. Resurrection from the grave is what Jews of Jesus' day *would naturally have meant* by the term "raised from the dead" (even though they could have *understood* alternative theories). And in the absence of compelling evidence for the claim that they had some other theory in mind (which evidence, as I have argued, is not forthcoming), the proper conclusion is that the New Testament writers had bodily resurrection in mind.

But to return to the main theme of this chapter, once we understand the implications of bodily transformation, we have a way of interpreting and unifying the quite disparate New Testament accounts of the resurrection.[19] Properly interpreted, all the New Testament accounts of the resurrection of Jesus present it as a case of bodily transformation rather than of resuscitation or of spiritual resurrection, despite the different ways they describe it. The proper conclusion, then, is that Christians ought to continue to affirm the traditional doctrine that Jesus was bodily raised.

18. On this point, see Brown, *The Virginal Conception and Bodily Resurrection of Jesus*, p. 76. Jewish apocalyptic literature contains clear references to immortality (e.g., Wisdom 3:1-8), and there are references to disembodied existence as well (see 1 Enoch 9:3, 10; 22:3; 2 Esdras 7:75-101; Apocalypse of Moses 32:4).

19. William L. Craig makes this point carefully and thoroughly in *Assessing the New Testament Evidence for the Historicity of the Resurrection of Jesus* (Lewiston, N.Y.: Edwin Mellen Press, 1989); see especially pp. 147, 158, 328-30, 359, 395.

4

Resurrection and the Empty Tomb

*The accounts of the empty grave, of which Paul still knows nothing,
are legends.*

Rudolf Bultmann[1]

*Today however historical criticism has made the empty tomb a dubious
factor and the conclusions of natural science have rendered it suspect.*

Hans Küng[2]

I

Traditional Christian belief about the resurrection of Jesus includes the
claim that the tomb in which he was buried was empty on Easter
morning. Despite differences in the details of their accounts of the
discovery of the empty tomb, all four Gospels report that it was empty.
"He is not here; for he has risen," says the angel to Mary Magdalene
and the other Mary in Matthew 28:6; similar notions are expressed in
the other Gospels (Mark 16:6; Luke 24:5; John 20:2).

Despite this, the tradition of the empty tomb is frequently criticized.
It is natural to expect those who doubt that Jesus was raised from the

---

1. Bultmann, *Theology of the New Testament*, vol. 1, trans. Kendrick Grobel
(New York: Scribner's, 1951), p. 45.
2. Küng, *On Being a Christian*, trans. Edward Quinn (New York: Pocket Books,
1976), p. 366.

dead to deny that the tomb was empty. But what is interesting about the contemporary theological scene is that some theologians who want to affirm in some sense or other that Jesus was raised either deny or struggle mightily to deemphasize the empty tomb. Why is this? Why does the empty-tomb tradition come in for so much criticism? The reasons are complex and fascinating. What I hope to do in this chapter is take a hard look at the arguments that are given for and against the tradition. Let me reveal here that I am one who wants to affirm the empty tomb; accordingly, I will try to reply to the objections that are typically raised against it. I will grant that these objections are interesting and thoughtful, but in the end I will argue that they are not convincing. I maintain that for both historical and theological reasons, Christians ought to continue to hold that Jesus' tomb was empty.

It is important to stress the narrowness of the scope of this chapter. I want to consider only arguments for and against the claim of the four evangelists that Jesus' tomb was found empty on Easter morning. Clearly there is a strong logical connection between the empty tomb and other concepts, such as bodily resurrection, and they are usually affirmed or denied together.[3] But having discussed bodily resurrection in Chapter 3, I will not do so here. I shall assume that the empty tomb, if it occurred, was a historical event in every relevant sense of the word and can be investigated historically. But since the empty tomb by itself does not entail the resurrection of Jesus, I will say little here about the complex matter of linking historical judgments to theological affirmations or to Christian faith.

II

Is the empty-tomb tradition believable? There are five major arguments that are typically given against it. First let me state them as fairly and strongly as I can; then I will reply to them. Some of them are closely related; the distinctions I make among them (especially the second, third, and fourth arguments) are somewhat artificial. Furthermore, the

3. Some recent scholars separate them, however. Barnabas Lindars, for example, affirms bodily resurrection but denies the empty tomb; see "Jesus Risen: Bodily Resurrection but No Empty Tomb," *Theology* 89 (March 1978): 90-96. Luis M. Bermejo, on the other hand, affirms the empty tomb but denies bodily resurrection; see *Light beyond Death: The Risen Christ and the Transfiguration of Man* (Anand, India: Gujarat Sahitya Prakash, 1985).

arguments aim in different directions — some, for example, attempt to show that the purported event of the empty tomb did not in fact occur; others attempt to show that even if it did, the empty tomb did not and should not play any important role in Christian faith or proclamation.

1. *The empty-tomb tradition is unreliable because the four Gospels, which are our only sources of the tradition, give contradictory reports about it.* In order to explore this argument, let us take a thorough and rather ruthless look at the apparent discrepancies.

a. The Gospels do not agree on the people who visited the tomb. Matthew mentions only Mary Magdalene and "the other Mary"; Mark mentions Mary Magdalene, Mary the mother of James, and Salome; Luke mentions Mary Magdalene, Joanna, and Mary the mother of James; and John mentions Mary Magdalene (although the "we" in 20:2 can sensibly be taken to imply that others were present).[4]

b. The Gospels do not agree on the time of the visit. All agree that it occurred on the first day of the week; Matthew elaborates by saying it was after (or late on) the Sabbath toward dawn; Mark says that it was very early on the day after the Sabbath and that the sun had risen; Luke says that it was early and at first dawn; and John says that it was early and still dark.

c. The Gospels do not agree on the purpose of the women's visit. Matthew says that it was merely to see the tomb; spices are not mentioned (perhaps given the stone and the guards, the women knew they would not be able to embalm the body); Mark says it was to anoint the body with aromatic spices bought the day after the Sabbath (16:1); Luke implies it was to anoint the body with spices and ointments the women had prepared before the Sabbath (23:55; 24:1); and John mentions no reason for the visit at all (perhaps because Nicodemus and Joseph of Arimathea are said to have anointed the body before the burial).

d. The Gospels do not agree on the location of the stone when the women arrived. Matthew seems to imply that it was in place when they arrived but that the angel rolled it away in their presence; Mark, Luke, and John say that the women arrived to discover the stone already rolled away.

---

4. See William L. Craig, "The Historicity of the Empty Tomb of Jesus," *New Testament Studies* 31 (January 1985): 53. See also Raymond E. Brown, *A Risen Christ in Eastertime* (Collegeville, Minn.: Liturgical Press, 1991), p. 66.

e. The Gospels do not agree on whether there was a guard at the tomb. Matthew states that there was such a guard, while the other Gospels mention no such thing.

f. The Gospels do not agree on the personages the women saw or on their location. Matthew mentions an angel of the Lord who sat on the stone outside the tomb; Mark mentions a young man in a white robe who was inside the tomb sitting on the right. Luke mentions two men in dazzling apparel who were standing inside the tomb. John (a bit later in the story — 20:12) mentions two angels who were sitting outside the tomb.

g. The Gospels do not agree on what the personages said to the women; the synoptic Gospels basically agree (with a few minor but interesting differences), but John's record of the message delivered by the two angels is quite different.

h. The Gospels do not agree concerning the reaction of the women. Matthew says they went away quickly with fear and great joy to tell the disciples. Mark says they fled trembling and astonished and told no one about what they had seen. Luke says the women left and told the disciples (who did not believe them). John says that Mary Magdalene ran to tell Peter and the Beloved Disciple that the body was missing.

2. *The story of the empty tomb is a late development in the pre-Gospel period, and so it is probably unreliable.* This claim is actually the fountainhead of most contemporary criticism of the tradition of the empty tomb. There are several reasons for regarding it as late.

a. The story of the empty tomb is not so much as mentioned in Paul's writings, which are our earliest records of Christian belief about the resurrection of Jesus. (I will treat the absence of any mention of the empty tomb in Paul's epistles as a separate argument below.)

b. The empty tomb is not mentioned in the speeches Luke attributes to Peter, Stephen, and Paul in Acts. While not considered by most scholars an early document, the book of Acts, and in particular the sermons attributed by Luke to the apostles, may well give vital clues to the earliest Christian beliefs about the resurrection, and the empty tomb is not mentioned.

c. The crucial text for the empty tomb is obviously Mark 16:1-8. (According to the vast majority of scholars, Mark was the first of the four canonical Gospels to be written and had a major influence on both of the other synoptic Gospels, apparently including what they say about the empty tomb.) And at least some scholars believe that Mark 16:1-8 was formulated long after the events themselves, does not fit with what precedes it, and played a secondary and quite subordinate role in the apostolic kerygma.[5] Furthermore, some scholars are troubled by what look like internal inconsistencies or at least improbabilities in Mark's account, such as the plan of the women (in hot Palestine) to anoint a body that had already been dead for parts of three days and their failure to consider, prior to their arrival at the tomb, how they were going to enter a tomb blocked by a large stone.[6]

A slightly different version of this second argument against the empty tomb runs as follows: the empty-tomb tradition was not originally meant as history — that is, it was not meant to state facts about the tomb in which Jesus was buried. It was instead a way of elaborating, explaining, or announcing the affirmation that "Jesus is risen" that arose in the Christian community in the period prior to the writing of Mark's Gospel.[7] The empty tomb, then, is best seen not as a report of a fact but as a product of the resurrection appearances of Jesus, as a legendary elaboration of the appearances that grew up long afterward. The body of Jesus was probably just somehow lost — burned or thrown into a common grave — or the location of the tomb in which it had been buried was forgotten.

3. Closely related to the above argument is this one: *The story of the empty tomb is a legendary addition to the earliest Christian proclamation of the resurrection, invented for apologetic purposes.* Several factors support this claim.

a. As we have seen, the Gospels deviate sharply from each other to a surprising degree on the details of the empty-tomb story, and there is evidence of the tradition developing and expanding in the later Gospels (e.g., concerning the guards at the tomb in Matthew; Peter's running to the tomb in John; Jesus' appearance to Mary Magdalene and the other Mary or to Mary Magdalene alone in Matthew and John; Joseph of Arimathea's being described as a follower of Jesus in Matthew and John; the disciples being increasingly involved in the story of the empty tomb).

b. The empty tomb is clearly the sort of story we might expect the early Christians to have seized upon because of its obvious apologetic

5. See, e.g., Bultmann, *The History of the Synoptic Tradition,* trans. John Marsh (New York: Harper, 1963), pp. 284-90.

6. Walter Kasper mentions these points and concludes that "we must assume therefore that we are faced not with historical details but with stylistic devices intended to attract the attention and raise excitement in the minds of those listening" (*Jesus the Christ* [London: Burns & Oates, 1976], p. 127).

7. Küng suggests this in *On Being a Christian,* pp. 364-65.

value. As all scholars grant, the resurrection was crucial to early Christian proclamation, a proclamation that was subject to severe criticism by those who rejected it. Thus it is not difficult to imagine the origin of the story of the empty tomb because of its obvious apologetic value — "If Jesus was not raised from the dead, then where is his body?" Christians could have asked their enemies.

c. In Mark's Gospel (written at a time when the story of the empty tomb was perhaps not yet widely known), the empty tomb is attested to only by a few women who keep silent about what they had seen (16:8). But in Matthew, written perhaps a generation later, when (perhaps because of the influence of Mark's Gospel) the empty-tomb story was widely known, the women are reported to have immediately hurried to tell the disciples the news (28:8). This, too, is witness to the late and legendary character of the tradition.[8]

4. The second and third arguments are supported by a fourth: *The case for the reliability of the empty-tomb tradition is seriously weakened by the fact that Paul, the earliest and therefore most reliable of our sources about the resurrection of Jesus, does not mention it.* The closest Paul comes to mentioning the empty tomb in any of his extant writings is the brief phrase "he was buried" in 1 Corinthians 15:4 (a phrase that is meant — so critics of the empty tomb say — only to emphasize the reality of Jesus' death and not to testify to a separate event). Since this epistle is our earliest record of the resurrection (most scholars date it at about A.D. 54, or about twenty-four years after the events), this too supports the notion that the empty tomb is a later development, unheard of in the early days. For it seems that Paul would hardly have omitted reference to something so crucial to the case for the resurrection of Jesus, a case he tries hard to make in 1 Corinthians, had he known about it. Or perhaps Paul knew of the empty-tomb reports but rejected them because they seemed to support a crudely physicalist conception of the resurrected body of Jesus, in contrast to his own more nuanced notion of a "spiritual body." At any rate, Paul probably believed that Jesus' "old body" remained decomposing in the tomb.

5. The final argument tries to deemphasize rather than disprove the empty tomb: *The empty tomb played no significant role in the faith of the earliest believers and should play no significant role in ours either.* Even from the Gospels themselves it seems clear that the faith of the disciples in the resurrection of their Lord was originally based not on the empty

---

8. This conjecture is put forward by Gordon Kaufman in *Systematic Theology: A Historicist Perspective* (New York: Scribner's, 1968), p. 419n.

tomb but on what they took to be his appearances to them. And the stories of the appearances contrast rather sharply with those of the empty tomb, as Hans Küng points out:

> The stories of the tomb are concerned originally only with the women and not with the disciples, the appearance statements with the latter and not the former. The stories of the tomb describe appearances of angels and not of Christ, the appearance statements again the opposite. The stories of the tomb are narratives (artistically elaborated to some degree) about astonished listeners and were perhaps used in the readings at the eucharist; the appearance statements in their oldest versions are summaries in catechism form for learning by heart (probably in catechetical use).[9]

Reginald Fuller argues that the disciples came to believe that Jesus was risen on the basis of appearances to them in Galilee. They then returned to Jerusalem and for the first time heard the women's story about the empty tomb. Naturally, they welcomed it as consistent with their own new belief, and presumably incorporated it into their preaching. Fuller goes on to say of the empty tomb that "the disciples were apparently not interested in it as a historical fact and so we hear nothing of their having checked it. They were interested only in using it as a vehicle for the proclamation of the resurrection. For the disciples, faith in the resurrection did not rest upon the empty tomb, but upon their revelatory encounters with the Risen One."[10] Furthermore, Gordon Kaufman argues that if we take the appearance stories as primary, we can easily account for the growth of the empty-tomb tradition. Unsophisticated early Christians, especially those to whom Paul's concept of a "spiritual body" was incomprehensible, would accept the story of the empty tomb as something naturally entailed by their belief that Jesus had risen.[11]

9. Küng, *On Being a Christian*, p. 364.

10. Fuller, *The Formation of the Resurrection Narratives* (Philadelphia: Fortress Press, 1970), p. 171. In the light of Luke 24:24, it is hard to credit Fuller's claim that "we hear nothing of their having checked it."

11. There are other and in my opinion less impressive arguments against the empty tomb. (1) Some claim for theological reasons that our resurrection must be like Christ's; since the tombs of Christians who have died are not empty (despite the fact that they will some day be resurrected), Jesus' resurrection must not have involved an empty tomb either. But in reply, two questions need simply be asked: first, is it an acceptable procedure to deduce a historical fact from a theological

III

Let me now try to respond to these arguments.

1. As to the first, I believe that few of the discrepancies among the Gospel accounts of the empty tomb present serious problems; plausible harmonizations (i.e., ones that do not involve special pleading) can be suggested without great difficulty. For example, the term "young man" in Mark and Luke was a conventional way to refer to an angel (Luke himself makes this identification in 24:23).[12] For another example, perhaps the women arose and left for the tomb while it was still dark and arrived after sunrise. On the other hand, I will grant that some of the discrepancies are difficult if not impossible sensibly to harmonize — such as the location of the stone when the women arrived (here Matthew differs from the other Gospels) and the reaction of the women (Mark alone among the evangelists has the women keeping silent).[13]

But the main point I wish to make is this: despite differences in details, the four evangelists agree to an amazing degree on what we might call the basic facts. All unite in proclaiming that *early on the first day of the week certain women, among them Mary Magdalene, went to the tomb; they found it empty; they met an angel or angels; and they were either told or else discovered* (Mary Magdalene in the fourth Gospel) *that Jesus was alive.* There is also striking agreement between John and at least one of the Synoptics on each of these points: *the women informed Peter and/or other disciples of their discovery, Peter went to the tomb and found it empty, the risen Jesus appeared to the women, and he gave them instructions for the disciples.*

---

point, especially a controversial one? Second, why must Jesus' resurrection be like ours in every respect? New Testament writers do take Jesus' resurrection as a promise and model of ours, but nowhere do they suggest that our resurrection must be like his in all respects. (2) Hans Grass suggests, following a vague reference in a speech that Luke attributes to Paul (Acts 13:27-29), that Jesus' body was buried by his enemies. He accordingly dismisses as legendary the burial by Joseph of Arimathea and the empty tomb. But in reply to this argument, it need only be asked whether it is proper to base such a bold theory on such a vague reference, itself subject to a variety of interpretations. The grounds for Grass's theory seem flimsy indeed. For a good discussion of these arguments, see Gerald O'Collins, *The Resurrection of Jesus Christ* (Valley Forge, Pa.: Judson Press, 1973), pp. 39, 90-91, 96.

12. See also 2 Macc. 3:26, 33; Josephus, *Antiquities,* 5.8.2; Gospel of Peter 9.

13. For a balanced and sensible critique of the approach that some biblical scholars take to the discrepancies in the empty-tomb accounts, see Eleonore Stump, "Visits to the Sepulcher and Biblical Exegesis," *Faith and Philosophy* 6 (October 1989): 353-77.

Furthermore, although it would be misleading to place great emphasis on this argument, it may be that the discrepancies themselves lend credence to the basic facts, showing as they do that a variety of Christian interpretations of the empty tomb, at many points quite independent of each other, all agree on these basic facts.[14]

2. Is the empty tomb a late tradition? I find the argument unconvincing. For one thing, exactly how do critics of the empty tomb go about deciding that a given document or passage is "late"? I will grant that there do appear to be instances in which a convincing case can be made that one document is later than another because of evidence of literary dependence. But when it comes to dating various strata, pericopes, or traditions in the Gospels (e.g., deciding that a given text in a "late" Gospel reflects an "early" tradition, or the like), there is typically a good deal less cause to be confident.[15] Though some comparative datings are based on carefully crafted linguistic arguments, others seem based more substantially on critical assumptions about what sorts of things might have been expressed by "early" believers and what could have been expressed only by "later" believers. Notice the circular argument in the following imagined but perhaps not unrecognizable dialogue between a critic and a defender of the empty tomb:

DEFENDER: The empty tomb is taught in this text.

CRITIC: That text is a late text, and can therefore be discounted.

DEFENDER: How do you know it is a late text?

CRITIC: Well, it presupposes a late theology — specifically, a physical view of the resurrection.

DEFENDER: How do you know that physical views of the resurrection weren't taught in early texts?

14. Even secular historian Michael Grant, who affirms the empty tomb but not the resurrection as historical, argues that discrepancies in secondary details do not affect the historical core of a narrative; see *Jesus: An Historian's Review of the Gospels* (New York: Scribner's, 1977), pp. 176, 200. For a good discussion of the limitations of the argument about the positive apologetic significance of the discrepancies, see Peter Carnley, *The Structure of Resurrection Belief* (Oxford: Oxford University Press, 1987), pp. 46-47. I do not agree with Carnley's contention that there is only one source of belief in the empty tomb, but his warning is well taken nonetheless.

15. As Pheme Perkins puts it, "Frequently the judgment about which form of a story is likely to be older is difficult to make" (*Resurrection* [Garden City, N.Y.: Doubleday, 1984], p. 169; see also p. 196).

CRITIC: Well, because they just weren't. Among the New Testament texts that talk about the resurrection, only the later ones push physical views of the resurrection.

DEFENDER: But how do you know they are the later ones?

CRITIC: Obviously because they are the ones that push the conceptions, such as physical views of the resurrection, that only developed later.

But far more importantly, if the empty tomb is a late tradition, we are entitled to wonder why early Jewish criticism of the resurrection of Jesus never disputed it (a point I will discuss further below). If the tradition developed late, I would think it likely that critics of the resurrection would have disputed the claim. That they did not do so suggests to me that the empty tomb was a fact agreed upon by all parties early in the game. Furthermore, if the tradition had developed late, it would also seem plausible to expect that it would contain much more kerygmatic coloring (e.g., citing proofs from prophecy, use of christological titles, etc.) than in fact it does.[16]

Also, it has been convincingly argued that the empty-tomb stories have linguistic features indicative of early tradition.[17] The stories incorporate various Semitic expressions and customs that may suggest an early Palestinian setting — for example, "on the first day of the week" (Mark 16:2), "angel of the Lord" (Matt. 28:2), "Miriam" (as opposed to "Mary"; Matt. 28:1 — Codex Alexandrinus and other sources), "[answering] said" (Matt. 28:5), and "bowed their faces to the ground" (Luke 24:5). I do not wish to place great emphasis on this point; it is, after all, hard to prove that such expressions could not or would not have been used in, say, a late first-century Diaspora text. Still, the existence of Semitisms in the empty-tomb stories is worth noting.

Why, then, is the empty tomb not referred to in the speeches that Luke attributes to the apostles in Acts? There is, I believe, an available explanation that is more plausible than the idea that stories of the empty

---

16. William L. Craig argues that the empty-tomb tradition was part of the pre-Markan passion story and is accordingly very old indeed (*Assessing the New Testament Evidence for the Historicity of the Resurrection of Jesus* [Lewiston, N.Y.: Edwin Mellen Press, 1989], pp. 197-201, 360-61).

17. See Robert H. Stein, "Was the Tomb Really Empty?" *Themelios* 5 (September 1979): 20. See also E. L. Bode, *The First Easter Morning* (Rome: Biblical Institute, 1970), pp. 6, 58, 71.

tomb had not yet developed in the early period. To the extent that the speeches in Acts accurately reflect the earliest period of Christian proclamation, it may be that the empty tomb was not mentioned because it did not have to be mentioned — that is, because it was a widely known fact, undisputed by all parties. The question for the people of that period was not "Was the tomb empty?" but rather "*Why* was the tomb empty?" Furthermore, although the empty tomb is not explicitly mentioned, it seems clearly presupposed in Peter's sermon in Acts 2. See especially verses 27-29, in which Jesus, who because of his resurrection "was not abandoned to Hades, nor did his flesh see corruption," is contrasted to King David, whose tomb "is with us to this day." The implication seems to be that Jesus' tomb is empty while David's is not. (See also Paul's sermon in Acts 13:29-37, which is susceptible to precisely the same reading.)

Finally, what about the theory that the empty-tomb stories in the Gospels are legendary products, written much later, of the earlier appearance stories? The problem with this claim is that there are many differences between the appearance stories and the empty-tomb stories, and the connections between them are tenuous. Accordingly, most interpreters believe that the two traditions have independent origins, that the one did not cause the other. The earliest appearance text, 1 Corinthians 15:3-8, contains several themes not found in Mark 16:1-8, the earliest empty-tomb text (e.g., explicit citation of tradition, the appeal to the Scriptures, the reference to the death of Christ "for our sins," the use of the title "Christ" as a proper name, and the list of six appearances). Likewise Mark 16:1-8 contains themes not mentioned in 1 Corinthians 15:1-8 (e.g., the purpose of the women's visit to the tomb, their discovery of the empty tomb, the angel and its message, and the promise that Jesus would appear to the disciples in Galilee).[18] About the only point of connection between the two texts is their common affirmation of Jesus' resurrection.

3. Is the empty tomb an apologetic legend? Again I am doubtful. The empty-tomb tradition just does not have the characteristics we would expect it to have if it were an invented apologetic device, designed to convince readers that Jesus really rose. For one thing, the empty tomb does not play an apologetic role in the New Testament (though I have little doubt that early Christians used it apologetically). Far from being

---

18. Gerald O'Collins marshals the evidence effectively. See *Jesus Risen* (New York: Paulist Press, 1987), pp. 125-27. See also Perkins, *Resurrection,* pp. 84-94.

presented as an irrefutable argument for the resurrection, the empty tomb is rather depicted as an enigma, a puzzling fact that no one at first is able to account for.[19] (Note Luke 24:22-23: "Moreover, some women of our company amazed us. They were at the tomb early in the morning and did not find his body." Cf. John 20:1-2, 13.) With the possible exception of the Beloved Disciple in the fourth Gospel (see John 20:8), *nobody* in the New Testament comes to believe in the resurrection of Jesus solely on the basis of the empty tomb — not Peter, not Mary Magdalene, not any of the other women. Only the appearances of Jesus himself moved these people to believe that he was alive. In other words, the fact that the empty-tomb stories in the Gospels produce only puzzlement and ambiguity rather than proof attests to the primitive and non-apologetic character of the tradition.

The second reason for doubting that the story of the empty tomb is an apologetic legend is that it is bad apologetics. If the story is an apologetic legend invented by later Christians, why is it that the story is made to hang so crucially on the testimony of women, whose evidence was not legally admissible in Jewish proceedings? (This must have constituted something of an embarrassment to those men in Jesus' party who were later to become leaders of the church — while they were hiding, it was the women who found that Jesus was risen.) If the story is an apologetic legend invented by later Christians, why does it (in Mark's original version) lead only to fear, flight, and silence on the part of the women? If the story is an apologetic legend invented by later Christians, why is it so openly admitted that some of Jesus' followers were suspiciously in the vicinity of the tomb early on the morning of the discovery of the empty tomb? And why is there no mention made of any thorough investigation of the tomb or its environs, or of some verifying word from Joseph of Arimathea? As an apologetic argument, this one seems weak.

The third reason for denying that the story of the empty tomb is an apologetic legend is, as noted above, that the emptiness of the tomb seems to have been conceded by all parties, friend and foe alike. I frankly suspect that the tomb *was* checked. The disciples themselves would surely have rushed there to verify or falsify the women's story

---

19. According to Perkins, "The restraint of the Markan story makes it evident that the empty tomb itself is ambiguous and that it is not immediately viewed as evidence for the Resurrection" (*Resurrection*, p. 123). See also Murray Harris, *Raised Immortal* (Grand Rapids: William B. Eerdmans, 1983), pp. 41-44, 62-64.

(again, see Luke 24:24), and later the enemies of the incipient Christian movement would doubtless have searched thoroughly in their effort to disprove the claims of the early Christians.[20] There is no record in any early anti-Christian polemic of anyone's suggesting that the tomb was not empty; critics focused on arguments that the disciples had stolen the body.[21]

It should be noted that I am presupposing here my earlier argument against the claim that the empty-tomb tradition is late. Naturally, the points I have just made will not be convincing to those who believe that the tradition was, for example, invented by Mark and that his Gospel was written outside Palestine during or after the Jewish war. By that time the location of the tomb could have been forgotten and verification would have been difficult. The crucial point here is that the Gospels all claim that the location of Jesus' tomb was known to the women and to the disciples (Mark 15:47; Matt. 27:61; Luke 23:55; John 20:1). This claim is embedded in the story of the burial of Jesus — which is considered historically credible by the vast majority of scholars — and not just in the resurrection accounts. So the claim that the location of the tomb was known should be rejected — or so I would argue — only for very compelling reasons indeed.[22]

To put it radically, it may be that the claim that the empty tomb is an apologetic legend is *itself* an apologetic legend — a legend suggested in defense of the view that Jesus was not really raised or was raised in some nonbodily sense. It is true that Christian apologists have used the story of the empty tomb in support of the claim that Jesus was bodily raised. But that does not make the story legendary. To show that a given story does or can play an apologetic role in somebody's belief system says nothing about its historical accuracy.

In this regard, note Matthew's story of the guard at the tomb (Matt. 27:62-66; 28:4). This story does seem to play an apologetic role in

20. The theory that the disciples had fled to Galilee and so were not around to check has been shown to be utterly implausible. Hans Von Campenhausen dismisses it as "a legend of the critics" (*Tradition and Life in the Church*, trans. A. V. Littledale [London: William Collins, 1968], p. 79).

21. See Raymond E. Brown, *The Virginal Conception and Bodily Resurrection of Jesus* (New York: Paulist Press, 1973), p. 22. See also Justin Martyr's *Dialogue with Trypho the Jew* (ca. A.D. 150), in which opponents of the resurrection still seem to grant the empty tomb.

22. See Craig, *Assessing the New Testament Evidence for the Historicity of the Resurrection of Jesus*, p. 352.

Matthew's Gospel, but that fact by itself does nothing to discredit it. Is the story a "legendary accretion"? I do not know. I have always thought that one point in its favor is, oddly, its own improbability; for the story would seem to have been apologetically useless to the writer of the first Gospel unless it were either widely known to be true or else completely uncheckable. But if the story is an apologetic legend, that will have to be shown on grounds other than the mere fact that the story answers certain objections (e.g., the slander that the disciples stole the body) that might be raised against the claim that the tomb was empty. Furthermore, in a similarly curious way, the story of the guard at the tomb — whether it actually occurred or is an apologetic invention of the later church — constitutes a powerful argument for the reliability of the empty-tomb tradition. For the telling of the story of the guard at the tomb is quite senseless unless the tomb of Jesus really was empty. Those who denied the claim that Jesus was raised from the dead were evidently not able to deny that the tomb was empty.[23]

4. What about Paul's purported ignorance of the empty tomb? It is quite correct that the apostle does not mention the empty tomb per se; not even his words "he was buried" (1 Cor. 15:4) explicitly refer to it. However, it does not follow from this that Paul had never heard of the empty tomb, or that he disagreed with the empty-tomb stories, or that he nowhere *implicitly* referred to the empty tomb, or even that the empty tomb was not part of early Christian proclamation. Some critics seem to come dangerously close to espousing the following obviously invalid inference:

1. Paul was the earliest New Testament author to proclaim the resurrection.
2. Paul did not mention the empty tomb.
3. Therefore, the empty tomb was not part of the earliest Christian proclamation of the resurrection.

Why is it, then, that Paul does not explicitly refer to the empty tomb? Are there other, better alternatives to the assertion that he had never heard of it or else that he disagreed with it? Certainly. In general I imagine Paul did not discuss the empty tomb because, given his

23. I owe this point to Professor Robert Gundry, in conversation. See also William L. Craig, "The Guard at the Tomb," *New Testament Studies* 30 (April 1984): 279, 281.

audience in Corinth, he did not find it necessary or helpful to do so. I can think of three possible explanations. (1) Perhaps Paul, always at pains to prove that he was a true apostle and equal with Peter, James, and the others, was reluctant to mention an aspect of the resurrection story in which he had had no part (unlike the appearances of Jesus, with one of which Paul was honored — 1 Cor. 15:8). (2) Perhaps Paul knew that the Corinthians already knew about the empty tomb and understood its importance and so felt that the story did not need to be repeated. Indeed, 1 Corinthians 15:1 suggests a belief on Paul's part that he had already convinced the Corinthians of the truth of Jesus' resurrection (on his initial visit there), and so perhaps he did not feel a need to compile all the evidence again. If, as I have argued, the empty-tomb tradition is old, it would be odd indeed if Paul had never heard of it. (3) Perhaps Paul believed the empty tomb, by itself, could be explained (e.g., by theft of the body) and that it was the appearances that were crucial. It does seem that anyone like Paul to whom the risen Jesus had personally appeared would naturally stress the appearances over the empty tomb as evidence of the resurrection. Any one of these explanations — some of which can be combined with each other — seems to me more plausible than the highly improbable claim that Paul either had never heard of the empty tomb or else disagreed with it.

But does Paul *implicitly* refer to the empty tomb in 1 Corinthians 15:4, where he mentions Jesus' burial? I believe it is quite probable that he does. Paul's own view of the nature of the resurrection, in my opinion, *requires* that the tomb be empty (which is the reverse of what is sometimes claimed). This is because his simile of the plant growing from the seed (1 Cor. 15:35-43) entails material continuity between the one and the other. That is to say, Paul's view would seem to imply that Jesus' body could not still be decomposing in the tomb, because it had been transformed into — it *became* — Jesus' resurrection body (just as the seed becomes the plant).[24]

Furthermore, the fact that the tomb was empty seems clearly entailed by the claims (explicitly made by Paul) that Jesus died, was buried, and was raised from the dead. It is possible, of course, to imagine survival-of-death theories that involve death, burial, and new life with the corpse still in the grave. But such theories would not agree with Jewish notions of resurrection — nor with Paul's. (There were of course

24. See also Rom. 8:11, in which Paul seems to equate resurrection with the Spirit giving life to a mortal body.

Jewish theories of *survival of death* that did not involve bodily resurrection, such as Enoch's or Elijah's translation to heaven and the immortality-of-the-soul doctrine of the Wisdom of Solomon, but these are not theories of *resurrection*, as Paul's explicitly is.) There is little evidence, for example, in favor of the claim that Paul had in mind some nonbodily notion of resurrection (such as the concept of spiritual resurrection) that did not require an empty tomb. So Paul's own belief that Jesus was raised from the dead, if it is correct, *entails* that the tomb was empty. Perhaps he did not mention the empty tomb because his understanding of resurrection entails the empty tomb as a matter of course.

My own view, then, is this: If it is true (1) that first-century Jews would naturally have believed that resurrection means bodily resurrection (as most scholars assume), and (2) that there is no convincing reason to believe that Paul had in mind some nonbodily theory, and (3) that the claim that Jesus was bodily raised entails the claim that the tomb was empty, and (4) that Paul was clever enough to recognize this logical implication, then I believe it is safe to say that Paul's reference to the burial of Jesus did indeed reveal knowledge of and commitment to the tradition of the empty tomb.[25] Thus I conclude that the fact that Paul nowhere explicitly refers to or discusses the empty tomb is not a compelling argument against it.

5. I have no quarrel with much of the fifth argument. As already noted, I happily agree that the faith of the earliest believers was based on the appearances rather than the empty tomb. But surely the first question we want to ask is not whether the empty tomb should be emphasized as part of Christian faith today but rather whether there is good reason to believe that Jesus' tomb was empty. Once we answer the second question, we can perhaps return to the first. (I believe the empty tomb does have certain theological implications, an issue that I will discuss briefly below. But I would think it curious indeed if someone who believes that the tomb was empty should try to belittle it or suggest that it has no place in contemporary Christian teaching.)

Another thing I find curious is the question of whether the stories of the appearances or the story of the empty tomb should, so to speak, take priority. Gordon Kaufman claims that if we regard the appearances as taking priority we can explain the growth of the empty-tomb tradition, but that it is much harder to explain the appearance stories on the basis

25. On these matters, see Brown, *The Virginal Conception and Bodily Resurrection of Jesus*, p. 70; Fuller, *The Formation of the Resurrection Narratives*, p. 73.

of the empty-tomb tradition.[26] Perhaps Kaufman is correct here. But why do we have to choose between the appearances and the empty tomb? Why should one or the other be regarded as "primary" (whatever that means)? Why not accept both that the tomb was empty and that there were resurrection appearances?

Finally, Reginald Fuller's claim that the disciples were not interested in the empty tomb as a historical fact but only as a vehicle for proclamation seems almost ridiculous. The statement certainly has rather startling implications, not the least of which is that the disciples must have been rather obtuse. Imagine, say, Peter in part basing what he took to be *the* crucial item of Christian proclamation — the resurrection of Jesus — on a historical claim (the empty tomb) the truth value of which he did not care about. Even if he thought he had another irrefutable proof of the claim (the appearances), this would be a foolish procedure indeed. How absurd to suggest that the disciples, preaching the resurrection in an environment hostile to their message, had no interest in the truth of the claim that Jesus' tomb was empty.[27]

IV

There are also two robust arguments in favor of the empty tomb that have not, to my mind, been refuted. Both are implicit in much that I have already said.

1. *The tradition of the empty tomb enjoys very broad support in the New Testament.* As we have seen, it is found in all four Gospels (it is significant that both the Synoptics and John stress it), with possible indirect references in Acts and 1 Corinthians. Furthermore, the fact that it is found in Mark, John, and Matthew's special source (i.e., material Matthew did not gain from Mark or Q) demonstrates the broad support the empty tomb receives from independent traditions. And the discrepancies between the accounts in the Gospels argue against the claim that the other

26. Kaufman, *Systematic Theology*, pp. 419-20n.

27. "It would be quite arbitrary to exclude the element of apologetic from the announcement of the kerygma, where the kerygma is understood in some religiously pristine sense as 'pure announcement' or proclamation," says Peter Carnley. "Indeed, such a thing may never have existed. The evidence suggests that the early Christians may always have proclaimed arguments" (*The Structure of Resurrection Belief* [Oxford: Clarendon Press, 1987], p. 140).

evangelists, or even the other synoptic evangelists, wrote about the empty tomb solely under the influence of Mark.

It is possible to claim, I suppose, that Matthew, Luke, and John wrote about the empty tomb only under the influence of Mark, and that the discrepancies are all due to editing.[28] But I think the evidence for multiple sources — sources other than Mark — for the empty-tomb tradition is far more compelling, (1) because the discrepancies are too numerous and too sprawling to have resulted from simple editing, and (2) because many of them do not seem to be redactional (i.e., it is difficult to imagine what theological purpose there could have been for introducing them).

As noted above, I believe that those New Testament scholars who argue that the empty tomb is a late tradition have not succeeded in making their case. They have not succeeded in pinpointing a period, let alone a document, in which Christians believed in the resurrection but not the empty tomb. And if it were true that the empty tomb was a late addition to Christian proclamation, this ought to be evident in the New Testament. But all the relevant sources either affirm or presuppose the empty tomb.

A good example of what I am talking about is the association of Joseph of Arimathea with the tomb in which Jesus was buried. It is significant that this figure, who so far as we know held no position and played no role in the early Christian movement, figures so prominently in all four Gospels. No critic has been able to show that this Joseph was a late apologetic invention of the church. Certainly the references to him have the ring of truth (see Mark 15:43-46; Matt. 27:57-60; Luke 23:50-53; John 19:38-42). As Robert Stein argues, "The historicity of the empty tomb is supported by the fact that a specific tomb, which was known in Jerusalem as Joseph of Arimathea's tomb, was associated with the burial of Jesus."[29]

2. *Early Christian proclamation of the resurrection of Jesus in Jerusalem would have been psychologically and apologetically impossible without safe evidence of an empty tomb.* The psychological point is that the earliest disciples, good Jews and believers in bodily resurrection as they undoubtedly were, would have found it psychologically impossible to preach that Jesus had

---

28. This seems to be Carnley's position; see *The Structure of Resurrection Belief,* pp. 46-47.

29. Stein, "Was the Tomb Really Empty?" p. 11. See also Grant, *Jesus: An Historian's Review of the Gospels,* p. 175.

been raised from the dead and was alive had they had to contend with the presence of his corpse. Or, if this *were* possible, then, as William L. Craig argues, early Christian preaching about the resurrection would have taken on an entirely different character than it in fact did.[30] The apologetic point is that the apostles would have been quite unable to convince anyone that Jesus was alive had the body been available.

The counterargument that Jews had a taboo-like fear of contact with cadavers, and that this would have prevented anybody's checking the tomb, is feeble.[31] A few weeks after the crucifixion, Jerusalem was apparently seething with reports of Jesus' resurrection. The Jewish authorities, who wanted at all costs to stamp out the growing Christian movement, would have wasted no time checking the tomb, taboo or not. If worse came to worst, they could have convinced Gentile allies to do the job. Perhaps they would not even have had to exhume the corpse — simply pointing to the location of the tomb would have sufficed. But the Jewish polemic against the resurrection shows that they could do neither.

In other words, without safe and agreed-upon evidence of an empty tomb, the apostles' claims would have been subject to massive falsification by the simple presentation of the body. As I have already suggested, there is no convincing evidence that by the term *resurrection* the early Christians meant something akin to modern "spiritual" notions of resurrection that allow the continued presence of the corpse. We can infer, then, that the apostles' proclamation of the resurrection was successful precisely because (among other things) nobody was able to produce the corpse. The tomb was empty and the body nowhere to be found.

Of course it is possible to *imagine* scenarios that would account for their inability to produce the body. Perhaps Jesus was buried in an unmarked or even a mass grave by a Roman functionary and two underlings who three days later, without having told anyone how they had disposed of the body, were transferred back to Rome. Hans Küng has suggested that

> the disciples (returned from Galilee?), numbering no more than a
> hundred and twenty even according to Luke's possibly exaggerated

30. Craig, "The Historicity of the Empty Tomb of Jesus," p. 57.
31. E. Hirsch presents this counterargument; see Wolfhart Pannenberg, *Jesus — God and Man,* 2d ed., trans. Lewis L. Wilkins and Duane A. Priebe (Philadelphia: Westminster Press, 1968, 1977), pp. 100-101.

and idealized estimate, did not start at once to proclaim the risen Christ, but only several weeks after Jesus' death (the Lucan date for Pentecost assumes fifty days). All this made verification difficult, particularly since the proclamation can scarcely have created much of a stir at the beginning or called for public control in a city of perhaps twenty-five to thirty thousand inhabitants. The story of the empty tomb therefore must not be seen as the recognition of a fact.[32]

The implication here is that, contrary to the impression one receives in the early chapters of Acts, the Christian claim that Jesus had been raised did not become a matter of public controversy until perhaps years after the events immediately following the crucifixion and that by then the tomb in which Jesus was buried had been forgotten. In an exchange with D. M. MacKinnon, G. W. H. Lampe asserted along these lines that "even assuming that Jesus' grave was known, which is by no means certain, it seems very possible that neither party was interested in it, or regarded the truth of Easter as dependent on it, until long after the event: until the period of the controversies reflected in Matthew, which would not arise until the empty tomb had become important in Christian thought about the resurrection."[33] This argument is often combined with the theory mentioned above that the disciples fled to Galilee immediately after the crucifixion and did not return to Jerusalem till later, perhaps much later. Barnabas Lindars speculates that the empty-tomb story arose in connection with the unsuccessful attempt to locate the body of Jesus when, much later, the disciples returned to Jerusalem.[34]

But as we have already noted, the flight-to-Galilee aspect of this argument has been thoroughly discredited. Moreover, the story of Joseph of Arimathea's involvement in the burial of Jesus seems so strongly supported and inherently trustworthy that it renders the argument for an unknown tomb quite implausible. What point would there have been to the early church to claim that Jesus' tomb was empty if it was only made years after the events themselves? Such a claim would have been

---

32. Küng, *On Being a Christian,* pp. 364-65.

33. Lampe, in *The Resurrection: A Dialogue* (Philadelphia: Westminster Press, 1966), p. 53. See also R. R. Bater, "Toward a More Biblical View of the Resurrection," *Interpretation* 23 (January 1969): 50.

34. Lindars, "Jesus Risen," pp. 93-94. Carnley argues along these lines as well; see *The Structure of Resurrection Belief,* p. 55.

apologetically valueless by then; opponents could always object that the tomb was simply lost. So the church's affirmation that Jesus' tomb was empty has the earmarks of a claim made very early indeed. As to Küng's suggestion, it too presupposes the flight to Galilee immediately after the crucifixion. But it seems clear that the location of the tomb was established *before* the return to Galilee. Furthermore, a sensible reaction to Küng's scenario is to admit that the location of an important person's tomb might be lost in fifty years — but in fifty days? And if Luke is correct (why doubt him?), the apostles' preaching *did* create a public stir almost immediately, and the authorities became involved immediately as well. (It is hard to give a precise number of days or weeks, however, because Acts 2:43-47, which forms a bridge between the account of the events on the day of Pentecost and the account in chap. 3 of the activity of Peter and John that provoked the authorities, is vague on the question of how much time has passed.)

At any rate, the point is that such scenarios, while possible, are highly improbable, being grounded in such scant evidence. What evidence is available (e.g., the references to Joseph of Arimathea, the testimony of the women, the presupposition of the empty tomb in early anti-Christian polemic) supports the claim that the location of Jesus' tomb was known. And if it was known, then, given the evident success of the apostolic preaching, there must be a strong presumption that it was empty.

V

Is it important for Christians to affirm that Jesus' tomb was empty? Fuller thinks not. What is crucial, he says, is the affirmation "he is not here; God has raised him," not the empty tomb. "Whether the women's story was based on fact, or was the result of mistake or illusion, is in the last resort a matter of indifference."[35] I do not agree with Fuller on this point. In my opinion, the empty-tomb tradition has three important theological ramifications for Christians.

First, the empty-tomb tradition rules out all reductive theories of the resurrection (i.e., theories which explain the meaning of the Christian affirmation that "Jesus is risen" in terms that do not involve a dead man living again). The New Testament tradition of the empty tomb, in

35. Fuller, *The Formation of the Resurrection Narratives*, p. 179.

short, entails that resurrection is something that happened to Jesus rather than something that happened to the disciples.

Second, the empty-tomb tradition makes it clear that the person who was raised was the same person as the person who died. I do not claim that such an identification logically requires the empty tomb, for I disagree with those philosophers who hold that personal identity always requires bodily continuity. Still, it was the fact that Jesus was *bodily* raised, a truth underscored by the empty tomb, that made possible his recognition (albeit with some difficulty in some of the instances) by the disciples. This was a virtual sine qua non of the Christian message in order to rule out misidentifications of the Risen One — assertions that he was an angel, or some new divine being, or just a "subjective vision." The person who was raised had to be the same beloved Lord who had died.

Third, the empty-tomb tradition distinguishes the Christian view of resurrection from dualist, spiritualist theories of the immortality of the soul. To put the point emphatically, the Christian resurrection claim is an *empirical* claim: it entails the life after death of *living bodies* (although of a transformed sort) that can be seen and touched.[36] The raised will be living bodies that are materially related to their old bodies (just as, in Paul's simile, the seed is materially related to the plant that it produces). Christian resurrection does not provide a docetic or Platonic "escape" from bodily life. The resurrection does not mean that, much to our pleasant surprise, we human beings turn out to have an indestructible aspect that survives death. It means rather that death has been defeated by a miraculous and decisive intervention by God.

An even larger point follows: on the Christian view, the whole of creation is to be redeemed in Christ, not just its spiritual or "higher" aspects (see Rom. 8:19-23). Christianity does not follow the pattern of a Greek or Oriental dualism in asserting that the divine cannot come into relation with concrete corporeal reality.[37] All creaturely existence is to be reconciled to God — even corruptible physical bodies. Christianity says a decisive No to religions and philosophies that aim to liberate our true spiritual essence from its fleshly prison.

36. Thomas Torrance grasps this fact more clearly than anyone else; see *Space, Time, and Resurrection* (Grand Rapids: William B. Eerdmans, 1976). "It is the empty tomb that constitutes the essential empirical correlate in statements about the resurrection of Christ," he says (p. 141).

37. See Torrance, *Space, Time, and Resurrection*, p. 81.

VI

The proper conclusion, then, is that Jesus' tomb was empty. The arguments against it are not convincing, and the strongest of the arguments for it have not been successfully answered. The traditional Christian belief with which we began, that the tomb of Jesus was discovered empty on Easter morning, is one that Christians ought to continue to affirm. As Karl Barth wisely put it, "Christians do not believe in the empty tomb but in the living Christ," but that does not imply "that we can believe in the living Christ without believing in the empty tomb."[38]

Does this mean that we have proved the resurrection? Of course not. The empty tomb, by itself, does not prove the resurrection. It is a necessary but not sufficient condition for the bodily resurrection of Jesus: if the tomb was not empty, Jesus was not bodily raised; but the empty tomb itself does not prove that Jesus *was* bodily raised. As in the days after Pentecost, the crucial question today is *why* the tomb was empty. Perhaps the tomb was empty because of quite natural circumstances that are now unknown. That option is always available to the skeptic. My own view is that the tomb was empty because God miraculously raised its occupant from the dead.

---

38. Barth, quoted by O'Collins in *The Resurrection of Jesus Christ*, p. 97.

5

General Resurrection and Dualism

I

One traditional Christian view of survival of death runs, in outline form, something like this: On some future day all the dead will be bodily raised, both the righteous and the unrighteous alike, to be judged by God; and the guarantee and model of the general resurrection (i.e., the raising of the dead in the last days) is the already accomplished resurrection of Jesus Christ from the dead.

My aim in this chapter is to explain and defend this basic view of resurrection. There are many ways in which it might be understood, of course, and perhaps more than one is coherent and even plausible from a Christian point of view. I shall defend one particular interpretation of the theory — an interpretation advocated by many of the Church Fathers, especially second-century Fathers, as well as by Augustine and Aquinas.

After a brief introduction to the issues, I will discuss in turn what I take to be the three most important claims made in the version of the theory that I wish to defend. Then I will consider one typical aspect of the traditional theory that has important philosophical as well as theological ramifications — namely, the notion that our resurrection bodies will consist of the same matter as do our present earthly bodies. Finally, since the version of the theory that I wish to defend envisions a period of existence in a disembodied state, I will defend the theory against some of the arguments of contemporary philosophers who find the very notion of disembodied existence incoherent.

II

There are several ways in which the basic concept of resurrection sketched in the opening paragraph can be fleshed out. One option is to understand the nature of the human person, and hence the nature of resurrection, in a basically materialist or physicalist way. Perhaps human beings are essentially material objects; perhaps some version of identity theory or functionalism is true. This option is not without its attractions; indeed, there was a time when I would have accepted it. But since it is no longer my preferred way of defending the notion of resurrection, I am going to defer discussion of it to another context, in Chapter 6.

Another option is to collapse talk of resurrection into talk of the immortality of the soul. A closely related strategy (and, as we have seen, a popular one in recent theology) is to interpret resurrection in a spiritual rather than bodily sense (if this in the end differs significantly from immortality). Such a view will doubtless be based on some version of mind-body (or soul-body) dualism. (People who endorse "spiritual" views of the resurrection often insist that they are talking about the resurrection of *the whole person,* but somehow the body seems typically to be left out.) Let us define dualism as the doctrine which says (1) that human beings consist of both material bodies and immaterial souls and (2) that the soul is the essence of the person (the real you is your soul, not your body). It then can be added that the body corrupts at death and eventually ceases to exist, but the soul is essentially immortal.

It is surprising (to me at least) that so many twentieth-century Christian thinkers are tempted toward some such notion as this. For it is quite clear, in both Scripture and tradition, that classical dualism is not the Christian position. For one thing, the biblical view is not that the soul is the essence of the person and is only temporarily housed or even imprisoned in a body; human beings seem rather to be understood in Scripture as psycho-physical entities, as unities of body and soul. For another, the notion that the body is essentially evil and must be escaped from (an idea often associated with versions of classical dualism) was condemned by virtually every orthodox Christian thinker who discussed death and resurrection in the first two hundred years after the apostolic age. The Christian idea is rather that the body was created by God and is good; the whole person, body and soul alike, is what needs to be saved. Finally, as I have already suggested, the biblical notion is not that we survive death because immortality is simply a natural property of souls; if we survive death, it is because God miraculously gives us life. Apart from God's intervention, death would mean annihilation for us. Thus Irenaeus says, "Our survival forever comes from his greatness, not from our nature" (*Against Heresies,* 5.3.2).

It would be interesting to explore this option further, and especially to consider why so many recent and contemporary Christian theologians are drawn to it, how they might distinguish "spiritual resurrection" from immortality of the soul, and how they might defend the theory against criticisms such as those just noted, but this would take us too far afield. As I have suggested, my aim here is to explore and defend a third way of understanding the traditional Christian notion of resurrection, a theory held in one form or another by virtually all (but not quite all) of the Church Fathers who discussed resurrection.[1] I will call this theory "temporary disembodiment."

This theory of resurrection is based on a view of human nature which says that human beings are essentially material bodies *and* immaterial souls; the soul is separable from the body, but neither body nor soul alone (i.e., without the other) constitutes a complete human being. Thus Pseudo-Justin asks,

> Is the soul by itself man? No; but the soul of man. Would the body be called man? No, but it is called the body of man. If, then, neither of these is by itself man, but that which is made up of the two together is called man, and God has called *man* to life and resurrection, He has called not a part, but the whole, which is the soul and the body. (*On the Resurrection,* chap. 8)

What this theory says, then, is that human beings are typically and normally psycho-physical beings, that the soul can exist for a time apart from the body and retain personal identity, but that this disembodied existence is only temporary and constitutes a radically attenuated and incomplete form of human existence.

I call the theory temporary disembodiment because it envisions the following scenario: We human beings are born, live for a time as psycho-physical beings, and then die. After death we exist in an incomplete state as immaterial souls. Some time later in the eschaton, God

1. See Harry A. Wolfson, "Immortality and Resurrection in the Philosophy of the Church Fathers," in *Immortality and Resurrection,* ed. Krister Stendahl (New York: Macmillan, 1965), pp. 64-72. See also Lynn Boliek, *The Resurrection of the Flesh* (Grand Rapids: William B. Eerdmans, 1962).

miraculously raises our bodies from the ground, transforms them into "glorified bodies," and reunites them with our souls, thus making us complete and whole again.

Belief in temporary disembodiment has several theological and philosophical advantages. For one thing, many Christian thinkers have seen a comfortable fit between it and the view of human nature expressed in the Bible, the Pauline writings particularly. The apostle seems to hold that human beings consist of both material bodies and immaterial souls, that the body is not merely an adornment or drape for the soul but that it is indeed good, since it can be the temple of the Holy Spirit (1 Cor. 3:16-17; 6:19-20), and that the soul is in some sense separable from the body (2 Cor. 5:6-8; 12:2-3). What the body does is provide the soul with a vehicle for action in the world, for the expression of intentions and desires; and the soul provides the body with animation and direction.[2]

For another thing, the theory seems to offer a tidy way to reconcile the traditional view that the general resurrection does not occur until the eschaton with Jesus' statement to the good thief on the cross, "*Today* you will be with me in Paradise" (Luke 23:43). The explanation (which naturally goes far beyond Jesus' simple statement) is as follows: the thief would be with Jesus in paradise that very day in the form of a disembodied soul, only to be raised bodily much later. The theory may also help resolve a similar tension that is sometimes said to exist in Pauline thought, with texts such as 1 Corinthians 15 and 1 Thessalonians 4 pointing toward the idea of a future, eschatological resurrection (with those who die beforehand existing until then in a kind of bodiless sleep) and texts such as 2 Corinthians 5:8 and Philippians 1:23 suggesting the idea that death for the Christian is an immediate gain since one is immediately at home with the Lord. Of course, this would leave unresolved the issue of how one could simultaneously be both "at home with the Lord" and "in an incomplete state."

Finally, this theory would seem to be more helpful than others with regard to resolving the problem of personal identity after death. At least this theory does not introduce the difficulty of a temporal gap in the existence of persons — although it does assume a gap in their existence as complete, unified persons. (For this reason, it will be necessary to explore the philosophical problem of personal identity in much

---

2. See Robert H. Gundry, *Soma in Biblical Theology: With Emphasis on Pauline Anthropology* (Cambridge: Cambridge University Press, 1976), p. 159.

more detail in Chap. 6, where I defend a "gap-inclusive" notion of resurrection.) In temporary disembodiment there is no moment subsequent to our births in which you and I simply do not exist: we exist either as whole persons (soul-bodies) or as mere souls at every moment until eternity.

III

There are three main aspects of temporary disembodiment that require discussion both from a philosophical and from a theological perspective. Let me now consider them in turn. The first is the notion that after death the soul exists for a time (i.e., until the resurrection) in an intermediate state without the body. The second is the notion that at the time of the parousia the body will be raised from the ground and reunited with the soul. And the third is the notion that the body will then be transformed into what is called a "glorified body."

The first main claim of temporary disembodiment, then, is that after death the soul temporarily exists without the body. This differs from physicalist concepts of resurrection (of which I have more to say in Chap. 6), which hold that the person does not exist at all in the period between death and resurrection. Temporary disembodiment need not be based on classical dualism as defined earlier, but it is based on one tenet of classical dualism — namely, the claim that human beings consist (or in this case at least normally consist) of both material bodies and immaterial souls. (The soul is not said to be the essence of the person, however, and is said to survive death not because immortality is one of its natural properties but because God causes it to survive death.)[3]

Almost all Christians believe that people exist in some kind of interim state between death and resurrection, but beyond this point there are many theological differences. Some, for example, think of the interim state as purgatorial in nature, and others do not. Some hold that spiritual change (e.g., repentance) is possible during the interim period, and others do not. Some think the soul rests or sleeps, that it is not active or conscious during the interim period, and others do not. It is not part of my purpose to express an opinion on either of the first two items of disagreement. However, on the third I will argue that the soul is conscious

3. See Wolfson, "Immortality and Resurrection in the Philosophy of the Church Fathers," pp. 56-60, 63-64.

in the interim state. The biblical metaphor of sleep (Luke 8:52; 1 Cor. 15:20) is not to be taken as a literal description. If that were the case, it would be difficult to make sense of the notion of a disembodied thing being in the presence of God ("Today you will be with me in Paradise"). If a soul is neither physically present nor in any sense aware of the presence of God, in what sense can it be said to be in his presence?[4] Furthermore, since sleeping seems essentially to be a bodily activity, the claim that a soul sleeps at the very least needs considerable explanation.

The state of being without a body is an abnormal state of the human person. This points to one of the clear differences between temporary disembodiment and immortality of the soul, for the second doctrine (at least in versions of it influenced by Plato) entails that disembodiment is the true or proper or ideal state of the human person. On the theory we are considering, however, the claim is that a disembodied soul lacks many of the properties and abilities that are normal for and proper to human persons. Disembodied existence is a kind of minimal existence.

Which properties typical of embodied human persons will disembodied souls have and which will they lack? Clearly they will lack those properties that essentially involve corporeality. They will not be able to experience bodily pains and pleasures. They will not be able to perceive their surroundings (using the spatial word "surroundings" in a stretched sense) — at least not in the ways in which we perceive our surroundings (i.e., through the eyes, ears, etc.). They will not be able to engage in bodily activities. Taking a walk, getting dressed, playing catch — these sorts of activities will be impossible.

But if by the word "soul" we mean in part the constellation of those human activities that would typically be classified as "mental," then the claim that our souls survive death entails the claim that our mental abilities and properties survive death. This means that human persons in the interim state can be said to have experiences, beliefs, wishes, knowledge, memory, inner (rather than bodily) feelings, thoughts, language (assuming memory of earthly existence) — in short, much of

---

4. It does not seem to make sense to speak of some disembodied thing x being "in the presence of" some other thing y, where "in the presence of" means "in the spatial vicinity of." The notion could be coherently understood, however, as something like "being acutely aware of and sensitive to." But since this sense, too, is ruled out by the concept of spiritual sleep, I am unable to provide a sensible construal of the notion of a disembodied and unconscious person being in the presence of God.

what makes up what we call personality. H. H. Price, in his classic article "Survival and the Idea of 'Another World,'" argues convincingly that disembodied souls can also be aware of each other's existence, can communicate with each other telepathically, and can have dreamlike (rather than bodily) perceptions of their world.[5]

But Aquinas argues that the disembodied existence of the person in the interim state is so deficient that attainment of ultimate happiness is impossible. No one in whom some perfection is lacking is ultimately happy, for in such a state there will always be unfulfilled desires. It is contrary to the nature of the soul to be without the body, Aquinas says, and he takes this to mean both that the disembodied state must only be temporary and that the true bliss of the human person is only attained after reembodiment (i.e., in the general resurrection). "Man cannot achieve his ultimate happiness," he says, "unless the soul be once again united to the body."[6]

IV

The second main claim of the theory that I am calling temporary disembodiment is that at the general resurrection the body will be raised from the ground and reunited with the soul. As the second-century writer Athenagoras says, "There must certainly be a resurrection of bodies whether dead or even quite corrupted, and the same men as before must come to be again. The law of nature appoints an end . . . for those very same men who lived in a previous existence, and it is impossible for the same men to come together again if the same bodies are not given back to the same souls. Now the same soul cannot recover the same body in any other way than by resurrection."[7]

As Athenagoras stresses, the idea is that each person's selfsame body will be raised; it will not be a different and brand-new body but

5. Price, "Survival and the Idea of 'Another World,'" in *Language, Metaphysics, and Death*, ed. John Donnelly (New York: Fordham University Press, 1978), pp. 176-95. I do not wish to commit myself entirely to Price's theory; among others, John Hick has detected difficulties in it (see *Death and Eternal Life* [New York: Harper & Row, 1976], pp. 265-77). But Price's main point — that disembodied survival of death is possible — seems to me correct.

6. Aquinas, *Summa Contra Gentiles*, 4.79.11.

7. Athenagoras, *Embassy for Christians and the Resurrection of the Dead*, trans. Joseph H. Crehan (London: Longmans, Green, 1956), pp. 115-16.

the old body. Echoing the argument of very many of the Fathers, Aquinas notes the reason for this: "If the body of the man who rises is not to be composed of the flesh and bones which now compose it, the man who rises will not be numerically the same man."[8] Furthermore, in the resurrection there will be only one soul per body and only one body per soul. As Augustine puts it, "Each single soul shall possess its own body."[9] Were this not the case — that is, if souls were to split and animate more than one body or if one body were to be animated by more than one soul — the problem of personal identity would be unsolvable, and the Christian hope that we will live after death would be incoherent.

The Fathers and Scholastics insisted, then, that both body and soul must be present or else the person does not exist, or at least does not exist fully or completely or in a state capable of ultimate happiness. "A man cannot be said to exist as such when the body is dissolved or completely scattered," says Athenagoras, "even though the soul remain by itself."[10] And Aquinas agrees: "My soul is not I, and if only souls are saved I am not saved, nor is any man."[11] Thus the Christian hope of survival is not merely the hope that our souls will survive death (although it is significant that they will do so in a temporarily disembodied form) but rather the hope that one day God will miraculously raise our bodies and reunite them with our souls.

What is it, then, that guarantees personal identity in the resurrection? What is it that ensures that it will really be *us* in the kingdom of God and not, say, clever replicas of us? Aquinas argues as follows: since human beings consist of bodies and souls, and since both souls and the matter of which our bodies consist survive death, personal identity is secured when God collects the scattered matter, miraculously reconstitutes it a human body, and reunites it with the soul.[12] This seems to me to be a powerful argument. If God one day succeeds in doing these very things, personal identity will be secure. It will be us and not our replicas who will be the denizens of the kingdom of God.

8. Aquinas, *Summa Contra Gentiles*, 4.84.7.

9. Augustine, *The Enchiridion on Faith, Hope, and Love,* ed. Henry Paolucci (Chicago: Henry Regnery, 1961), 87.

10. Athenagoras, *Embassy for Christians and the Resurrection of the Dead,* p. 115.

11. Aquinas, quoted by P. T. Geach in *God and the Soul* (London: Routledge & Kegan Paul, 1969), p. 22.

12. Aquinas, *Summa Contra Gentiles,* 4.81.

V

The third main claim of temporary disembodiment is that in the resurrection the old body will be transformed into a "glorified body" with certain quite new properties. In order to explain this claim, let me briefly review some points I made in Chapter 3. The notion that resurrected persons will have glorified bodies is based primarily on Paul's discussion of the resurrection in 1 Corinthians 15, and secondarily on the unusual properties that the risen Jesus is depicted as having in some of the accounts of the resurrection appearances (e.g., the apparent ability of the risen Jesus in John 20 to enter a room despite the fact that the doors were locked). In 1 Corinthians 15, Paul notes that some ask how the dead are raised and what kind of body they will have. He answers that their new "glorified" or "spiritual" bodies *(soma pneumatikon)* will be a transformation of the old bodies rather than a *de novo* creation (much as a stalk of grain is a transformation of a seed of grain — it exists because of changes that have occurred in the seed and can be considered a new state of the grain). Further, Paul argues, while the old or natural body is physical, perishable, mortal, and sown in weakness and dishonor, the glorified body is spiritual, imperishable, immortal, and sown in strength and honor. The first body is in the image of the man of dust; the second body is in the image of the man of heaven.

As I suggest in Chapter 3, the term "spiritual body" might be misleading; it should not be taken as a denial of corporeality or as a last-minute capitulation to some version of the immortality of the soul as opposed to bodily resurrection. By this term, Paul means not a body whose stuff or matter is spiritual (whatever that might mean) or an immaterial existence of some sort; rather, he means a body that is fully obedient to and dominated by the Holy Spirit. "Flesh and blood cannot inherit the kingdom of God," says Paul (1 Cor. 15:50). What enters the kingdom of heaven, then, is not this present weak and mortal body of flesh and blood but the new glorified body. This new body is a physical body (Paul's use of the word *soma* implies as much),[13] and it is materially related to the old body (taking seriously Paul's simile of the seed), but

13. See Gundry, *Soma in Biblical Theology*, pp. 164ff. For more on this and other points made in this paragraph, see also C. F. D. Moule, "St. Paul and Dualism: The Pauline Concept of Resurrection," *New Testament Studies* 12 (January 1966): 106-23; and Ronald J. Sider, "The Pauline Conception of the Resurrection Body in I Corinthians XV,35-54," *New Testament Studies* 21 (April 1975): 428-39.

is a body transformed in such ways as make it fit to live in God's presence. If by the term "physical object" we mean an entity that has spatio-temporal location and is capable of being empirically measured, tested, or observed in some sense, then my argument is that the new body of which Paul speaks is a physical object.

Temporary disembodiment, then, entails that human souls can animate both normal earthly bodies and glorified resurrection bodies. Continuity between the two bodies is provided by the presence of both the same soul and the same matter in both bodies. "Nor does the earthly material out of which men's mortal bodies are created ever perish," says Augustine; "but though it may crumble into dust and ashes, or be dissolved into vapors and exhalations, though it may be transformed into the substance of other bodies, or dispersed into the elements, though it should become food for beasts or men, and be changed into their flesh, it returns in a moment of time to that human soul which animated it at the first and which caused it to become man, and to live and grow."[14] The matter of our present bodies may be arranged differently in the resurrection, he says, but the matter will be restored.

Many of the theologians of the early church and of the medieval period also stressed the perfection of the glorified body. They maintained that it will be free of every bodily defect. It will be fully controlled by the spirit of God and thus immune to evil. It will not suffer. It will not grow old or die. It will have "agility" — which, as noted above, is an ability like that of the risen Jesus to come and go at will, unimpeded by things like walls and doors. It will exist in a state of fulfilled desire. It will need no material food or drink but will be nourished by the elements of the eucharist.[15]

VI

Is the picture of resurrection just presented coherent? Is it plausible? The main objections that have been raised against it in recent philosophy revolve around the problem of personal identity. Some philosophers argue that, so far as disembodied existence is concerned, this problem cannot be solved. They contend that if it is some immaterial aspect of me that

14. Augustine, *The Enchiridion on Faith, Hope, and Love*, 88.
15. See Irenaeus, *Against Heresies*, 5.2.3; Augustine, *The Enchiridion on Faith, Hope, and Love*, 91; Aquinas, *Summa Contra Gentiles*, 4.83-87.

survives death, it will not be me that survives death. Since the view of survival of death that I am defending essentially involves a period of disembodied existence, I will try to defend the view against these sorts of objections. But a prior problem must be considered first — whether the Fathers and Scholastics were correct in their strong claim (I will call this claim "the Patristic theory") that if it is to be me in the kingdom of God, the very matter of my original earthly body must be raised. After discussing this point, I proceed to consider the arguments of those philosophers who oppose the notion of disembodied existence because of the problem of personal identity.

Why did Aquinas and the Fathers who influenced him insist that the same matter that constituted my old body must be raised? Let us see if we can construct an argument on their behalf. Like many arguments in the area of personal identity, it involves a puzzle case. Suppose that I own a defective personal computer which I rashly decide to try to repair myself. Having taken it apart (there are now, say, sixty separate computer components scattered on my workbench), I find that I am unable to repair it. I call the outlet that sold me the computer, and the manager suggests I simply bring all sixty components to the store for repair. I do so, but through a horrible series of misunderstandings and errors, the sixty pieces of the computer are then sent to sixty different addresses around the country. That constitutes the heart of my story, but there are two separate endings to it. *Ending number one:* It takes three years for everything to be sorted out, for the pieces to be located and collected in one place, for the repairs to be made, and for the parts to be reassembled and restored, in full working order, to my desk. *Ending number two:* After three years of trying in vain to locate and collect the scattered pieces, the manager gives up, collects sixty similar parts, assembles them, and the resulting computer ends up on my desk.

I do not wish to raise the interesting question of whether my computer *existed* during the three-year period. I am concerned only with the related question of whether the computer now located on my desk is *the same* computer as the one that was there three years ago. So far as ending number one is concerned, it seems most natural to affirm that the computer I now possess is indeed the same computer as the one that I possessed before. The computer may or may not have had a gap in its existence (i.e., a period when it did not exist), but it seems clear that identity has been preserved here. So far as ending number two is concerned, it seems most natural to deny that the computer I now possess is the same computer as the one that I possessed before. Furthermore, we would doubtless insist on this denial even if all of the sixty components the manager used to construct the computer I now possess were qualitatively indistinguishable from the sixty old components. What I now have is a qualitatively similar but numerically different computer.

Now I doubt that the Church Fathers often pondered personal identity test cases involving computers, and it is obvious that personal computers are different from human beings in many striking ways. But it was perhaps *the sort* of insight arrived at above that led them to take the strong stand that they took on the resurrection. Only if God reassembles the very particles of which my body once consisted will it be me who is raised. If other particles are used, the result will be what we would call a replica of me rather than me.

But despite the above argument, does it still not seem that Aquinas and the Fathers in their strong stand have made the solution to the problem of personal identity more difficult than it need be? Even granting the point that some of the particles of the matter of which our bodies consist will endure for the requisite number of years, why insist that God must re-collect it — that very matter — in the resurrection? For surely in the interim state it will be us (and not soul-like replicas of us) who will exist without any body at all; surely the Fathers and Scholastics insist on this much. Thus the presence of the soul alone must suffice for personal identity; what philosophers call the memory criterion (which is typically taken to include not just memory but all one's "mental" characteristics and properties) must suffice by itself. Identity of memory, personality, and other "mental" aspects of the person are sufficient conditions of personal identity. To admit this much is not necessarily to abandon the traditional notion that the soul is not the whole person and that the whole person must be raised; it is merely to insist that the existence of my soul entails *my* existence. Otherwise talk of my existence in the interim state is meaningless.

I do not claim that the Patristic theory is logically inconsistent. It is possible coherently to hold that when I die my soul will be me during the interim period but that it will no longer be me if my soul in the eschaton animates a body consisting of totally new matter, even if the new body is qualitatively indistinguishable from the old one. Perhaps an essential property of my soul is that it can animate only *this* body — where "this body" means in part a body consisting of *these* particles. So if *per impossibile* my soul were to animate a different body, the result would not be me. Or perhaps every configuration of particles that can possibly constitute a human body has as one of its essential properties that it can be animated by one and only one particular soul. But while logically consistent, this view seems to me exceedingly difficult to defend.

So far as the problem of personal identity is concerned, it is accordingly not easy to see why a defender of temporary disembodiment could not dispense with all talk of God one day re-collecting the molecules, atoms, quarks, or whatever of our bodies. Perhaps human beings in this regard are unlike computers. Why not say that God can award us brand-new bodies materially quite unrelated to (although qualitatively similar to) the old ones? If the existence of the soul is sufficient for personal identity, and if the human soul never at any moment subsequent to its creation fails to exist, it will be us who exist after the resurrection in the kingdom of God whether or not our old bodies are reconstituted.

Furthermore, it needs to be noted here that identity of particles of bodily matter does not seem necessary to preserve the identity of an ordinary human person even during the course of a lifetime. As Frank Dilley notes, "We constantly replace our atoms over time and there is no reason to think that an eighty year old person has even a single atom in common with the newborn babe. If a person maintains personal identity over a process of total atom-by-atom replacement, it is difficult to see why such identity would not be preserved through a sudden replacement of all the atoms at once."[16]

Dilley's argument seems plausible, but we should notice that it does not necessarily follow. Perhaps gradual replacement of all the individual atoms of a human body is consistent with personal identity while all-at-once replacement of them is not. Perhaps some strong sort of material continuity is needed. One of the difficulties encountered by philosophers who discuss personal identity is that different persons' intuitions run in different directions. For example, in a slightly different connection, Peter van Inwagen argues that sameness of person requires both (1) sameness of atoms and (2) regular and natural causal relationships between those atoms, and so if God were now to try to raise Napoleon Bonaparte from the dead by omnisciently locating the atoms of which his body once consisted and miraculously reassembling them, the result would not be Napoleon.[17] I do not agree with van Inwagen here; I see no convincing

16. Dilley, "Resurrection and the 'Replica Objection,'" *Religious Studies* 19 (December 1983): 462.

17. Van Inwagen, "The Possibility of Resurrection," *International Journal for Philosophy of Religion* 9 (1978): 119.

reason for his second stipulation. I raise the point merely to show that van Inwagen's intuitions run in a different direction than Dilley's. Since Dilley's case of sudden-replacement-of-all-the-atoms-at-once seems to constitute something *un*natural and *ir*regular, van Inwagen would doubtless deny that in such cases personal identity would be preserved.

What if there were, so to speak, some natural way of reassembling persons out of totally new matter? Derek Parfit considers in detail a series of test cases involving an imagined teletransporter, a machine that is designed to send a person to distant places like Mars by (1) recording the exact state of all the body's cells (including those of the brain), (2) destroying the body and brain, and (3) transmitting the information at the speed of light to Mars, where (4) a replicator creates out of new matter a body and brain exactly like the old one.[18] Suppose Parfit enters the machine and is "teletransported to Mars." Would the resulting Parfit-like person on Mars *be* Parfit? Here again our intuitions might differ, even in this relatively simple case (i.e., apart from considerations of such complications as the original Parfit somehow surviving on earth or fifteen Parfit-like persons somehow appearing on Mars). Those who, like the Church Fathers and Aquinas, hold to some strong requirement about material continuity will deny that it is Parfit. Those who stress the memory criterion are free to affirm that Parfit is now on Mars, as are those (e.g., John Hick) who believe that identity is exact similarity plus uniqueness. Those who think that identity is exact similarity plus the right kind of causal origin or causal ancestry might go either way, depending on whether they think the operation of a teletransporter constitutes an appropriate sort of causal origin for the Parfit-like person on Mars.

The moral of the story thus far is that the Fathers and Aquinas may be right in what they say about resurrection, but it is not clear that they are right. Their position may be consistent, but it does seem implausible to hold both (1) that it will be me in the interim period without any body at all (i.e., the presence of my soul is sufficient for personal identity) and (2) that it will not be me in the eschaton, despite the presence of my soul, if the body that my soul then animates consists of new matter. There may be other (perhaps theological) reasons why we

---

18. Parfit, *Reasons and Persons* (Oxford: Oxford University Press, 1986), pp. 199-200. I mention here only the most simple of the test cases involving teletransportation that Parfit discusses. Nor will I consider in this chapter what I take to be the central theses of Part 3 of his book.

should hold that it must be the very matter of our old bodies that is to be raised, but so far as the problem of personal identity is concerned, a strong case can be made that it will not matter.

Recent and contemporary Christian theologians who discuss resurrection seem for the most part to have departed from the Patristic theory. The more common thesis is that our glorified bodies will be wholly different bodies, not necessarily consisting of any of the old matter at all. As John Hick, an articulate spokesperson for this new point of view, says, "What has become a widely accepted view in modern times holds that the resurrection body is a new and different body given by God, but expressing the personality within its new environment as the physical body expressed it in the earthly environment. The physical frame decays or is burned, disintegrating and being dispersed into the ground or the air, but God re-embodies the personality elsewhere."[19] Frequently connected with this view is an exegetical claim — namely, that by the term "the body" St. Paul meant not the physical organism but rather something akin to "the whole personality." What will be raised from the dead, then, is not the old body but rather the *person,* and in being raised the person will be given a brand-new body by God.

It is not hard to see why such a view has come to be widely adopted. (1) As noted above, personal identity does not seem to require the resurrection of the same matter of which the old body consisted. (2) The Patristic theory seems to many contemporary Christians to be scientifically outmoded and difficult to believe; the idea that in order to raise me God must one day cast about, locate, and collect the atoms of which my earthly body once consisted seems to many people absurd. (3) Many such theologians want to hold in any case that the kingdom of God is not spatially related to our present world, that it exists in a space all its own, and so it can contain no material from this spatio-temporal manifold.

I am unable to locate any philosophical or logical difficulties in the "modern" theory. It seems to me a possible Christian view of resurrection, and it can fit smoothly with the other aspects of the traditional notion that I am calling temporary disembodiment. Are there any theological reasons, then, for a Christian to retain the old theory and believe that the matter of our old bodies will be raised? Two points should be made here. The first is that the most natural reading of 1 Corinthians 15 is along the lines of the Patristic theory. Paul seems to be suggesting there that the old body *becomes* or *changes into* (rather than

19. Hick, *Death and Eternal Life,* p. 186.

is replaced by) the new body, just as a seed becomes or changes into a plant. Thus, just as there is material continuity between the seed and the plant, so there will be material continuity between the old body and the new; the plant is *a new form of* the seed. Note also Paul's use in verses 42 and 43 of the expression "*It* is sown . . . *it* is raised . . . ," as if the one thing (a human body) is at one time in a certain state and at a later time in another state (see also vv. 53, 54).[20] Furthermore, as noted already, Paul's use of the term *soma* reveals that what he had in mind was a body; it is simply a lexical mistake to say that he merely meant "the whole personality" or some such thing.[21]

The second point has to do with the difficulty that God will face in collecting the atoms, quarks, or whatever fundamental particles human bodies consist of. This may well be the oldest philosophical objection ever raised against the Christian notion of resurrection. Virtually every one of the Fathers who discussed resurrection tried to answer it, as did Aquinas. Such scenarios as this were suggested: What if a Christian dies at sea and his body is eaten by various fishes who then scatter to the seven seas? How can God later resurrect that body? Or what if another Christian is eaten by cannibals, so that some of the material of her body becomes the material of their bodies? And suppose God later wants to raise all of them from the dead, cannibals and Christian alike. Who gets what particles? How does God decide?

The move made by virtually all of the Fathers in response to this objection is to appeal to omnipotence. You and I might not be able to locate and reconstitute the relevant atoms of someone's body, especially after many years or even centuries have passed, but God can do this very thing. And as long as (1) the basic constituents of matter (e.g., atoms) endure through time (as contemporary physical theory says they normally do) and (2) it is merely a matter of God locating and collecting the relevant constituents, I believe the Fathers were right. An omnipotent being could do that.

But with the cannibalism case and other imaginable cases in which God must decide which constituent parts shared at different times by two

---

20. Commenting on Paul's argument in 1 Corinthians 15:53, Tertullian says, "when he says '*this* corruptible' and '*this* mortal,' he utters the words while touching the surface of his own body" (*On the Resurrection of the Flesh*, 51).

21. Gundry makes this point convincingly; see *Soma in Biblical Theology*, p. 186. See also Sider, "The Pauline Conception of the Resurrection Body in I Corinthians XV,35-54," pp. 429-38; and Bruce Reichenbach, "On Disembodied Resurrection Persons: A Reply," *Religious Studies* 18 (June 1982): 227.

(or even two thousand) separate persons go where, the matter is more serious. The problem does not seem insoluble, but much more needs to be said. Perhaps some constituent parts of human bodies are essential to those bodies and some are not. That is, perhaps God will only need to collect the essential parts of our bodies and use them, so to speak, as building blocks around which to reconstruct our new bodies. And perhaps omnipotence must accordingly guarantee that no essential part of one person's earthly body is ever a constituent part, or an essential constituent part, of someone else's body. If these stipulations or ones like them are followed (e.g., Augustine's idea that atoms will be raised in that human body in which they *first* appeared),[22] it still seems that the Fathers were correct — an omnipotent being will be able to raise us from the ground.

Reacting against these and similar patristic appeals to omnipotence in order to rationalize resurrection, Paul Badham argues as follows:

> Given belief in a once-for-all act of creation on the pattern of Genesis 1, then the act of resurrection cannot be difficult for an all-powerful God. Given that God made the first man by direct action, the restoration of a decomposed man becomes an easy task. Given that man consists of particles, it is easy to believe that omnipotence could reassemble these particles. But today each of these premises has lost its validity, and hence the conclusions drawn from them cannot stand. That man as a species is part of a slowly evolving process of life and in every respect continuous with the processes of nature from which he has emerged does not provide a congenial background for the idea of resurrection. Further, our increasing knowledge of the incredible complexity and constant changing of our physical components makes it difficult to see the resurrection as simply involving the re-collection of our physical particles. We are not composed of building bricks but of constantly changing living matter.[23]

It is not easy to see exactly what Badham is getting at with these arguments. Of course he is right that human bodies are incredibly

---

22. Augustine, *The Enchiridion on Faith, Hope, and Love*, 88. See also *The City of God*, 22.20.

23. Badham, *Christian Beliefs about Life after Death* (London: Macmillan Press, 1976), p. 50. Despite my disagreement with him on this point, I must admit that Badham does successfully rebut several unconvincing patristic arguments about bodily resurrection.

complex and that they consist of constantly changing living matter. But does this deny — or indeed does contemporary physics deny — the idea that our bodies consist of particles? I think not. Furthermore, it is hard to see how a commitment to evolutionary theory (a commitment I make) undercuts the ability of an omnipotent being to raise human beings from the dead. Perhaps it does undercut the sort of simplistic argument that we occasionally find in the Fathers to the effect that since God already did the difficult job of creating human beings *de novo* by assembling the particles of their bodies, God can also do the far easier job of reassembling them in the eschaton.[24] But surely claims about what is easy and what is hard for an omnipotent being to do are suspect anyway. The point that the Fathers were making is that whatever difficulties resurrection presents can be overcome by an omnipotent being. I believe that point still stands and is not rendered improbable or implausible by evolution.

VII

Several philosophers have argued in recent years that the concept of disembodied existence is incoherent or at least that no disembodied thing can be identified with some previously existing human person. Antony Flew, Bernard Williams, D. Z. Phillips, Terence Penelhum, and John Perry, among others, have jointly presented what might be called the standard arguments against survival of death in disembodied form.[25] P. T. Geach has similarly argued against the notion of *permanent* disembodied existence, though he supports something like the theory that I am calling temporary disembodiment.[26] Now, I am inclined to hold that the standard arguments have been successfully answered by defenders of disem-

---

24. See, e.g., Irenaeus, *Against Heresies*, 5.3.2; and Tertullian, *On the Resurrection of the Flesh*, 11.

25. For Flew's argument, see "Immortality," in *The Encyclopedia of Philosophy*, ed. Paul Edwards (New York: Macmillan, 1967); the articles collected in Part III of *The Presumption of Atheism and Other Essays* (London: Elek/Pemberton, 1976); and *The Logic of Mortality* (Oxford: Basil Blackwell, 1987). For Williams's argument, see *Problems of the Self* (Cambridge: Cambridge University Press, 1973). For Phillips's argument, see *Death and Immortality* (New York: St. Martin's Press, 1970). For Penelhum's argument, see *Survival and Disembodied Existence* (New York: Humanities Press, 1970). For Perry's argument, see *A Dialogue on Personal Identity and Immortality* (Indianapolis: Hackett, 1978).

26. See Geach, *God and the Soul*, pp. 17-29.

bodied existence;[27] that is to say, I believe the notion of survival of death (and even permanent survival of death) in disembodied form is intelligible and logically possible. Furthermore, one result of recent discussion of the puzzle cases in the area of personal identity is that many philosophers are now prepared to defend the notion that we can imagine cases in which the memory criterion will suffice by itself. But since the arguments of Flew, Williams, Phillips, and Penelhum have been discussed thoroughly in the journals, let me instead focus on the case John Perry makes in his excellent little book *A Dialogue on Personal Identity and Immortality.*

Perry seems, in this dialogue, to speak primarily through the character of Gretchen Weirob, a mortally injured but still lucid philosopher who does not believe in life after death. Weirob seems to present three main arguments against the conceivability or possibility of survival of death. All are versions of arguments that we find elsewhere in the literature, but the virtue of Perry's work is that they are presented with great clarity and vividness. Perry's first argument has to do with the soul and personal identity, the second concerns memory and personality identity, and the third is an argument about the possibility of duplication of persons.

The first argument says that immaterial and thus unobservable souls can have nothing to do with establishing personal identity. Personal identity does not consist in sameness of soul, for if it did, we would never know who we are or who others are. Since souls are not observable, no thesis having to do with souls is testable (not even the thesis, "My soul is I"). So I cannot know whether other human beings have souls, or even whether I have a soul; I have no idea whether I have one soul or several, or whether I have one soul for a time and then later a different soul. Thus there are no criteria for determining what constitutes "the same soul" and hence no way to make informed judgments about it. We might simply on faith assume criteria such as "Same body, same soul" or "Same mental traits, same soul," but since we never independently observe souls, there is no way to test these principles and thus no reason to think that they apply. But since we evidently are able to make

27. For examples of this defense, see Richard L. Purtill, "The Intelligibility of Disembodied Survival," *Christian Scholar's Review* 5 (1975): 15-26; and Paul Helm, "A Theory of Disembodied Survival and Re-embodied Existence," *Religious Studies* 14 (March 1978). See also Bruce Reichenbach, *Is Man the Phoenix? A Study of Immortality* (Washington: University Press of America, 1983).

correct personal identity judgments about persons, it follows that personal identity has nothing to do with souls. Personal identity must instead be based on bodily criteria. Thus, concludes Perry, no thesis about my survival of death via the survival of my soul is coherent.

Perry's second argument is that the memory criterion of personal identity, which those who believe in immortality must rely on, is never sufficient to establish personal identity. This is because of the obvious fact that memory is fallible. Without some further criterion, we will never be able to distinguish between apparent memories and genuine memories. In fact, believers in immortality are committed to a kind of circularity — they claim that genuine memory explains personal identity (i.e., a purported Jones in the afterlife really is Jones only if the purported Jones genuinely remembers from Jones's point of view events in Jones's past), and they claim that identity marks the difference between apparent and genuine memories (the purported Jones can have genuine memories of events in Jones's past only if the purported Jones *is* Jones; otherwise the memories are merely *apparent* memories). Thus, again, the thesis that our souls survive death, which must rely on the memory criterion of personal identity, is incoherent.

Finally, Perry argues that the thesis of survival of death through immortality is rendered incoherent by the possibility of multiple qualitatively identical persons in the afterlife. As Weirob puts it,

> either God, by creating a Heavenly person with a brain modeled after mine, does not really create someone identical with me but merely someone similar to me, or God is somehow limited to making only one such being. I can see no reason why, if there were a God, He should be so limited. So I take the first option. He would create someone similar to me, but not someone who would *be* me. Either your analysis of memory is wrong, and such a being does not, after all, remember what I am doing or saying, or memory is not sufficient for personal identity. Your theory has gone wrong somewhere, for it leads to absurdity.[28]

When told by one of the discussants that God may well refrain from creating multiple qualitatively identical persons in the afterlife and that if God does so refrain, the immortality thesis is coherent, Weirob replies that a new criterion has now been added: What suffices for personal identity

28. Perry, *A Dialogue on Personal Identity and Immortality*, p. 3.

(i.e., what makes it such that the purported Jones in the afterlife *is* Jones) is not just memory but rather memory plus lack of competition. This opens an odd way for someone to be killed in the afterlife, she remarks: God need only create, so to speak, an identical twin to Jones, and then *neither* would be Jones — Jones would then not have survived death. This would rather oddly make identity depend on something entirely extrinsic to the person involved. And if memory does not secure personal identity where there are two or more Joneses in the afterlife, it does not secure personal identity at all. Weirob concludes that it is best simply to abandon any thought of survival of death — when my body dies, I die.

Perry's first argument in favor of the notion that survival of death is incoherent is based on an element of truth, but he uses it in an erroneous way. Throughout his book he seems illicitly to jump back and forth between talk about criteria of personal identity and talk about evidence for personal identity. It is surely true that the soul is not observable, except in the sense that observation of a person's behavior is usually evidence of personality or of the state of the soul.[29] So the presence or absence of a soul or of a certain soul is not something for which we can successfully test, at least not directly. What this shows, I believe, is that the soul does not provide *evidence for* personal identity. We cannot, for example, prove that a given person really is our long-lost friend by proving that this person really has our long-lost friend's soul. But it still might be true that the soul provides *a criterion of* personal identity. That is, it still might be the case that the person really is our long-lost friend if this person and our long-lost friend have the same soul. It might even be true to say that a purported Jones in the afterlife is the same person as the Jones who once lived on earth if the purported Jones has Jones's soul. How we might test for or come to know this is another matter. Perhaps only God can know for sure who has what soul. Perhaps the rest of us will never know — at least apart from divine revelation — whether the purported Jones has Jones's soul. But it can still be true that if they have the same soul, they are two different temporal episodes of the same person.

And the claim that personal identity consists in or amounts to the presence of the soul does not rule out the possibility of our making reliable personal identity judgments on other grounds, as Weirob seems to claim it does. Those who believe in the possibility of disembodied existence need not deny that there are other criteria of personal identity (e.g., if a person has the same body as my long-lost friend, this person

---

29. I owe this point to W. S. Anglin.

is my long-lost friend) and other ways of producing evidence in favor of or against personal identity claims.

Perry's second argument is also based on an element of truth — memory certainly is fallible; we do have to distinguish between apparent memories and genuine memories. So unless I have access to some infallible way of making this distinction, the mere fact that the purported Jones seems to remember events in Jones's life from Jones's point of view will not establish beyond conceivable doubt that the purported Jones is Jones (although it might count as evidence for it). As above, however, this does not rule out the possibility that memory is a criterion of personal identity. If the purported Jones does indeed remember events in Jones's life from Jones's point of view, then the purported Jones is Jones.

It is sometimes claimed that the memory criterion is parasitic on the bodily criterion and that use of the memory criterion never suffices by itself to establish identity. But such claims are surely false. We sometimes do make secure identity claims based on the memory criterion alone — e.g., when we receive a typed or printed letter from a friend. We hold that it is our friend who wrote the letter solely on the basis of memories and personality traits apparently possessed by the author of the letter that seem to be memories and personality traits that our friend has or ought to have. Of course if doubts were to arise, we would try to verify or falsify the claim that our friend wrote the letter by the use of any evidence or criterion that might seem promising. We might check the letter for fingerprints; we might try to see if it was written on our friend's typewriter; we might even telephone our friend and ask whether she wrote the letter. This is not to suggest that we must always rely on the bodily criterion; there may well be cases in which we try to verify an identity claim originally based on the bodily criterion by means of memories. It is simply to suggest that in cases of doubt we will be inclined to look at both sorts of criteria.

But in cases where the bodily criterion cannot be used (e.g., during the interim period postulated in temporary disembodiment), can identity claims rationally be made? Can we ever be sure that a disembodied putative Stephen Davis *is* Stephen Davis? The problem is especially acute since memory is notoriously fallible. Without recourse to the bodily criterion, how can we distinguish between actual memories and purported memories? Of course, so far as a *criterion* of personal identity is concerned, the quick response to this objection is the assertion that God will ensure that our apparent memories are genuine memories. And that will suffice. So far as *evidence* of personal identity is concerned, I would argue that secure identity claims can be made without resort to the bodily criterion in cases in which there are very many memories from very many different people that cohere together well. The context makes all the difference. If there are, say, one hundred disembodied souls all wondering whether everyone else is in fact who he or she claims to be, it would be irrational to deny that their memories are genuine if those memories all fit together, confirm each other, and form a coherent picture. Doubt would still be conceivable but not rational. And something like this is precisely what defenders of temporary disembodiment claim will occur during the interim period.[30]

The third or duplication argument is one that critics of disembodied existence frequently appeal to, but I will not discuss it here. Formulating a reply to this objection is my principal aim in Chapter 7. Let me then close this section with one further point.

Although the view I am defending in this chapter — temporary disembodiment — does not require the coherence of any notion of permanent disembodiment (such as the doctrine of the immortality of the soul), I nevertheless hold both temporary and permanent disembodiment to be coherent. As we have already noted, Geach argues strongly that only temporary disembodiment is coherent, that the problem of the personal identity of a disembodied person is manageable only on the basis of an assumption of its capacity or potential to be reunited with a given body at some point. Otherwise, he says, disembodied minds cannot be differentiated.[31] If Geach is right, only temporary disembodiment is coherent; immortality of the soul is not. Or at least those who believe in immortality of the soul must add an item to their theory — perhaps something about a permanently disembodied soul permanently retaining the (forever unrealized) *capacity* to be reunited with a given body.

VIII

It should be evident by this point that I do not consider what I have been calling the Patristic theory to be normative for Christians today. The "modern" theory seems to me an acceptable interpretation of

---

30. I will not try to answer Perry's charge of circularity, because I believe Parfit has decisively done so with the notion that he calls quasi-memories. See *Reasons and Persons*, pp. 220ff.

31. Geach, *God and the Soul*, pp. 23-28.

resurrection. God's ability to raise us from the dead in the eschaton does not seem to depend on God's ability to locate and reunite the very particles of which our bodies once consisted. Nevertheless, the Patristic theory also constitutes an acceptable understanding of resurrection for Christians. The standard objections to it are answerable, and the most natural exegesis of 1 Corinthians 15:35-50 supports it. Furthermore, I would argue that respect for Christian tradition must grant great weight to views held by virtually all the Church Fathers unless there is serious reason to depart from what they say. It seems to me quite possible that God will one day raise us from the dead in the very way that the Fathers and Aquinas suggest.

My overall conclusion is that the theory of resurrection that I have been considering (which can be interpreted in either the Patristic or the "modern" way) is a viable notion for Christians. Temporary disembodiment seems eminently defensible, both philosophically and theologically. I do not claim that it is the only viable option for Christian belief about life after death; I do claim that it is an acceptable way for Christians to understand those words from the Apostles' Creed that say, "I believe in . . . the resurrection of the body."

Much contemporary philosophy tends, in its understanding of human nature, in a behaviorist or even materialist direction. No one who believes in temporary disembodiment can embrace philosophical materialism, but such believers can have great sympathy with any view that says that a disembodied person would hardly be a human person in the full sense of the term. Both philosophical materialists and those who believe in temporary disembodiment can accept the notion that a disembodied person is only a minimal person, a mere shadow of a true human person.

Christians can accordingly embrace the notion that full and true and complete human life is bodily life. That is why they look forward to "the resurrection of the body." The central idea here is that death disassembles us for a while, and then God (either in the Patristic or the "modern" way) puts us back together again. In a sense, then, we human beings are God's artifacts.[32] The unity over time of an artifact (e.g., my computer) is a function in part of natural processes of behavior and change *and* of the intentions of its creators and users. (I will consider the role of the divine intention in personal identity in detail in Chap. 6.) In any case, the idea is that at some time after death, God will reconstitute

32. This idea was suggested to me by Richard Warner.

us in a new and perfected way. As Pseudo-Justin says, "In the resurrection the flesh shall rise entire. For if on earth He healed the sickness of the flesh, and made the body whole, much more will He do this in the resurrection, so that the flesh shall rise perfect and entire" (*On the Resurrection,* chap. 4).

6

General Resurrection and Physicalism

I

In the introduction to this volume, I noted that the standard Christian view of general resurrection presupposes some version of mind-body or body-soul dualism. This is the view I defended in Chapter 5. However, I am also of the opinion that the Christian view of resurrection is viable even on a materialist or physicalist basis — that is to say, even if human beings are essentially and entirely material objects. I will attempt to defend that assertion in this chapter.

Suppose there is a person x who lives from T1 to T2 (i.e., is born at T1 and dies at T2). And suppose there is a person y who begins living at T3. Suppose further that y claims to be x resurrected from the dead. Let us say that y seems to be sincere; seems to know the meanings of such words as *person, death, resurrection,* and the like; seems to have a personality similar to x's; and seems to have x's memories. In short, let us suppose that y passes all our tests with flying colors and seems, so far as we can tell, to *be* x. (If we preferred we could also add, in order to make the case relevant to Christian resurrection claims, that y's body is in some ways remarkably similar to but in some ways different from x's body.)[1]

---

1. I make this parenthetical remark because (1) the Gospels seem to imply that Jesus' body after his resurrection was both similar to and different from his pre-resurrection body and (2) Jesus' resurrection from the dead is typically taken by Christians as the basis for and model of our resurrection (see Phil. 3:10-11, 21; Rom. 6:5; 1 Cor. 15:20-23).

If all this occurred, the question before us would be: Is y the same person as x? That is, is y correct in y's claim to be x resurrected from the dead?

We can imagine that there are several possible answers to our question. (1) We might decide that y is definitely x, and hence that y is correct in claiming to be x. (2) We might decide that while we cannot be certain, given the arguments and evidence available, it seems more likely than not that y is x. (3) We might decide that it is impossible to make a rational decision in this case, that the evidence is balanced pro and con, perhaps, or that there are simply too many other equally good explanations of the situation available besides resurrection, and hence, although there *is* an answer to our question, we just can't know or be reasonably sure what it is. (4) We might decide that in cases like this there just *is no* answer, that if compelled to make a choice we cannot do much better than, say, flipping a coin to decide whether to regard y as x. (5) We might decide that while we cannot be certain, given the arguments and evidence available, it seems more likely than not that y is not x. (6) Or, we might decide that y is definitely not x, and hence that y is incorrect in claiming to be x.

My own view, for which I will argue in this chapter, is that in the case we have envisioned, a person can rationally hold option (1) — that y is x. But it needs to be noted that the issues here are thorny and complex, with many ramifications in various areas of philosophy and theology. There are no easy answers.

To see that this is the case, let me mention several questions that seem so powerfully relevant to our simple question ("Is y the same person as x?") that we may not be able to answer it till we answer them.

1. What exactly does it mean to say that one thing, A, is identical to or is the same thing as B?
2. Is temporal continuity required for identity, or are temporal gaps allowable? For example, in order for the sycamore tree that exists in my front yard today to be identical to the sycamore sapling my wife and I planted there eleven years ago, must the tree have existed at every temporal moment between eleven years ago and today, or could there have been temporal gaps in its existence (i.e., moments when it did not exist)?
3. In cases like that of y and x, in which one human being claims to be another (now dead) human being, are striking and even indefeasible memory and character similarities sufficient to establish

identity, or is some kind of bodily continuity required as well or instead?

4. Since in resurrection cases both bodily changes and temporal gaps seem part of the picture (we die at a given point and are resurrected years or centuries later in a new form), is the bodily criterion of personal identity satisfied in such cases?

5. How much qualitative change is compatible with numerical identity (i.e., is there an upper limit of qualitative change past which there is no longer numerical identity)?

6. How do we handle the many test cases that can be suggested in order to evaluate or even challenge the claim that y is x? For example, what do we say if there are two people, y and z (or even seven or fifty people), who with equal plausibility claim to be x resurrected? Or how do we explain hypothetical cases of brain transfer, fission of persons, fusion of persons, or the like?

II

We will return to several (but not all) of these issues later; for now, let me sketch two possible ways in which the Christian claim that the dead will be raised in the eschaton might be understood. Other models than these have been suggested by Christian thinkers,[2] but the two that I will discuss seem to be the two most obvious alternatives. I call the two views "temporary disembodiment" and "temporary nonexistence."

As we saw in Chapter 5, *temporary disembodiment* is based on metaphysical dualism — the notion that human beings consist, or at least normally consist, of both material bodies and immaterial souls, and that the soul is the essence of the person (the real Davis is Davis's soul, not Davis's body). The theory runs as follows: A given human being Jones is born, lives as a soul incarnate in a body, and dies; when the body dies, Jones's soul goes on existing in an incomplete, disembodied state with God until the general resurrection in the eschaton; at that point Jones's body is raised and permanently reunited with Jones's soul.

2. There is, e.g., the theory that bodily resurrection occurs immediately after death; see Murray Harris, *Raised Immortal* (Grand Rapids: William B. Eerdmans, 1983). Harris makes an impressive case, and his exegesis of 2 Corinthians 5:1-10 is careful and interesting, but I will not discuss the thesis of immediate resurrection (despite the fact that it might be useful for monistic theories such as I am discussing in this chapter) because I consider it inconsistent with the main thrust of Scripture.

As we also noted in Chapter 5, there are several strong points that commend this theory to us. First, there is no temporal gap for us to have to worry about: Jones exists at all the temporal points between Jones's birth and the general resurrection. Second, if the real Jones is Jones's soul, then Jones's premortem and postmortem bodies do not have to be at all similar; Jones's resurrection body can be a whole new body, and it will still be Jones. (As we also saw in Chapter 5, this is not the traditional Christian view — similarity between the two bodies is usually stressed — but it does seem at least a possible answer to standard anti-resurrection arguments that ask how a body dead for, say, a thousand years can possibly be reconstituted.) Third, as noted, temporary disembodiment solves a sticky theological problem — how it can be true both that the general resurrection will not occur until the eschaton (which seems to be taught in the Bible) and that Jesus said to the thief on the cross, "Today you will be with me in Paradise." The solution — as we saw above — is that the thief was and is with Jesus in paradise in the form of a disembodied soul; his body will be raised later. But temporary disembodiment (or at least temporary disembodiment with continuing consciousness in the disembodied state) has what some philosophers would consider a weakness — it is based on metaphysical dualism (entailing disembodied existence, the soul being the essence of the person, etc.).

Temporary nonexistence (which has some affinities with the theological view called "soul sleep") is neutral vis-à-vis dualism or materialism. The theory runs as follows: A given person, Smith, is born and then dies; after Smith's death, Smith simply does not exist until the eschaton, when God raises Smith from the dead. This theory too seems to have several strong points. First, there is no need to worry about such dualistic doctrines as immortality or disembodied existence. The word *soul* can still be used, though probably not as indicating a substance — for example, the soul might be considered the principle of life (i.e., living beings are beings with souls). Second, as mentioned, temporary nonexistence is compatible with metaphysical materialism, which might be an exceedingly vital strong point if some version of materialism turns out to be philosophically preferable to dualism. Third, defenders of temporary nonexistence argue that a theological point in its favor is that certain New Testament texts seem to suggest it. But this theory too has a weak point — the existence of the temporal gap between Smith's two periods of existence. Some argue that the existence of the gap requires that the two Smiths are not identical or at least that we have no good reason to insist that they are identical.

Let us now turn to the question of the relationship between a person's earthly and resurrection bodies. The limits of acceptable Christian views on this question might be said to be set by Paul's words in 1 Corinthians 15:51: "We shall all be changed." The phrase "shall all be changed" indicates that each resurrected person will change qualitatively — that is to say, no resurrected person will have all the same properties as before. And since Paul says that it is *"we"* who "shall all be changed," we can assume that it will still be "us" after the change — that is to say, the person who has changed will be the same person as the person before the change; the person will not have changed numerically. So resurrected persons will be both the same (in the sense of numerical identity) and not the same (in the sense of qualitative identity) as the premortem persons who are resurrected. Now it is impossible for x and y to be numerically identical without some significant degree of qualitative similarity, so I take it that resurrected persons must share at least some properties with the premortem persons with whom they are identical.

But what are the possible views that are available here? How might Christians claim that one's premortem body is related to one's resurrection body? (Let us call the two bodies B1 and B2 respectively.)

One possibility is to say that B1 and B2 are qualitatively identical (i.e., have all their properties in common). But this theory seems outside the limits of acceptable Christian views noted above. Following the New Testament accounts and statements, Christian thinkers have always stressed that B2 is in some ways qualitatively different from B1. Furthermore, not even my own premortem body at a given point and that same body, say, a year later have all their properties in common. So this first view is too strong.

A second possibility suggested by this last point is that B1 and B2 are as qualitatively similar as, say, two different temporal episodes of a person's premortem body. Perhaps B2 is no more different from B1 than is a person's body at a given time and that same person's body, say, a few years later. But there is a theological difficulty here too — this view seems closer to resuscitation than resurrection. The Christian view is that in the resurrection one's premortem body is *transformed*. This view, then, is to be rejected too because it amounts to resuscitation rather than resurrection.

The most radical theory that might be suggested would say that B1 and B2 are not at all qualitatively similar. But this introduces radical problems as well. For one thing, it falls outside the bounds of acceptable

Christian views of the resurrection mentioned earlier. For another, it is difficult to see how numerical identity can be affirmed in the absence of any or at least some significant degree of qualitative identity. If B1 and B2 are as different as (or more different than), say, Napoleon's body and Roosevelt's body, we would be hard pressed to explain how the one was the other raised from the dead.

We seem forced, then, toward some version of the less radical view that B1 and B2 are at least in some ways quite qualitatively different and yet have in common some significant number of properties. Naturally, this raises the question of precisely how continuity is to be preserved, since Christian thinking holds that B2 just *is* B1 resurrected, and not someone else. And here too there appear to be several possibilities:

1. Perhaps what provides continuity is not any bodily similarity — though there may in fact be qualitative similarity between B1 and B2 — but rather the soul. That is to say, perhaps B2 is B1 resurrected rather than another person altogether in virtue of the fact that B1 and B2 share the same soul. (Naturally, this is a theory that will be attractive to dualists.)
2. Perhaps what provides continuity is the fact that many physical qualities or components (e.g., myriads of atoms, the structure of myriads of atoms, genetic makeup, physiognomy, or the like) are held in common.
3. Perhaps what provides continuity is the sharing of just one component (one atom, say) that constitutes the essence of the person. Possibly each person possesses some physical particle that constitutes that person's individual essence; if so, God can raise B1 from the dead merely by preserving this particle and making it the basis of B2.
4. Perhaps what provides continuity is the sharing of just one component, where that component does not necessarily constitute any individual essence. That is to say, perhaps B2 is B1 resurrected rather than another person altogether because God preserves, say, some one atom of B1's body and uses it as the kernel or nucleus of B2.
5. Perhaps what provides continuity is not a physical particle but rather the fact that B2 has precisely B1's genetic and bodily makeup (the same color hair, blood type, fingerprints, physiognomy, etc.)

III

We have been discussing, in effect, what philosophers call the problem of personal identity. This is the problem of establishing criteria for identifying and reidentifying things, especially persons, over time. Some philosophers think of it as an epistemological problem. They see it as the problem of *how we can tell* that some past thing x is numerically identical to (i.e., is the same thing as) some present thing y. I prefer to see it as a metaphysical problem — specifically, a problem of explaining what numerical identity between x and y *involves* or *consists in*, of specifying the conditions that must be satisfied for it to be true that x is y.

I will discuss here the problem of personal identity only as it concerns human persons. The principles or criteria of identity for such things as galaxies, trees, chairs, atoms, or quarks (let alone for properties, relations, propositions, or possible worlds) will surely be quite different. I will specify four criteria of personal identity, each of which is somewhat complex and will require discussion. The relationships among the four, also complex, will require further discussion.

It should be noted, however, that it is probably impossible to come up with a set of criteria that cover all possible situations in which the problem of personal identity arises, even concerning human persons. We can imagine test cases in which our concepts would be so strained beyond usefulness that we would be unsure what to say; we would be unable to tell whether x is identical to y. We can even imagine test cases in which personal identity even seems to be indeterminate, in which there seems to be no answer to the simple question "Is x the same person as y?"[3] (This is not to suggest that all personal identity questions are unanswerable, however; in more ordinary cases, I would argue that there is an answer and that it can be known.)

3. See Parfit, *Reasons and Persons* (Oxford: Oxford University Press, 1986), pp. 233, 238, 260, 264. A related point should be made here: because of the difficulties philosophers have encountered in supplying necessary and sufficient conditions for personal identity, some philosophers (Parfit and others) have abandoned the concept of personal identity per se and have instead chosen to speak about "what matters most" in survival or about a person's "closest continuer." My point is that such options are not available to Christian philosophers because Christian teachings entail that *we* (the very persons that we are) will survive death. So the question for Christian philosophers is not something like "Under what conditions will some future person preserve what matters most to me?" but rather "Under what conditions will some future person be the same person as me?"

I do not pretend that the following brief analysis constitutes a full treatment of this thorny and controversial topic. I do, however, think it constitutes a defensible analysis that can be helpful in discussions of those problems of personal identity that typically interest philosophers of religion, especially those concerning the survival of death of human persons. In what follows I will speak of identity between some past person P1 and some present person P2; their bodies I will call B1 and B2, respectively.

Criterion 1: *Striking psychological (i.e., memory and personality) similarities and/or continuity between P1 and P2 with the right kind of causal relationship between the memories and personality of P1 and the memories and personality of P2.* Along with many contemporary philosophers, even some who tend toward some version of physicalism, I am inclined to hold that certain imaginable test cases lead strongly toward the conclusion that this first criterion can take priority over the second. That is, there are cases where Criterion 1 (together, as I will argue, with Criteria 3 and 4) is sufficient for personal identity — whether Criterion 2 is satisfied or not.

It should be noted that the above word "striking" is intentionally ambiguous. So far as *evidence* of personal identity is concerned, the similarities in most cases will have to be extensive and dramatic (i.e., before we will believe that P1 is P2). But so far as a *criterion* of personal identity is concerned, the condition might conceivably be satisfied if even one memory is held in common (this might be important, e.g., in the case of the resurrection of an infant or a severely retarded person). So I am arguing that if P2 has just *one* genuine memory in common with P1 (and as long as Criteria 3 and 4 are also satisfied), P1 is P2.

It should also be noted that the notion of "the right kind of causal relationship" is equally ambiguous, and I do not intend to explore in detail the question of what sorts of causal relationships are compatible with personal identity and what sorts are not. I mention the point because we can imagine cases in which P2 genuinely shares a memory or even many memories from P1's life from the perspective of P1 but in which we would be inclined to deny that P1 is P2. This might be our inclination, for example, if P2 has the relevant memories only because some small portions of P1's long dead but medically preserved brain were transplanted into P2's brain.

Criterion 2: *Striking bodily similarities and/or material continuity between B1 and B2 with the right kind of causal relationship between them.* The right kind of causal relationship is again difficult to specify. If B2 is the result of changes that have occurred in B1 — that is, if B2 is a new state of B1 — Criterion 2 is surely satisfied. But then Peter van Inwagen asks, What if God here and now in front of van Inwagen the adult philosopher creates a replica of van Inwagen's ten-year-old self, using atoms that were part of the ten-year-old's body but are not part of the adult philosopher's body?[4] Who is van Inwagen? Apparently each could truly say, "I am van Inwagen." Well, I believe that an omnipotent being could do the very thing envisioned here, but that fortunately (so I believe) God hasn't and won't. In this case, considerations of causality and spatio-temporal continuity are crucial. We can see that the adult philosopher is van Inwagen since his body has the right kind of causal relationship with all earlier van Inwagen bodies; the ten-year-old (being a *de novo* creation of God) is the impostor.

Now as noted above, Criterion 2 does not seem a necessary condition of personal identity. Perhaps (if dualists are right, for example), P2 can be P1 even if P2 has no body at all. Furthermore, we can imagine test cases in which there is no material continuity between B1 and B2 (e.g., Parfit's teletransporter)[5] but in which the truth seems to be that P1 is P2.

Criterion 3: *Uniqueness.* Our concept of a human person includes the notion that there is but one instance of each person. If there were, *per impossible,* two qualitatively identical human beings standing before us (or two human beings as qualitatively identical as possible — their location could not be the same, for example), we would nonetheless consider them numerically distinct. We would understand that we were seeing two different individuals. Thus some present person P2 can be numerically identical to some past person P1 only if there is, so to speak, only one P2. If P1 dies and five years later there appear six virtually qualitatively identical persons all claiming with apparent sincerity and cogency to be P1 raised from the dead, we would be puzzled indeed.

Such an eventuality (especially if such events became common and if there were some sort of acceptable causal explanation available) might cause us radically to revise our concept of a human person. For example, we might then allow for the idea of mechanical replication of persons

4. Van Inwagen, "The Possibility of Resurrection," *International Journal for Philosophy of Religion* 9 (1978): 120.
5. Parfit, *Reasons and Persons,* pp. 199ff.

or something of the sort. Most probably (and this is what Criterion 3 would require), we would simply deny that P1 has survived death. We would assert that none of the six P2s is numerically identical to P1. (Criterion 4 might help us find our way out of the impasse; we will come to that point presently.)

There is a difficulty with Criterion 3, however. As several authors have pointed out, the criterion specifies a property that P2 must have in order to be P1 that is wholly extrinsic to P2. The implication is that there are cases in which the answer to the question of whether P2 is numerically identical to P1 will depend not on P2 (i.e., not on any of P2's intrinsic properties) but on whether there is any competition for P2ness. As John Perry's character Gretchen Wierob suggests, this would give God an odd way of killing someone: in order to ensure that P1 has not survived death, all God need do is create multiple qualitatively identical replicas of P2 in the afterlife.[6] However, I am going to defer detailed consideration of this difficulty to Chapter 7.

Criterion 4: *The will of God*. Following R. T. Herbert, I claim that P2 is not P1 unless it is God's will that P2 be P1.[7] This is a radical claim; controversial theological concepts are rarely raised these days in discussions of apparently purely logical issues. Accordingly, let me back up a bit and make some brief theological points before returning to personal identity.

Christians typically believe that God is both the Creator and the Sustainer (or Preserver) of all existing contingent things. The fact that God is Creator means that we can say of any contingently existing thing x that x exists because God has caused it to exist. The fact that God is Sustainer means that we can say of any contingently existing thing x that x continues to exist, and continues to exist *as x*, because God causes it to do so (see Neh. 9:6; Col. 1:17; Heb. 1:3).[8] If God were, so to speak, to withdraw ontological support from x, x would cease to exist. Everything in the universe depends here and now on God; no contingent thing has the inherent ability to continue existing

6. Perry, *A Dialogue on Personal Identity and Immortality* (Indianapolis: Hackett, 1978), p. 35.

7. R. T. Herbert, *Paradox and Identity in Theology* (Ithaca, N.Y.: Cornell University Press, 1979), pp. 150-55. Herbert's chapter entitled "The General Resurrection" is an excellent study that has influenced me at several points.

8. "By preservation," says Charles Hodge, "is meant that all things out of God owe the continuity of their existence, with all their properties and powers, to the will of God" (*Systematic Theology*, vol. 1 [New York: Scribner's, 1895], p. 575).

or to continue existing as the thing it is.[9] The will of God is the glue of the world.[10]

In *Being Human . . . Becoming Human*, German theologian Helmut Thielicke (in a rather different context) makes a compelling point. He argues that our identity as human beings is not based primarily on our own properties or creaturely nature but on the initiative of God, who recognizes and upholds us as the individuals we are. "Self-consciousness and self-determination," he says, "are not of our own making but something assigned to us by creation. . . . Human identity is finally grounded in the history that God has initiated with the human race, so that the essence of humanity is being addressed and called and chosen by God. . . . The constancy of our identity is the constancy of God's faithfulness."[11] My continuing integrity through time as the person that I am, then, is based in the first instance not on my own properties but on the fact that God sustains and upholds me as that being by recognizing and calling me.

Now, the doctrine of divine preservation need not imply any sort of pantheism or divine idealism. Stones, trees, human beings, and the like are real objects existing as things separate from God. They are not just ideas in the mind of God. The point is simply that at every moment

9. On my proposed analysis of personal identity, the will of God may well be the "further fact" or "boundary line" that Parfit says he needs to resolve difficult cases of personal identity but is unable to find (*Reasons and Persons,* pp. 210, 239, 242, 277-79). The will of God makes human beings (contrary to Parfit's view) "separately existing entities" (p. 240), and hence renders personal identity (*pace* Parfit) a deep "further fact" that genuinely matters. It is true that there are conceivable test cases in which personal identity is indeterminate, in which the question "Is x the same person as y?" has no answer apart from arbitrary stipulation. But it cannot be the case that personal identity does not matter and that what really matters (as Parfit argues) is "psychological connectedness and/or continuity with the right kind of cause," where "the right kind of cause could be any cause" (p. 215). What if there turns out to be psychological connectedness between me today and a bar of soap in the twenty-first century — if the bar of soap has my memories, believes itself to be me, thinks and feels the way I do, and the like. (Don't ask me how this could possibly happen: Parfit is the one who says that any sort of causation will do.) Would the future existence of this bar of soap be nearly as good to me as my survival of death? I hardly think so. If someone were to convince me that the above scenario will occur, I would be more puzzled than comforted.

10. Or, to borrow the words of J. L. Mackie, "the cement of the universe." See his book of that title (Oxford: Clarendon Press, 1974).

11. Thielicke, *Being Human . . . Becoming Human* (Garden City, N.Y.: Doubleday, 1984), p. 89; cf. pp. 90-91, 134-36, 169.

we would not exist or would not retain our integrity as the things we are apart from God's power. The world would be radically Heraclitean apart from the divine intention that it be stable and enduring. The will of God holds the world together, makes of it a cosmos rather than pure chaos or even nothingness. The divine intention is a required aspect of identity, then, not just in cases of gaps in the lives of persons but in the case of all the enduring things that make up the world. Without God's intention that the computer on which I type this sentence be the same thing it was five minutes ago, it would not be that thing (despite near-exact qualitative identity).[12]

How are the four criteria related? I argue that the only necessary conditions of identity for human persons are Criteria 3 and 4. Neither 1 nor 2 is by itself necessary, but *either* 1 or 2 (or both) must be satisfied in all cases of personal identity. Although, as I argued, Criterion 1 can take priority over Criterion 2, we can imagine cases in which P1 is numerically identical to P2 despite the fact that there are no relevant kinds of psychological connections between them (which is why I claim there are cases in which the satisfaction of Criteria 2, 3, and 4 will suffice for personal identity).

Suppose there is a person Smith who is afflicted with some severe and rare form of amnesia that causes Smith occasionally to lose *all* personality characteristics and memories (both memories of past experiences and memories of how to do things) for three seconds before returning to normalcy again. Now if Criterion 1 is a necessary condition of personal identity, then during the relevant three-second period the truth is that the person who is suffering from this horrible malady is not the same person as the normal person of a few seconds before. And that seems an unacceptable result. Here it seems the fact of the matter is that the two are the same; the satisfaction of Criteria 2, 3, and 4 is sufficient.

Thus I claim there are two sufficient conditions for the numerical identity of human persons — the satisfaction of Criteria 1, 3, and 4, or the satisfaction of Criteria 2, 3, and 4. By this I am not saying that all four of the stipulated criteria can or do count as *evidence* of personal

12. The doctrine of divine preservation does not imply that God is the cause of everything that happens in the sense that whatever occurs occurs because God wills it to occur. God has chosen to follow the policy of sustaining or preserving us even in our evil deeds, despite the fact that it is not God's will that we commit them. That is to say, God has given us the power to act in ways contrary to God's will.

identity: I do not claim that we must know or be sure that the three necessary criteria are satisfied before we can ever make a secure identity claim. For example, we will rarely if ever have access to the will of God in cases in which personal identity is at issue (although it is conceivable that the divine will might be revealed to us). And, as noted, apart from those esoteric puzzle cases beloved of philosophers, we quite reasonably assume there are never any numerically distinct but qualitatively identical items of any kind in the world. So the criterion of uniqueness need never be mentioned in actual personal identity cases (i.e., involving existing things). Furthermore, so far as making a judgment of personal identity is concerned, we can quite often formulate a rational belief (e.g., that P1 either is or is not P2) on the basis of bodily evidence alone, or psychological evidence alone (which is why I did not feel it necessary to mention Criterion 4 in Chap. 5). Still, my claim is that personal identity consists in, is not present without, or involves the satisfaction of either Criteria 1, 3, and 4 or Criteria 2, 3, and 4.

My most controversial point, however, is perhaps the one about the will of God, and I should say something more about it. I need to make clear first that I am *not* saying that in personal identity cases God investigates matters thoroughly, sees what the truth is (say, that P1 is P2), and then "wills" accordingly. Rather, I am saying that the will of God is a constitutive factor in determining what the truth in fact is. Suppose that in some personal identity case, Criteria 1, 2, and 3 were all satisfied but Criterion 4 was not. Then, I would say, P1 is not P2; P2 is a mere replica of P1 (where a "replica of P1" is an entity without P1's history who exists after P1's death and who is physically and behaviorally indistinguishable from P1; such a being would be indistinguishable from P1 in normal ways, but would nonetheless not be P1). Would the will of God make any difference to observers of P1 and P2 who wonder whether P1 is P2? Possibly not. Unless God's will were made known to them, they might, quite rationally but mistakenly, conclude that P2 is P1. But to put the point bluntly, what makes an apparent replica of Jones Jones is God's will that it be Jones. And to turn momentarily to the epistemological issue, it follows that there are imaginable cases in which we would have to know the will of God before we could know whether P2 is P1.

A test case: Suppose Jones dies at T1 and that at T2 *two* replicas of Jones come to exist, Jones1 and Jones2. I suspect that identity could be established here without mentioning God if there were a causal relationship that existed between Jones and one but not the other of Jones's replicas — if one of them, for instance, resulted from regular and predictable changes that occurred in Jones's body and the other inexplicably appeared out of the blue. But what if no such relationship obtained? Let us suppose further that God intends that Jones1 be (a continuation of the life of) Jones and that Jones2 not be (a continuation of the life of) Jones. What then? Now, I do not believe that any such multiple-replica case has ever occurred or will ever occur. Nevertheless, if, *per impossible*, such a case were to occur, I would hold that Jones1 is Jones and that Jones2 is not.

Or what if Criteria 1, 2, and 3 were satisfied but 4 was not? For example, what if a unique candidate for Napoleonhood appeared before us looking, acting, and apparently thinking, feeling, and remembering just as Bonaparte himself should do if he were raised from the dead? I claim that this person would be Napoleon only if Criterion 4 were also satisfied — that is, only if it were God's will that he be Bonaparte raised from the dead. Apart from the satisfaction of Criterion 4, he would be a mere replica. Of course if we had no knowledge of the divine will, we would doubtless be within our intellectual rights in regarding him as Napoleon; such an identification would be rational but mistaken.

It is important to note that in ordinary cases, and even in some test cases, we can make secure identity claims without mentioning God. I hold that personal identity and indeed the integrity of all objects through time is in part a function of the divine intention. But especially in cases involving no temporal gap, rational identity claims can be made without appeal to theological considerations.

But what if we ask the opposite question: What if Criteria 1, 2, and 3 were not satisfied but Criterion 4 was? Could God merely by willing it make it such that the left shoe I am now wearing is numerically identical to Julius Caesar (e.g., is Julius Caesar raised from the dead)? Of course not; that would be logically impossible. To repeat: personal identity consists in and is not present without the satisfaction of either Criteria 1, 3, and 4, *or* 2, 3, and 4; the three criteria are singly necessary (in the case of the first two, the disjunction "1 or 2" is what is singly necessary) and jointly sufficient conditions of personal identity.

IV

Having discussed temporary disembodiment in Chapter 5, I will not do so here. As I have noted, my aim in this chapter is to consider the alternative of temporary nonexistence. I want to see if a Christian understanding of resurrection is possible on the basis of a purely physicalist understanding of human nature. Of course I do not hold that the notion of an incorporeal person is incoherent, for I believe that God is an incorporeal person. But perhaps dualism concerning human beings will turn out to be false; perhaps some version of identity theory or functionalism will turn out to be true; perhaps human beings are essentially material objects. As I state in the introduction to this book, this is not my own view. Still, so far as we know, it *might* be true, and if it is, we might naturally wonder whether the Christian notion of survival of death by bodily resurrection would be viable.

As we have seen, temporary nonexistence entails a temporal gap in personal existence: if a given person Jones is born, lives, dies, and is resurrected, Jones will not exist in the period between Jones's death and resurrection. But serious difficulties apparently emerge in this picture of human existence. Some philosophers have strongly argued that the existence of the gap rules out (or, alternately, makes entirely unverifiable and thus optional) personal identity. If what appears to be Jones is resurrected at some time (say two weeks or two hundred years) after Jones's death, then it is not really Jones but a mere replica of Jones who lives. And if it is not really Jones who will live in the resurrection world but someone else, the Christian hope that we will be raised from the dead and live with God is groundless.

The question, then, is whether spatio-temporal continuity is required for personal identity or whether temporal gaps are allowable. The critic of resurrection will claim that without spatio-temporal continuity there can be no personal identity. Is this correct? Before looking at various arguments that such critics present, let us note in a preliminary way that there are several responses that defenders of resurrection might make. One is to ask, as George Mavrodes does, exactly what spatio-temporal continuity consists in, and to argue, as Mavrodes skillfully does, that no answer is available that does not beg important questions.[13] Another is to present a notion of resurrection (one combined with some version of the doctrine of the immortality of the soul, perhaps) that involves no temporal gap, or at least to argue, as Philip Quinn does, that, properly understood, the notion of resurrection satisfies the critic's requirement of spatio-temporal continuity.[14] A third is to admit that resurrection (or at least some orthodox versions

13. See Mavrodes, "The Life Everlasting and the Bodily Criterion of Identity," *Nous* 2 (March 1977): 27-39.
14. See Quinn, "Personal Identity, Bodily Continuity and Resurrection," *International Journal for Philosophy of Religion* 9 (1978): 101-13.

of it) entails the existence of a gap and argue that personal identity is nevertheless possible. It is this third approach that I will take.

What are the arguments against the claim of some resurrectionists that persons are what we might call gap-inclusive? That is, what are the arguments in favor of the claim that spatio-temporal continuity is required for personal identity? We are all familiar with certain gap-inclusive items. We have no problem, for example, with the notion that two different episodes of *Sesame Street* are episodes of one and the same television program, despite being separated by a gap of, say, a whole day. Rivers that periodically run dry, wars that persist despite cease-fires or lulls in the fighting, dramas with intermissions, and serialized stories that break between episodes are all apparently gap-inclusive. Even persons of a sort can be said to be gap-inclusive: we have no trouble identifying the character George Smiley in John Le Carre's *Tinker, Tailor, Soldier, Spy* with the George Smiley of the same author's *Smiley's People*.[15] (Here, incidentally, is a case in which intention — in this case the intention of the author — appears to be crucial in establishing identity. We are convinced that the Smiley of the one novel *is* the Smiley of the other in large part because we are convinced that that is what Le Carre intended. And one secure way of establishing identity would be to ask the author if that is what is intended.) But the critic of resurrection denies that this sort of thing can also be true of *real living* persons (or once living persons). Let us consider five arguments in favor of that denial.

1. One of the major arguments in favor of the idea that personal identity always requires spatio-temporal continuity (i.e., can allow no gaps) was first stated by Thomas Reid.[16] The claim is that things (and certainly persons) can come into existence only once. So if x ceases to exist, then no later individual y can be numerically identical to x. Otherwise, two extremely odd results would follow: (1) x would exist after having ceased to exist, and (2) x would have had an existence before x's existence began. These implications of "gap-inclusivity" are so conceptually odd — so the argument goes — as to force us to embrace the

15. There are admitted difficulties with some of these examples. Does a television program *cease to exist* when it is not on the air? Does a temporarily nonexistent Smiley *return to existence* when Le Carre publishes another novel about the British master spy? The problem of personal identity for such entities seems particularly difficult.

16. Reid, *Essays on the Intellectual Powers of Man* (Cambridge: M.I.T. Press, 1969), p. 340. See also book 2, chap. 27 of John Locke's *Essay concerning Human Understanding*.

idea that personal identity requires an uninterrupted continuity of existence. But the natural reply to Reid is that his argument begs the question against the position of the defender of temporary nonexistence. It is true that something can *first* begin to exist only once; but why deny that something (that has ceased to exist) can legitimately be said to "come into existence" on more than one occasion?[17] Furthermore, as I have just argued, some sorts of things (rivers, wars, etc.) *are* gap-inclusive. Why not persons too? It will not do simply to insist that they are not.

2. Sometimes critics merely seem to insist dogmatically that there can be no personal identity without spatio-temporal continuity. They assert that no claims to the effect that "This person here before me is my old friend Jones" can be true without bodily continuity between "this person" and "Jones." But this argument too (if it is an argument at all) surely begs the question. The resurrectionist will insist that resurrections constitute counterexamples to the crucial claim being insisted upon. In at least this one sort of case, the resurrectionist will say, there can be personal identity despite the presence of a temporal gap. The critics of resurrection will then argue that without spatio-temporal continuity, what we will have is not Jones but a replica of Jones. But again this begs the question against resurrection. If human persons are gap-inclusive creatures, or at least creatures whose existence can include *one* temporal gap, as resurrectionists claim, the criticism fails. By itself, this argument does not show us that persons are not gap-inclusive.

3. The critic may then ask what criterion of personal identity the resurrectionist is using. It cannot be the bodily criterion (or at least a criterion based on bodily continuity). So how then do we go about deciding that a given person in the resurrection world is Jones and not someone else? The resurrectionist replies that we decide primarily on the basis of personality, memory, and bodily similarity (e.g., recognizability as Jones, blood type, fingerprints, etc.). Terence Penelhum and others have responded to this assertion by arguing that use of the memory criterion of personal identity presupposes use of the bodily criterion.[18]

17. "If by 'beginning of existence' one means 'first moment of existence,' then an object with interrupted existence has only one beginning," says Baruch A. Brody. "If, however, one means 'first moment of existence after a moment of nonexistence,' then objects with interrupted existence have two beginnings of existence, but there is nothing incoherent with that" (*Identity and Essence* [Princeton: Princeton University Press, 1980], p. 80).

18. See Penelhum, *Survival and Disembodied Existence* (New York: Humanities Press, 1970), pp. 54-67.

We can verify memory claims only by appealing to bodily criteria, just as a detective might try to verify someone's alleged memory of Smith at the scene of the crime by checking for Smith's fingerprints there or the like. But this seems to present no serious difficulties for those who believe in resurrection. Even if Penelhum's claim is correct (and I believe it is), resurrectionists can allow for use of the bodily criterion of personal identity. The resurrected Jesus (supposedly the model for Christian views of the general resurrection) was, after all, physically recognized as Jesus (albeit usually with some difficulty), and his pre-resurrection wounds were examined. As Bruce Reichenbach points out, nothing here has ruled out the possibility of a gap.[19] Verifying memory claims may well require appeals to bodily criteria (i.e., to previous bodily existence), but it has not been shown that it requires continuous bodily existence.

4. Critics of resurrection might then retire to the more careful claim that the absence of spatio-temporal continuity makes entirely optional the identification of persons in the resurrection world with the pre-resurrection people they claim to be. Terence Penelhum, for example, argues that because of the gap we are not rationally compelled to say "It is Jones" rather than "It is a replica of Jones"; we can reasonably do either.[20] But surely this argument will be unconvincing to the denizens of the resurrection world. If in that world Christian claims about God's aims and promises are apparently verified, and if there is case after case of persons claiming (truthfully so far as anyone can tell after rigorous questioning and testing) to be persons who lived and then died in the pre-resurrection world, then, I say, Penelhum's argument will lose whatever force it has here and now. The context makes all the difference. Even if the observable facts, so to speak, are equally well explained by the replica hypothesis and the resurrection hypothesis, the context of the eschaton will settle the matter.

5. The critic might then reply: Yes, but even in the context envisioned, we can never know for sure whether it is Jones or a mere replica of Jones. Not even the purported Jones can know, since *ex hypothesi* the facts will be the same in either case. We might be able to *call* the person Jones and *treat* the person as Jones, but we will not be able to *identify* the person as Jones. But, as R. T. Herbert points out, this argument proves too much.[21] Since nobody has observed every moment of my life (i.e.,

19. Reichenbach, "Monism and the Possibility of Life after Death," *Religious Studies* 14 (March 1978): 32-33.
20. See Penelhum, *Survival and Disembodied Existence*, pp. 93-102.
21. Herbert, *Paradox and Identity in Theology*, pp. 169-70.

nobody has observed spatio-temporal continuity between the Claremont philosopher who was born in Lincoln, Nebraska, in 1940 and the person who is writing this paragraph), I might well here and now be a mere replica of Stephen T. Davis rather than Stephen T. Davis. You will never be able to know for sure. (God might know, but no one else ever will.) And this skepticism applies equally well to you and all your friends and relatives as well (assuming their lives, too, included periods in which nobody was watching). If this general skepticism about personal identity seems excessive, as surely it must, it will be excessive in the resurrection world too.

V

Finally, let me consider three objections that might be raised against the theses that are peculiar to this chapter — namely, temporary nonexistence and divine intention.

1. One theological difficulty that is associated with all temporary-nonexistence theories arises among Roman Catholic believers but not Protestants, being related to the Catholic notion of prayers for and intercession by the dead. Catholics traditionally distinguish among the Church Militant (Christians on earth), the Church Suffering (Christians in purgatory), and the Church Triumphant (Christians in heaven). Members of the Church Militant have an obligation to pray for members of the Church Suffering, it is said, and to ask for the intercession of the Church Triumphant. But it is difficult to imagine how one could meet either obligation if temporary nonexistence is a reality.[22]

In response, let me say that only part of the point being made here is valid. There is no conceptual or theological reason why we cannot implore God graciously to restore the dead to life or even pray that the dead be restored to life in God's presence. On the other hand, if it is the case that the dead (temporarily) do not exist, they obviously would not be able to intercede for anyone else. That much is indeed an implication of temporary nonexistence. Perhaps, then, this theory will be unattractive to most Catholics; perhaps Catholic theology is essentially dualist in its understanding of human nature and is accordingly committed to temporary disembodiment.

2. John W. Cooper argues that physicalist accounts of resurrection

22. This objection was pointed out to me by James Hanink.

confuse *identity* and *identification*. The first is the *fact* that, say, x is numerically identical to y, and the second is the *judgment* that x is numerically identical to y. Unless truth is a matter of convention (where thinking that x is identical to y makes x identical to y), we must distinguish between the ontological or factual question (whether x is in fact y) and the epistemological question (how one might legitimately come to judge that x is y). Now, says Cooper, on all monistic accounts of the resurrection (e.g., physicalist accounts such as temporary nonexistence), identity and identification amount to the same thing; "there is nothing more to the ontology of identity than identifiable personal characteristics."[23]

But while the distinction Cooper makes is surely apt, his objection to physicalist accounts of resurrection is unconvincing. It is of course impossible for x and y to have *all* their properties in common without being numerically identical to each other. Still, *judging* that their properties are identical is not the same as their properties *being* identical. But the physicalist can sensibly reply to Cooper that identification is the best or only evidence that we have for identity without claiming that it constitutes identity. Indeed, my central aim in this chapter has been to talk about identity, not identification. I have tried to stipulate criteria that, when satisfied, make it a fact that x is y. Some of these criteria might also be used to make rational judgments about identity, but their primary purpose is the former. If the criteria are satisfied for any x and any y, then x is numerically identical to y, whether anybody recognizes it or not.[24]

---

23. Cooper, "The Identity of Resurrected Persons: Fatal Flaw of Monistic Anthropology," *Calvin Theological Journal* 23 (April 1988): 31.

24. Cooper has acknowledged his agreement with me that " 'God's will is the glue of the universe,' but," he says, "I don't see how this makes uniqueness an essential rather than an accidental property or why it is plausible to think that God intends to conflate numerical identity and exact similarity" (*Body, Soul, and Life Everlasting* [Grand Rapids: William B. Eerdmans, 1989], p. 192n.). I say it is essential to every distinct entity that God wills it to be the thing that it is. It is a contingent fact that God has thus far steadfastly avoided creating any replicas of Stephen T. Davis (i.e., entities that are indistinguishable from me but are not me), but if uniqueness is one of my essential properties (and I agree that it is), then it is not a contingent fact that God has created no other me (i.e., a being numerically identical to me, as opposed to a mere replica); that is something that cannot be done. Finally, God does not on my theory conflate numerical identity with exact similarity; for one thing, my replica is *not* exactly similar to me precisely because (among, presumably, other things, such as life history) it fails to possess the property of "being willed by God to be Stephen T. Davis."

3. A final objection might be raised — this one directed against the use I have made of the notion of divine intention. It is surely true — so the objection might run — that in some cases intention is crucial in establishing identity (e.g., in the case noted above about identifying a strikingly similar character in two different novels), but surely in other cases intention is irrelevant. To borrow another example from van Inwagen, suppose one day your small daughter builds an elaborate pyramid-shaped structure out of toy blocks. Suppose that later, when she is out of the room, you accidentally knock it over. Not wanting your daughter to be hurt, suppose you then rebuild the structure exactly as she had made it. Suppose finally that your *intention* is that the pyramid you constructed be *the same* pyramid as that constructed by your child. Would it then be *the same* pyramid? Would it be a pyramid of which your daughter could be proud? Of course not — so the objection would run — it would be a new pyramid, very like the old one, a replica, if you will.[25] Similarly, it might be argued, God's intention cannot magically make B2 *be* B1 raised from the dead. The death of B1 and the ensuing temporal gap ensure that B2 is a replica of B1 rather than B1.

This argument seems sound with respect to objects such as block pyramids, but perhaps in this regard block pyramids are not like human persons. In any case, the defender of resurrection and divine intention will claim that the proposed analogy fails. Structures made of toy blocks are not like living persons; your relationship to the block pyramid you built is not like God's relationship to the living persons God creates; and above all, your relationship to the universe in which you created the block pyramid is not like God's relationship to this universe. The will of God is the glue of the world, but your will is not the glue of block pyramids.

We can conclude, then, that the arguments mentioned above do not disprove the claim that human persons are beings that can include a gap. The resurrectionist's claim is that we just don't know enough about the nature of human persons. Unlike wars and television programs, we are suspicious of the claim that persons are gap-inclusive, because we know little of the eschaton. If we had God's view, we might find nothing suspicious here; we might know that persons are gap-inclusive. We are perhaps like an amateur naturalist who is deeply interested in and knows a great deal about the cocoons to be found in the forest — who is in fact an expert on the structure and biochemistry of cocoons — but who

25. Van Inwagen, "The Possibility of Resurrection," p. 118.

is totally unaware that butterflies emerge from the cocoons. Our ignorance of the gap-inclusive nature of human existence is perhaps not entirely our fault. We just don't see people raised from the dead often enough to be used to the idea. We aren't familiar with the second stage of human lives, so to speak. But someday we will be.

Part of the problem that Christian philosophers must contend with when they set out to defend resurrection is that most philosophers quite naturally tend to criticize the notion on the basis of beliefs that are fitted to the world as we now experience it. (The belief that personal identity requires spatio-temporal continuity is one such belief.) So we need to ask such philosophers, What if the world, and thus our beliefs about it, changed? What if we suddenly became much more familiar with resurrection from the dead than we are now? (Christians think that one day this very thing will happen.) Then our eyes would be opened. We would be something like the knowledgeable but ignorant naturalist who suddenly discovers that cocoons open to yield butterflies. Then our concepts would change.

7

Uniqueness, Duplication, and Survival

I

In both of the preceding chapters, we noted an important objection that can be raised against resurrection or, indeed, against virtually any survival-of-death theory. This objection revolves around the notion of duplication — the possibility of multiple qualitatively identical (or nearly qualitatively identical) persons in the afterlife. Among other things, this possibility seems to play havoc with the notion that uniqueness is a criterion of personal identity. It is now time to consider the merits of this objection.

The first statement of the objection in the literature is that of Bernard Williams. Speaking of a person Charles, who seems, for all we can tell, to have become (a continuation of the life of) Guy Fawkes, Williams says,

> If it is logically possible that Charles should undergo the changes described, then it is logically possible that some other man should simultaneously undergo the same changes; e.g., that both Charles and his brother Robert should be found in this condition. What should we say in that case? They cannot both be Guy Fawkes; if they were, Guy Fawkes would be in two places at once, which is absurd. Moreover, if they were both identical with Guy Fawkes, they would be identical with each other, which is also absurd. Hence we could not say that they were both identical with Guy Fawkes. We might instead say that one of them was identical with Guy Fawkes, and that the other was just like him; but this would be an utterly vacuous manoeuvre, since

there would be *ex hypothesi* no principle determining which description was to apply to which. So it would be best, if anything, to say that both had mysteriously become like Guy Fawkes, clairvoyantly knew about him, or something like this. If this would be the best description of each of the two, why would it not be the best description of Charles if Charles alone were changed?[1]

Let us now suppose that there was a person named Smith who died some time ago. And let us suppose further that some people hold that Smith will survive death (i.e., that Smith is the same person as a certain person who will live forever in the afterlife). In resurrection terms, then, the problem that Williams raises is this: if it is possible for God to bring about a state of affairs in which it would seem that Smith has survived death and is identical to one who exists in the afterlife, then it is equally possible for God to bring about a state of affairs in which it seems that Smith is identical to two — or even two hundred — different people in the afterlife. That is, an omnipotent being could easily bring about the existence of two or two hundred qualitatively indistinguishable people in the resurrection world, all of whom seem also to be qualitatively indistinguishable from Smith.[2] This creates a serious problem, because identity is a transitive and symmetric relation — that is to say, if A is identical to B, and B is identical to C, then A is identical to C. Thus, if Smith is identical to Smith21 (one of the two hundred Smiths in the afterlife), and if Smith is also identical to Smith96 (another of them), then Smith21 and Smith96 (who exist simultaneously) are identical to each other, which is absurd. Since the survival thesis in such a case would be absurd, it would be equally absurd in the first case. The possibility of duplicates (i.e., of multiple qualitatively identical candidates for Smithhood) renders incoherent the thesis of survival of death.

---

1. Williams, "Personal Identity and Individuation," *Proceedings of the Aristotelian Society* 57 (1956-57): 332.

2. I am assuming here that the premortem Smith is one and only one person. This point needs to be mentioned, because some have argued that the premortem Smith is as many persons as Smith will later become — i.e., the premortem Smith is a "person stage" that shares two (or two hundred) distinct persons. The most noted defender of this theory is David Lewis; see his "Survival and Identity" and "Postscripts to 'Survival and Identity,'" in *Philosophical Papers* (New York: Oxford University Press, 1983), pp. 55-72, 73-77. I do not find this view plausible, however, and so do not propose to discuss it. It involves what I take to be far too great a distortion of our concept of a human person.

II

When pressed in this simple way, the duplication objection is not particularly impressive. For one thing, it seems to work best against theories that equate identity with exact or striking similarity. But this is an equation that I do not make; in my view (as explained in Chap. 6), identity equals striking similarity plus uniqueness and divine intention. For another, the objection turns out to fail even against similarity theories. Of course the claim that Smith has survived death would be difficult to believe if there were two — or two hundred — virtually qualitatively identical candidates for Smithhood, each claiming to be Smith with equal apparent sincerity and success. But what if there is in fact only one? Wouldn't Smith's survival then be believable? And isn't it open to defenders of resurrection to insist that there will be one and only one Smith in the afterlife? Surely you can't refute a thesis, or the possible truth of a thesis, merely by imagining possible worlds in which the thesis would be exceedingly difficult to believe. Survival of death, so it seems, might well make good sense if in the afterlife there is never more than one person who claims to be some premortem person. And since it is possible for there to be but one Smith in the afterlife, Smith's survival seems quite possible.

But what about Williams's deeper point — namely, that the mere logical possibility of duplication (as opposed to its actuality) renders belief in survival of death untenable? Put again in resurrection terms, the point is this: the mere fact that in the afterlife God logically *could* create two or more duplicates of Smith makes the belief that Smith — or any person — will survive death unbelievable. But it is difficult to accept that this claim is true, as John Hick has argued in the context of a discussion of resurrection:

> I freely grant that if there were two resurrection 'Mr. X's' neither of them could be identified as the same person as the earthly Mr. X, and that therefore, so far from there being two, there could not even be one. But I deny that the unrealized logical possibility of there being two resurrection 'Mr. X's' makes it logically impossible for there to be one. It is a conceptual truth that if there were one resurrected 'Mr. X' there could not be another; but this truth does not prohibit there being one and only one. The fact that if there were two or more 'Mr. X's', none of them would be Mr. X, does not prevent there being the only kind of resurrected 'Mr. X' that could exist, namely a single one.[3]

3. Hick, *Death and Eternal Life* (New York: Harper & Row, 1976), p. 292.

In John Perry's book *A Dialogue on Personal Identity and Immortality*, the protagonist Gretchen Weirob recognizes the weakness just pointed out in the duplication argument. After the argument is stated, one of Weirob's former students, Dave Cohen, says, "But wait. Why can't Sam [the college chaplain, another participant in the dialogue] simply say that if God makes one such creature [i.e., one Gretchen Weirob in the afterlife], she is you, while if he makes more, none of them is you? It's possible that he makes only one. So it's possible that you survive."[4] Cohen seems to be entirely correct here; the argument he offers on Sam's behalf in fact constitutes a simplified version of Hick's point.

One of the advantages of Perry's book, however, is that having stated the correct response to the initial version of the duplication argument, he moves the objection to a more profound level. Weirob goes on to argue (1) that a new criterion of personal identity — uniqueness (Weirob calls it "lack of competition") — has now been introduced; (2) that personal identity is now made to rely on a property of Weirob that is "wholly extrinsic" to her — namely, whether or not there are any competitors for Weirobhood around (i.e., whether or not a given candidate for Weirobhood in the afterlife is or is not Weirob surprisingly depends not entirely on her own properties but also on "the existence or nonexistence of other people"); and (3) that God now has an exceedingly odd way of killing someone: that in order to ensure that Weirob does not survive death, God need only create more than one duplicate Weirob in the afterlife.

Perry's third point is not quite correct as it stands. If Weirob survives death and then out of thin air God creates a second Weirob — a duplicate or replica Weirob — surely Weirob *has* survived death, and only the first afterlife Weirob is identical to the premortem Weirob. As I suggested in Chapter 6, this is because the first afterlife Weirob has the appropriate causal connections with the premortem Weirob — that is to say, they share the same history. The second afterlife Weirob would clearly be the impostor; we might not be able to tell the difference between the two (assuming God has done a skillful job of duplicating Weirob), but, having been created *de novo* in the afterlife, and not genuinely sharing Weirob's history, she would not be Weirob. A problem *would* exist, however, if after Weirob's death God were to bring it about that two or more Weirobs

4. Perry, *A Dialogue on Personal Identity and Immortality* (Indianapolis: Hackett, 1978), p. 33.

came simultaneously and through the same causal process to exist in the resurrection world. And the same problem would arise if God were to cause the one and only resurrected Weirob suddenly to divide into two virtually qualitatively identical Weirobs.[5]

But what exactly is wrong with saying that uniqueness or lack of competition is a criterion of personal identity? Lack of competition is a criterion that technically applies in this life as well as the next. We hardly ever bother to mention it because it rarely occurs to us that God has the ability to create multiple qualitatively identical persons here as well. The identity and continued survival of persons here and now depends on God refraining from exercising that ability. (Nor do puzzle cases about duplication need to involve God. Derek Parfit, for example, suggests a whole range of cases involving teletransportation, some of which we will consider a bit later.) Perhaps it *is* odd that God could prevent someone's survival in the way envisioned and that personal identity is here made in part to depend on something entirely extrinsic to the person. These facts are odd, but, as I will argue, they do not impugn the possibility of the survival thesis.

Christians strongly deny that there will be multiple qualitatively identical persons in the eschaton. If the existence of multiple replicas of a given person in the afterlife in some cases threatens personal identity and thus survival of death, then, necessarily, if God intends that a given person should survive death, God will not allow there to be any replicas of that person to exist in the afterlife. Christians would hold, however, that God has the power to create such persons, so it is perfectly fair for critics to ask how it would affect their advocacy of resurrection if God were to exercise this power.

5. This helps us to see what is right and what is wrong in David Wiggin's dictum "a malefactor could scarcely evade responsibility by contriving his own fission" ("Locke, Butler and the Stream of Consciousness: And Men as a Natural Kind," in *The Identities of Persons,* ed. Amelie Rorty [Berkeley and Los Angeles: University of California Press, 1976], p. 146). A malefactor who arranged to be duplicated in the sense that he continued to exist in the presence of a duplicate would still be responsible for his malefactions; the duplicate (who "remembers" doing them but did *not* do them) would not be. However, a malefactor could avoid being punished for his malefactions by arranging that he die and then be replaced by two qualitatively indistinguishable duplicates. If I am right, they should not be punished for his evil deeds, for neither would be identical to him. But of course this is no different from avoiding being punished for one's evil deeds by killing oneself, which even malefactors unskilled in the arts of duplication can manage.

I prefer to hold that the existence of multiple qualitatively identical Smiths in the eschaton would place far too great a strain on our concept of a human person for us to affirm that Smith has survived death (especially if the various replicas were to have the same causal history). Our concept of a person, as I have argued, includes a notion of uniqueness: there is and can be only one instance of each "person." Uniqueness is a criterion of personal identity. So I would argue at the very least that we would not know what to say if there seemed to be more than one Smith in the afterlife; perhaps our concept of a human person would have to be radically revised, especially if such events became common and there were some sort of plausible causal explanation available. As noted earlier, perhaps we might allow for mechanical duplication of persons or something of the sort.[6] More strongly, I would argue that Smith — the unique person who lived on earth — has not survived death.

So our concept of a human person includes the notion that there is but one instance of each person. If there were, *per impossibile,* two qualitatively identical human beings standing before us (or two human beings as qualitatively identical as possible — their location could not be the same, of course), we would nonetheless consider them numerically distinct. We would consider that we were seeing two different individuals. Thus some present person P2 can be numerically identical to some past person P1 only if there is, so to speak, only one P2.

III

There is a difficulty with this argument, however. As several authors, including Perry, have pointed out, the criterion specifies a property that P2 must have in order to be P1 — uniqueness — that is wholly extrinsic to P2. The implication is that there are cases in which the answer to the question of whether P2 is numerically identical to P1 will depend not on P2 (i.e., not on any of P2's intrinsic properties) but on whether there is any competition for P2ness.

Derek Parfit finds this difficulty so powerful that he makes it one of the two central reasons for which he abandons the notion of personal

---

6. Williams suggests that "it is possible to imagine a man splitting amoeba-like, into two simulacra of himself" ("Bodily Continuity and Personal Identity: A Reply," *Analysis* 21 [December 1960]: 47).

identity.[7] Citing Williams, he notes two requirements that any coherent theory of personal identity must satisfy:

> Requirement (1): Whether a future person will be me must depend only on the *intrinsic* features of the relationship between us. It cannot depend on what happens to other people.

> Requirement (2): Since personal identity has great significance, whether identity holds cannot depend on a trivial fact.[8]

Parfit views both requirements as plausible, fails to find a criterion of personal identity that satisfies both, and so gives up on the idea of personal identity. (Only the first requirement need concern us here; the existence of a replica of some person is certainly not a "trivial fact.")

It is easy to see why Parfit, Perry, and many other philosophers consider Requirement 1 plausible.[9] With that in mind, let us turn now to Parfit's notion of teletransportation. As we have already noted, a teletransporter is an imagined device that is designed to send people to distant places like Mars by (1) analyzing the state of all their cells here on earth, (2) communicating that information to a replicator on Mars, (3) destroying the earthly body, and (4) reproducing the person, now made of entirely new matter, on Mars. When all goes well, Parfit argues, our intuition would be that the person on Mars is (a continuation of the life of) the person who entered the teletransporter on earth. And I agree. Certainly the person who leaves the machine on Mars would take himself or herself to be the same person, and so, doubtless, would other people on either planet who knew what had happened.

But we can easily imagine lots of entertaining cases involving the uniqueness criterion in which personal identity would be problematical. Suppose our "space traveler" is named Smith. What if the machine on earth malfunctions and fails to destroy Smith's original body? Who then

---

7. The other main reason Parfit cites is the fact that in certain test cases he discusses, personal identity seems to be either undecidable or indeterminate.

8. Parfit, *Reasons and Persons* (Oxford: Oxford University Press, 1986), p. 267.

9. Requirement 1 seems so obvious to so many philosophers that it is rarely argued for. David Wiggins, for example, merely says, "What we need, if *identity* is what we want to elucidate, is a criterion which will stipulate that for a relation R to be constitutive of the identity of a and b, a's having R to b must be such that objects distinct from a or b are irrelevant to whether a has R to b" (*Sameness and Substance* [Cambridge: Harvard University Press, 1980], p. 96).

is Smith — the one on earth or the one on Mars? Or suppose the replicator on Mars malfunctions and *two* Smithlike creatures emerge from it. Which one is Smith? Or is neither Smith? We can also imagine the following case: Smith is being teletransported to Mars; so far as anyone on earth or Mars knows, all has gone according to plan; the sensible belief for everyone, then, is that Smith is now on Mars; however, unbeknownst to all the others, some clever scientists on Io have also picked up the signal and have replicated their own "Smith" on Io. Does this mean that Smith has not in fact survived, that the "Smith" on Mars is now only a replica of Smith (merely because another Smithlike person has appeared on one of the satellites of Jupiter)? Or what would it mean?

Again, Parfit's Requirement 1 does seem plausible. It does seem odd to suggest, as I have been doing, that since uniqueness is a criterion of personal identity, whether or not the "Smith" on Mars is Smith depends not entirely on "Smith's" intrinsic properties but on factors that are "wholly extrinsic" to "Smith." Nevertheless, I will argue that Requirement 1 is false. The suggestion noted is odd but not incoherent.

It is important to notice that there are perfectly innocuous cases in which x's having a given property or not having it depends not entirely on x but rather on the properties of some third person or thing. It may be that most properties of persons are not of this sort; it is likely that the preponderance of properties will be much more straightforward attributes such as *being healthy* or *being a carpenter* or *being sixty years old.* Whether or not x has properties like these depends, so to speak, on x's own nature and not on anyone or anything else. But what about properties like *being the shortest basketball player in the NBA* or *being the first person to climb K-2* or *being admired by the president of the United States* or *being a widow?* It would seem that whether or not x has these properties depends not entirely on x's intrinsic nature but on whether certain other people or things have certain other properties.

Notice that these are not instances of the weird or purely formal properties beloved of philosophers (e.g., *not being a prime number* or *being either a sewing machine or not a sewing machine* or *being grue*). These are genuine, concrete properties, properties of things that could well be mentioned in ordinary conversation. And the point is (to illustrate with just one of these properties) that God could easily make the NBA's shortest player no longer the NBA's shortest player not by doing anything to him (e.g., making him grow) but by bringing it about that an even shorter player plays in the NBA.

Those who defend uniqueness as a criterion of personal identity can simply suggest that such properties as *having survived death* or *being numerically identical to P1* belong in the second category. Whether or not one possesses them depends not only on what happens to oneself but on what happens to others as well. This is somewhat counterintuitive, I admit; our intuition is to believe that whether or not the x before us is numerically identical to the y who died depends on the properties of x and not on the properties of some third person z. I would argue that this is simply one area (there are others in philosophy) where our attempts to think clearly on some thorny problem lead us to surprising conclusions.

IV

But let us see if it is possible to argue, and not just suggest, that the identity or even survival of a person might be decided on the basis of a property that is (as Perry says) wholly extrinsic to that person. It will be useful to begin this effort by distinguishing among different sorts of properties.

First, here are some properties that I will call *nonrelational properties* of x:

1. x is healthy.
2. x is a carpenter.
3. x is sixty years old.

Intuitively they seem nonrelational because only one property-bearer — x — is mentioned in each statement. These properties are to be distinguished from what I will call *obvious relational properties,* such as

4. x is wearing a sweater;
5. x is taller than y;
6. x loves y,

where more than one property-bearer is mentioned.

Is it possible to suggest a criterion, one with at least some degree of clarity, for distinguishing between relational and nonrelational properties? Yes it is. I would argue that it is logically impossible truly to assert that a given property-bearer has a relational property without that assertion entailing that some other property-bearer possesses some other property. This, then, allows us to suggest the following formal definition:

> *A relational property of* x = (by definition) a property of x such that it is logically impossible for z truly to assert that x has it without z's assertion entailing that some property-bearer other than x or z — namely, y — has some other property.

It is logically impossible for me to assert that you have the property of wearing a sweater without my assertion entailing that the sweater has the property of *being worn by you;* it is logically impossible for you to assert that I have the property of being taller than my son without your assertion entailing that my son has the property of *being shorter than I;* and it is logically impossible for me to assert that you have the property of loving your mother without my assertion entailing that your mother has the property of *being loved by you.*

In the case of nonrelational properties, on the other hand, it is logically possible for someone to assert that a given property-bearer has such a property without that assertion entailing that any other property-bearer possesses any other property. Since healthiness, carpenterness, and sixty-year-oldness are not property-bearers (or substances, as older philosophers might have said), it is possible to assert that someone is healthy, or is a carpenter, or is sixty years old without those assertions entailing that any other property-bearer possesses any other property.

One rule-of-thumb test, then, is epistemological rather than metaphysical. It has to do with verification: a property of some property-bearer is relational if in verifying the claim that the property-bearer has the property in question one must verify that some other property-bearer has some other property. One cannot verify that x loves y without simultaneously verifying that y has the property of being loved by x; one can, however, verify that x is healthy, that x is a carpenter, or that x is sixty years old without verifying that any other property-bearer has any particular property.

Armed with this criterion, let us look at two other sorts of properties:

7. x is the NBA's shortest player.
8. x is the first person to climb K-2.
9. x is admired by the president of the United States.
10. x is a widow.

Although it may not be obvious at first, by the above criterion the properties mentioned in 7-10 are all relational. One cannot verify that x is the NBA's shortest player without checking on the height of all other NBA players; one cannot verify that x is the first person to climb K-2 without proving that no one else has previously climbed that mountain; one cannot verify that x is admired by the president without checking on the president's state of mind or dispositions; one cannot verify that x is a widow without showing that there is another property-bearer who has the properties of being male, of being dead, and of having been married to x at the time of his death.

This shows that there are some properties which are such that whether or not a given property-bearer has them is in part a function of whether or not certain other property-bearers have other properties. Whether or not x is a widow in part depends, as we have seen, on properties that are "wholly extrinsic" to x. One cannot verify the claim that x is a widow merely by observing x's intrinsic properties, without considering properties of other property-bearers.

Now let us consider two of what I will call *survival properties* of x:

11. x has survived death.
12. x is numerically identical to (i.e., is the same person as) y.

Are these properties relational or nonrelational? How might we go about deciding? If we follow the above definition of relational properties, these survival properties are relational. Any attempt to verify them (at least if uniqueness is a criterion of personal identity) would indeed involve checking on and verifying the properties of other property-bearers. As we have seen, in order to prove that x has survived death, it is necessary to prove that there are no competitors for xness in the afterlife. Again, it is logically impossible for z to assert that x is identical to y without that assertion entailing that there are no other equally good competitors for xness.

V

The claim that the identity of a person can be based in part on properties that are extrinsic to that person has been subjected to a variety of criticisms. Some philosophers believe that absurd consequences follow from this claim. Let me reply to three such criticisms that have appeared in the recent literature.

1. Peter Carruthers points out that identity is not an explicitly

comparative notion. You can be more or less tall or fast than somebody else, but you cannot be more or less identical to x than somebody else. There are degrees of height and speed but not of identity. In order to decide whether somebody is tall or fast, you may have to compare that person with other persons. But identity is not that sort of notion; identity is not a comparative notion. Thus, whether x is identical to y must depend only on facts about x and y.[10]

But this argument is not convincing, since there are obvious counterexamples to the principle that seems to undergird it — namely, the principle that for all noncomparative properties (e.g., identity with x), whether a person has such a property can depend only on that person. Widowhood is not a comparative notion either. There are no degrees of widowhood; one widow cannot be "more of a widow" than another widow. But whether or not a given woman is a widow does depend in part on the properties of other persons.

2. Doubtless the most important and oft-repeated criticism of extrinsicness has been summed up by Harold Noonan. The defender of extrinsicness, he says, "is committed to saying that of any pair of *equally good candidates* for identity with an earlier individual (than which there are no better), it is true of each pair that, if it had not existed, nor would the other."[11] Perhaps an example will help. Let's refer to me, writing this paragraph in 1992, as SD1. Now let's suppose that in 1996, I will divide into two qualitatively similar persons, SD2 and SD3. It does not matter what kind of division we are talking about, but here are two possibilities: (1) In 1996 SD1 simply divides, amoeba-like, into two virtually qualitatively identical persons (at least they would be virtually qualitatively identical at first), SD2 and SD3. (2) In 1996 SD1's body is destroyed by a duplicator, which creates two exact copies of SD1 — namely, SD2 and SD3 (assuming that this is technologically possible). Now let's call all the possible worlds in which SD1 is divided in 1996 (in either of the two ways) D-worlds, and all possible worlds in which SD1 is not divided in 1996 (and continues existing as SD1) ND-worlds.

Now, if uniqueness is a criterion of personal identity, it follows that in the D-worlds in 1996, SD1 has not survived and no longer exists. Neither SD2 nor SD3 is identical to SD1; they are individuals who are

---

10. Carruthers, *Introducing Persons* (Albany: State University of New York Press, 1986), p. 207.

11. Noonan, "Reply to Garrett," *Analysis* 46 (October 1986): 209.

quite distinct both from each other and from SD1. Here, then, is the criticism of extrinsicness implicit in Noonan's argument: notice how absurd it is that after the division SD2 can say to SD3, "Thank goodness you exist — that is to say, thank goodness the division occurred — because *if you did not exist, I would not exist.*"

Now I suggest that the statement "If you did not exist, I would not exist" sounds absurd because it is ambiguous. It might be taken to mean (when said by SD2) that if SD3 stopped existing, then SD2 would stop existing too, as if they were Siamese twins, or as if their fates were for some other reason closely linked. Or it might be taken to mean that if SD3 had never come into existence, then SD2 (the very body that constitutes SD2) would never have come into existence. Such notions certainly are absurd, but they are not entailed by extrinsicity. The second is ruled out because of the obvious possibility that the division occurs in 1996 but that SD3 does not survive it.

In both sorts of D-worlds, it is certainly true counterfactually that if SD3 had never existed (or even if SD3 had survived the division but only very briefly), then the body which in the D-worlds we call SD2 would be identical to SD1. It is also true that in all ND-worlds, there would be no "SD2." But so what? This is hardly a metaphysically interesting result. Consider again SD2's statement to SD3: "Thank goodness you exist . . . because *if you did not exist, I would not exist.*" If this statement means that SD2 exists only in worlds in which SD3 also exists, it is patently false. What is to say that SD2 could not survive nicely even if SD3 died a year after the division? If it means merely that SD2 exists only in worlds in which (1) the division occurs and (2) SD3 lives long enough after the division for it to be the case via the uniqueness criterion that SD2 is not identical to SD1 (i.e., SD2 is a unique individual), then SD2's statement is true. But why should this statement be taken as paradoxical or even puzzling? It seems rather to have the status of an obvious truth.

Suppose that we are living in a D-world after the division and that we have SD2 and SD3 before us. In such a situation, it would be possible for people to ask counterfactually, "Who or what SD-like person or persons would we have before us if the division had not occurred?" What would not follow is that SD2 (the very body that in 1996 makes up SD2) would not exist. What would follow, as we have seen, is that the person whom we call SD2 in the D-worlds would not be in the ND-worlds an individual distinct from SD1. (I am assuming here that problems connected with transworld identity can be solved — i.e., that it makes sense to identify some SD-like person in one possible world with some SD-like person in another.) That is, the person whom we call "SD2" in the D-worlds would simply be SD1 continuing to exist.

But it is important to see that the configuration of matter that in the D-worlds we call SD2 (that very body with its properties of height, age, abilities, etc.) *would* or at least certainly could still exist in the ND-worlds. There is of course this difference: the SD2 who exists after the division in the D-worlds is the causal descendent of just one-half of SD1's pre-1996 body; the SD1 who exists after 1996 in the ND-worlds is the causal descendent of the whole of SD1's predivision body. Still, by hypothesis, the body of SD2 in the D-worlds would have characteristics so strikingly similar to SD1's predivision body, and to SD1's post-1996 body in the ND-worlds, as to allow the inference that the body is the same.

3. Finally, Noonan makes the following point: if extrinsicness is allowed, then "events which constitute the origin of some entity of a certain kind in one situation, may not constitute the origin of that, or any entity of the kind, in a second situation, even though all the events constituting the history of that entity in the first situation remain present in the second."[12] And this, Noonan suggests, is incoherent. Take the individual SD2 in the D-worlds (i.e., in those worlds in which the division occurs and SD3 exists too). In all D-worlds, we can coherently consider the event of the division of SD1 in 1996 as the origin of SD2. But notice the fact that in that subset of the D-worlds in which the division occurs in 1996 but SD3 immediately dies (and in which we would accordingly almost certainly consider via the uniqueness criterion that SD1 simply continues to exist), the splitting would no longer be the origin of SD2. The origin of "SD2" in all such D-worlds is simply the birth, possibly years before, of SD1.

This third objection to extrinsicness is parasitic on the second. Accordingly, there is an air of question-begging about it, especially if my reply to the second objection is on target. In the light of that reply, let me simply add here that those who defend extrinsicness need not be bothered by the purportedly absurd conclusion that Noonan draws from their position, for they defend extrinsicness precisely because they hold that extrinsic and thus apparently causally irrelevant events can make a difference in some cases of identity. In the scenario envisioned, the SD body simply has a much longer history in the ND-worlds than we might have imagined had we attended only to the D-worlds.

12. Noonan, *Personal Identity* (New York: Routledge, 1989), p. 160.

It might be objected to the overall thesis of this chapter that the rejection of Requirement 1 in favor of the uniqueness criterion of personal identity carries with it a certain cost. It might be said that no survival claim such as "P1 [who lived and died] is the same person as P2 [a person in the afterlife]" could ever be verified. This is because there just might exist, in some distant corner of the afterlife, a second candidate for P1hood. This is a possibility that will always have to be entertained.

And it seems that this point, or at least part of it, is correct. There *will* always be such a possibility. Whether survival claims will be able to be verified depends, of course, on what is meant by "verify." To borrow a distinction that John Hick made years ago, if "verify" means "remove all possible doubt," then it will be impossible to verify survival claims, but if, on the other hand, it means "remove all rational doubt," then it surely will be possible to verify survival claims.[13] This will be true in the same way in which we today are able to verify such claims as "This is Smith here before us." We simply do not bother to worry about the logical possibility that last night Smith died and that God decided to create, simultaneously and through the same causal processes, two equal Smith duplicates, one of which, say, is here before me in Claremont and the other of which is in hiding in Paraguay.

In conclusion, I claim in this chapter to have made a strong case that such properties as "survives death" and "is identical to P1" are relational, that the uniqueness criterion of personal identity is plausible, that Parfit's Requirement 1 is false, and that the duplication objection to survival of death accordingly fails.

13. Hick, *Faith and Knowledge* (Ithaca, N.Y.: Cornell University Press, 1957), pp. 169-99.

8

Resurrection and Judgment

I

In Luke's version of the apostle Paul's speech before the Roman governor Felix, Paul affirms that "there will be a resurrection of both the just and the unjust" (Acts 24:15; see also Rom. 14:10). And the fourth evangelist records Jesus as similarly saying, "The hour is coming, and now is, when the dead will hear the voice of the Son of God. . . . Do not marvel at this; for the hour is coming when all who are in the tombs will hear his voice and come forth, those who have done good, to the resurrection of life, and those who have done evil, to the resurrection of judgment" (John 5:25, 28-29). In part because of these texts (as well as others), Christians have traditionally held that *all* human beings will be raised from the dead, not just the saved. The general resurrection of which I have been speaking in this book will be, according to Christian tradition, a universal resurrection.

But what will happen to people after the general resurrection? What will be the fate of "those who have done good" and "those who have done evil"? Christians have also traditionally believed that at least some people, after death, live eternally apart from God. Let us call those who believe this doctrine *separationists,* because they hold that these people are eternally separated both from God and from the people who are with God. Other Christians, who espouse the doctrine of universalism, believe that all human beings will ultimately live eternally with God (i.e., that no one will be eternally condemned).[1]

1. Among recent and contemporary Christians, Nicholas Berdyaev, Nels Ferré,

147

The debate between separationists and universalists is an important theological debate in and of itself. But it also seems to have many implications for other areas of theology (e.g., soteriology), for philosophy (e.g., with respect to the problem of evil), and for Christian life and practice (e.g., with respect to evangelism). Although I am sympathetic with the intentions of those who espouse universalism, I am not a universalist myself, and I will argue against the doctrine in this chapter. I will begin by presenting the strongest doctrine of universalism and the strongest arguments in favor of it of which I can think, and then I will reply to these arguments from a separationist standpoint and make a case for separationism. Finally, at the conclusion of the chapter, I want to make some remarks about the biblical concept of the wrath of God.

Before proceeding to these main points, however, let me make three points that will help put my arguments in context. First, the theological problem of universalism and the fate of those who remain ignorant of the gospel message should not be confused with the question of the salvific relationship between Christianity and the other religions of the world.[2] The two issues are related, but I can clarify the difference between them by pointing out that it is possible to be a Christian universalist and a religious exclusivist; equally, it is possible to be a Christian separationist and a religious pluralist. Second, I need to remind readers that I am a Christian of a fairly traditional theological persuasion. Among other things, this means that I accept the Bible as religiously authoritative. Thus I want to take seriously what the Bible seems to be saying on the topic of this chapter. I dissociate myself entirely from any view of Scripture that dismisses it as unimportant or that allows one to pick and choose whichever biblical texts one finds congenial.[3] Third, I will not discuss the theory known as annihilationism, which holds that God permanently destroys, rather than consigns to hell, those who reject

William Barclay, J. A. T. Robinson, and John Hick have all defended some form of universalism. Karl Barth has been accused of espousing the doctrine.

2. I have addressed this issue in "Evangelicals and the Religions of the World," *Reformed Journal* 31 (June 1981): 9-13.

3. Although I frequently quote and refer to texts from the Bible in this chapter with little reference to problems associated with context, dating, authorship, authenticity, tradition, redaction history, etc., I wish to note that I do not reject biblical criticism and believe I can defend the use I make of Scripture in the light of concerns biblical scholars might have. I more fully explain my own views about the theological authority of the Bible in *The Debate about the Bible* (Philadelphia: Westminster Press, 1977).

God. Although I do not have the space to defend my position in this book, I oppose annihilationism because I consider it contrary to the central thrust of the New Testament.[4]

Let me now sketch what I take to be a strong doctrine of universalism. God does indeed hate sin and does indeed judge sinners, but God's judgment is always therapeutic: it is designed to bring people to repentance. Thus God's wrath is an integral part of God's loving strategy for reconciling people to God. Some are reconciled to God in this life; some die unreconciled. But God continues to love even those who die apart from God and to work for their reconciliation. If there is a hell, it exists only for a time, until the last recalcitrant sinner decides to say Yes to God. It is *possible* that hell will exist forever because it is possible that some will deny God forever. But after death, God has unlimited time, arguments, and resources to convince people to repent. God will not force anyone into the kingdom; God always respects the freedom of God's creatures. But because of the winsomeness of God's love, we can be sure that God will emerge victorious and that all persons will eventually be reconciled to God. We are all sinners and deserve punishment, but God's love is so great and God's grace so attractive that eventually all persons will be reconciled to God. This, then, is what I take to be a strong version of universalism. Now, what about the arguments in its favor? Let me mention five of them.

1. *The Bible implies that universalism is true.* Many universalists are quite prepared to admit that their doctrine is not taught in the Bible and indeed that separationism seems much more clearly taught. Nevertheless, they do typically argue that universalism is at least implied or suggested in various texts. First, it can be pointed out that many texts suggest that it is God's intention that everyone be reconciled to God (see Rom. 11:32; 1 Tim. 2:4-6; 2 Pet. 3:9). Second, it can be shown that the work of God's grace in Christ was designed for the salvation of everyone (see 2 Cor. 5:14, 15; Tit. 2:11; Heb. 2:9; 1 John 2:2). Third, there are texts that proclaim God's total victory and say that everything will ultimately be reconciled to God:

> For as in Adam all die, so also in Christ shall all be made alive. (1 Cor. 15:22; cf. vv. 23-28)

4. Although I do not agree with everything that he says, Daniel P. Fuller effectively points out many of the exegetical and theological difficulties of annihilationism in *The Unity of the Bible* (Grand Rapids: Zondervan, 1992), pp. 196-203.

In Christ God was reconciling the world to himself. (2 Cor. 5:19)

For in [Christ] all the fulness of God was pleased to dwell, and through him to reconcile to himself all things . . . making peace by the blood of his cross. (Col. 1:19-20; see also Rom. 8:19-21; Eph. 1:10, 20-23)

Finally, there are texts that the universalists interpret as explicitly predicting that all will eventually be reconciled to God:

Then as one man's trespass led to condemnation to all men, so one man's act of righteousness leads to acquittal and life for all men. (Rom. 5:18)

Therefore God has highly exalted him and bestowed on him the name which is above every name, that at the name of Jesus every knee should bow, in heaven and on earth and under the earth, and every tongue confess that Jesus Christ is Lord, to the glory of God the Father. (Phil. 2:9-11; see also John 1:29; 3:17; 12:32, 47)

2. *How can God's purposes be frustrated?* Some universalists argue as follows: eternal sin and eternal punishment would obviously frustrate God's intention that no one be eternally lost. But if God is truly sovereign, how can any divine intention be frustrated? If separationism is true, some will eternally resist God, and it follows that God is at least a partial failure. Surely if God is omnipotent, nothing can eternally frustrate the divine aims; if it is God's aim that all be rescued, all *will* be rescued.[5]

3. *How can a just God condemn people to eternal torment?* Universalists frequently argue that no one deserves *eternal* punishment. Perhaps terrible sinners deserve to suffer terribly for a terribly long time. But surely sin should be punished according to its gravity; why do the damned deserve to suffer for an *infinitely* long time? They certainly do not cause anyone else (or even God) *eternal* sorrow or pain. Suppose we decide that some tyrant, say the emperor Nero, deserves to suffer a year in hell for every person he ever killed, injured, treated unfairly, insulted, or even inconvenienced. Suppose further that on this criterion he deserves to suffer for 200,000 years. The problem is that once he has served this sentence he will not have made even the slightest dent in eternity. According to

5. See, for example, J. A. T. Robinson, *In the End, God* (London: James Clarke, 1950), p. 107.

separationism, he must suffer forever. Is this just? It does not seem so. (And this is not even to speak of more run-of-the-mill sinners who perhaps never cause anyone serious harm.)

4. *How can the blessed experience joy in heaven if their friends and loved ones are in hell?* Obviously (so universalists will argue), they can't. People can know true joy and happiness in heaven only if everyone else is or eventually will be there too. If the blessed are to experience joy in heaven, as Christian tradition says they are, universalism must be true.

5. *What about the fate of those who die in ignorance of Christ?* Christianity has traditionally taught that salvation is to be found only in Christ. Jesus is reported as having claimed this very thing: "I am the way, and the truth, and the life; no one comes to the Father, but by me" (John 14:6). And this claim seems to dovetail well with standard Christian notions about sin and salvation: there is nothing we can do to save ourselves; all our efforts at self-improvement fail; all we can do is trust in God as revealed in Christ; those who do not know God as revealed in Christ are condemned. But surely — so universalists argue — the traditional notion is unfair. It is not right to condemn to hell those who die in ignorance of Christ.

Suppose there was a woman named Oohku who lived from 370-320 B.C. in the interior of Borneo. Obviously, she would never have heard of Jesus Christ or the Judeo-Christian God; she would never have been baptized, nor would she ever have made any institutional or psychological commitment to Christ or to the Christian church. She *couldn't* have done these things; she was simply born in the wrong place and at the wrong time. Could it be right for God to condemn this woman to eternal hell just because she was never able to come to God through Christ? Of course not. The only way that Oohku can be treated fairly by God is if universalism is true. God is just and loving; thus, universalism must be true.

II

These are the best arguments for universalism of which I can think. We now need to see how separationists will handle them and defend their own doctrine.

Let us begin with the biblical argument of the universalist. The first thing to notice is that separationists like me do not deny that God desires the salvation of all persons, that Christ's atoning work was designed to rescue everyone, or that all people have access to God's offer of salvation. No one is excluded from salvation by the initiative or plan of God.

Accordingly, the texts cited in connection with the first argument for universalism presented above do not tell against separationism. As to the texts that emphasize God's total victory and that universalists interpret as predicting universal salvation, the separationist replies that this is not their proper interpretation. To affirm that God is ultimately victorious over all enemies and that God's authority will one day be universally recognized is one thing. All Christians can agree on that. But to say that every person will eventually be reconciled to God is quite another; such an assertion can only be based on a surprisingly literalistic interpretation of such terms as "all," "all things," "every knee," and "the world" in the passages cited. It is odd that universalists, who typically protest against literalistic interpretations of the many texts that seem to teach separationism (see below), appear themselves to adopt a kind of literalism here. They need to approach the passages cited with a bit more hermeneutical subtlety; they need to ask (especially in the light of other texts) whether this is what these passages really mean. Indeed, I believe a convincing case can be made that the ultimate reconciliation of all things to God — which all Christians should affirm — includes divine judgment as well as blessing.

Furthermore, the fact that these "universalistic passages" appear in many of the same texts in which separationism seems clearly taught ought to make us doubt that universalists interpret them correctly. Three passages make this clear:

> For God sent the Son into the world, not to condemn the world, but that the world might be saved through him. He who believes in him is not condemned; he who does not believe is condemned already, because he has not believed in the name of the only Son of God. (John 3:17-18)

> Then as one man's trespass led to condemnation for all men, so one man's act of righteousness leads to acquittal and life for all men. For as by one man's disobedience many were made sinners, so by one man's obedience many will be made righteous. (Rom. 5:18-19)

> We have our hope set on the living God, who is the Savior of all men, especially of those who believe. (1 Tim. 4:10)

The passage from the Fourth Gospel shows, contrary to the universalist's interpretation of the "all" passages, that the Son's being the savior of "the world," whatever this means, is quite consistent with some people being condemned. Whatever Paul meant by the phrase "all persons" in the Romans passage, he was clearly not advocating universalism; otherwise he would not have gone on to say, twenty-eight verses later, "There is therefore now no condemnation *for those who are in Christ Jesus*" (Rom. 8:1, italics added), as if there *is* condemnation for those who are not in Christ Jesus. And the 1 Timothy passage shows that the sense in which God is the savior of "all persons" is not the same sense in which God is the savior of "those who believe." God is the savior of all people, but to those who believe, God is the savior in a different and special sense.

Moreover, separationists can produce a biblical argument of their own that is much more compelling. For the reality of hell — and even of eternal hell — is spoken of often in the New Testament (see Mark 9:43-50; Matt. 25:41, 46; 2 Thess. 1:7-9; Jude 6; Rev. 14:11; 19:3; 20:10) and seems inextricably tied to such major themes in New Testament theology as God, sin, judgment, atonement, and reconciliation. Thus it would seem that the introduction of universalism would require severe changes at various other points in traditional Christian theological systems. (In fact, it almost always does; e.g., upon close examination, I believe that many universalists tend toward Pelagianism.) Indeed, in the New Testament there seems to be a strong connection between the reality of hell and the need for atonement and a savior from sin (see, e.g., Matt. 25:41; 2 Cor. 5:10; 2 Thess. 1:8-9).[6] Furthermore, it seems methodologically odd for a person both to deny the reality of eternal hell and (because of biblical teaching and Christian tradition) affirm the reality of heaven, since both seem to stand on an equally firm exegetical and traditional foundation. It is clear that, for most universalists, philosophical considerations outweigh exegetical ones.

My reply to the biblical argument of the universalist, then, is that while it is possible to read a few New Testament (especially Pauline) texts as supporting universalism, a more careful analysis shows that not even those texts actually teach universalism. Furthermore, biblically oriented Christians believe that problematical passages on any topic should be interpreted in the light of the testimony of the whole of Scripture, and universalism — so I have argued — is inconsistent with that testimony.

---

6. Of course a universalist could respond that it is precisely because of the atoning work of Christ that all will be saved. But in fact, few universalists argue in this way. In any event, I believe my claim still stands on the basis of arguments from a traditional Christian understanding of God's grace, which I will develop shortly.

Let me confess that I would be greatly heartened if universalism were true. Like all Christians, I would find it wonderfully comforting to believe that all people will be citizens of the kingdom of God, and certain thorny intellectual problems, especially the problem of evil, might be easier to solve if universalism were true.[7] But as a matter of theological method, we cannot affirm a doctrine just because we would like it to be true. The fact is that separationism is taught in the Bible and that the so-called "universalistic passages" do not teach universalism. That is enough for me; that is why I am a separationist. Philosophical and theological arguments over what God should do are outweighed by the teaching of Scripture. God has revealed to us a doctrine of eternal judgment; we had best accept it. That God has not also revealed to us how to reconcile this doctrine with our understanding of God's love creates a theological problem that we must do our best to solve.

III

I will now briefly sketch the separationist doctrine that I support. It differs from some traditional theological accounts at two points: (1) for exegetical reasons, I do not believe that hell is a place of horrible fiery agony; and (2) while I believe that hell in some sense can be spoken of as punishment, I do not believe that it is a place where God, so to speak, gets even with those who deny God — which is to say, I do not believe that it is primarily a place of retribution.

We know little about hell. Much of what the New Testament says is clearly metaphorical or symbolic. For example, the New Testament uses the metaphor of fire to convey the suffering of people in hell. This image has been enormously influential in forming popular Christian conceptions of hell. But the metaphor need not mean that condemned people actually suffer the pain of burns. Mark 9:48 describes hell as a place where "the worm does not die" and "the fire is not quenched." Why take the second literally and not the first? I would say both are metaphors of the eternalness of hell.

The parable of the rich man and Lazarus in Luke 16:19-31 has been taken by some interpreters as a picture of the afterlife, but this does not seem sensible. It is a parable, a story designed to convey a certain

7. As, above all, John Hick has seen. See *Evil and the God of Love* (London: Macmillan, 1966), pp. 98, 113-20, 183, 377-81.

religious message, not a journalistic account. Furthermore, it is difficult to imagine that heaven and hell could be separated by a "great chasm" that could not be physically crossed but that would accommodate communication from one side to the other. There are many biblical metaphors for hell — for example, everlasting fire (Matt. 25:41), bottomless pit (Rev. 9:2), outer darkness (Matt. 8:12), destruction (Matt. 10:28), place of weeping and gnashing of teeth (Matt. 8:12), place of no rest (Rev. 14:11), place where the uttermost farthing must be paid (Matt. 5:26). None, I would argue, is a literal description. The doctrine that hell exists, then, is not the same thing as the pictures and images used to express it. This is not to say that we can simply dismiss these images; we have to take them seriously: hell is a terrible state, a place of incalculable loss. But a hermeneutic that takes these pictures literally is improbable.

Hell is separation from communion with God (2 Thess. 1:9). It is not separation from the presence of God, of course — that would mean hell would not exist, for nothing can exist apart from God. The biblical tradition denies that anything or anyone can ever be totally separated from God (see Ps. 139:7-12). But hell is separation from fellowship with God, the source of all true love, joy, peace, and light. It is not a place of agony, torment, torture, and utter horror (I reject the lurid and even sadistic pictures of hell envisioned by some Christian thinkers), but there is no deep or ultimate joy there. I believe its citizens know that they are separated from God and are accordingly miserable. Their great loss is something of which they will be at least dimly aware. To be apart from the source of love, joy, peace, and light is to live miserably.

Why are the damned in hell? I have already ruled out retribution or any notion of God's "getting even" with them.[8] To put it radically, I believe they are in hell because they choose to be in hell; no one is sent to hell against his or her will.[9] Sadly, some people choose to harden

---

8. It must be admitted that there are New Testament texts that can be taken (but in my opinion do not have to be taken) to imply that condemnation to hell is an act of vengeance or retribution on sinners (e.g., Matt. 5:22, 29; 8:12; 10:15; 2 Thess. 1:6-9; Heb. 2:2-3; 10:28-31; 2 Pet. 2:4-9, 12-13). Some even seem to suggest degrees of punishment corresponding to degrees of guilt (see Matt. 11:22-24; Luke 12:47-48; 20:47).

9. "To choose finally and for ever — unfathomable mystery of iniquity — to say 'No' to Jesus is to be held in a hell of one's own choosing and making," says Thomas F. Torrance. "It is not God who makes hell, for hell is the contradiction of all that is God" ("Universalism or Election?" *Scottish Journal of Theology* 2 [September 1949]: 317).

their hearts and live their lives apart from God and will continue to do so after death; some will doubtless do so forever. For such people, I suspect, living in the presence of God will seem worse than living in the absence of God. Allowing them to live forever in hell is simply God's way of continuing to grant them the freedom that they enjoyed in this life to say No to God. I nevertheless suspect that people in hell are deeply remorseful. Can people both freely choose hell over heaven, knowing that in their unrepentant state they would be unable to endure heaven, but still be full of remorse that they cannot happily choose heaven? I believe this is quite possible.

Is the existence of hell consistent with God's love and power? Yes, it is. Some Christians try to justify the existence of hell by speaking of it as the "natural consequence" of a life of sin.[10] I accept the notion that hell is the natural consequence of a life of sin (and it is in this sense that hell is a punishment), but I do not believe that this in itself would justify God in sending people to hell, for it does not justify the divinely ordained laws of natural or moral necessity that make hell the natural consequence of sin. I claim, to the contrary, that the people who are in hell are there because they freely choose it — that is, they freely choose not to live in God's presence. If God is to remain consistent with the divinely established desire for human beings to be free, God has no choice but to "give them up" (Rom. 1:24, 26, 28) to their own proud and perverse desires. In this sense, we can view hell as an expression not only of divine justice but of divine love.

IV

I have been replying to the biblical argument of the universalist. Now I must comment on the other universalist arguments.

How can God's purposes be frustrated? I agree that God desires the salvation of everyone, and so I acknowledge that separationism entails that at least some of God's desires are not satisfied: some people will be lost. How can this be, if God is sovereign? The answer is that God created us as free agents; God gave us the ability to say Yes or No to God. One of the risks that God ran in so doing was precisely that God's purposes

10. See John Wenham, *The Goodness of God* (Downers Grove, Ill.: InterVarsity Press, 1974), p. 38n.; and P. T. Geach, *Providence and Evil* (Cambridge: Cambridge University Press, 1977), pp. 128, 138-40, 147.

would be frustrated, and this, sadly, is exactly what has happened. God's will is flouted whenever anyone sins. It is not true that "God's will is always done." (Note that Jesus taught his disciples to pray "Thy will be done, on earth as it is in heaven" — which would certainly seem to imply the belief that God's will is not always being done on earth.) Furthermore, it seems that sovereignty entails only *the power* to impose one's will, not the actual imposition of it.

How can a just God condemn someone to eternal torment? In the first place, as already noted, I believe the citizens of hell are there because they freely choose to be there; they have hardened their hearts and would be unable to endure heaven. Unless one bows to God and makes the divine will one's own, heaven is too much to bear, and one chooses hell. Thus, as also noted, it is not only just but loving of God to allow them to live forever in hell. Second, hell may have the effect on many of strengthening their resolve never to repent. In hell they may continue to sin, and if it is right for evil-doers to experience the consequences of the evil deeds they do here and now, this should be true of the evil deeds they do after death as well. Eternal hell is morally justified for those who will eternally reject God (i.e., for those who will never cease freely to choose hell). Third, Christians believe that their salvation is a matter of grace alone; we deserve to be condemned, but out of love rather than sheer justice God forgives us and reconciles us to God. The notion of grace, then, is at the heart of the Christian good news. God loves us though we are unlovable; God accepts us though we are unacceptable; what we receive from God is infinitely better than what we deserve. But the thing to notice here is that if separationism is inconsistent with God's love — that is, if a loving God cannot consistently condemn anyone to hell — then our salvation (i.e., our rescue from hell) can no longer be a matter of grace; it must be a matter of our being justly freed from a penalty that we don't really deserve. In the end, universalism overturns the Christian notion of grace.

In a series of recent articles, Tom Talbott has defended universalism, arguing that it is consistent with the Christian Scriptures and that the doctrine of hell is inconsistent with the notion that God loves all persons.[11] Much that Talbott says is not relevant to the approach that I have taken in this chapter, so I will attempt no full-blown discussion of

---

11. See Talbott, "The Doctrine of Everlasting Punishment," *Faith and Philosophy* 7 (January 1990): 19-42; "Providence, Freedom, and Human Destiny," *Religious Studies* 26 (June 1990): 227-46; and "The New Testament and Universal Reconciliation," *Christian Scholar's Review* 21 (June 1992): 376-94.

his views.[12] One of his arguments, however, is aimed at what he calls the "moderately conservative theist," by which he means somebody who holds (as I do) that "some persons will, despite God's best efforts to save them, finally reject God and separate themselves from God."[13] So I will try to respond to Talbott's objection to this claim.

His contention is that the very idea of a rational agent freely choosing eternal damnation is "deeply incoherent." How could any rational person consciously and freely choose eternal damnation, he asks.[14]

But given the points I have made about the nature of hell, I fail to see any incoherence. Such a free choice of hell might be said to be objectively irrational if I am mistaken in my claim that anyone in an unredeemed state is quite incapable of enduring heaven. But who is to say that the damned must always make rational choices? I believe it is entirely possible that they might perceive the choice of hell to be in their best interests. Furthermore, I do not agree with Talbott that "over the long run . . . evil will always undermine and destroy itself."[15] There is a kind of evil — pride, rebellion, the refusal to submit one's will to God — that can feed on itself and grow rather than diminish. Nor do I agree with Talbott's notion that all evil is due to ignorance or illusion (which, Talbott says, in the afterlife God could rule out in the minds of the damned by a clear revelation).[16] No doubt some evil is due to ignorance, but I would argue that much of it is due to the kind of stubborn pride — a freely chosen bondage — that might only grow more rebellious and hard-hearted in the face of God's efforts.

How can the blessed be joyous if friends and loved ones are in hell? I do not have an adequate answer to this question. I expect that if I knew enough about heaven, I would know the answer, but I know little about heaven. The problem is perhaps less acute for me than for those separationists who believe that hell is a place of permanent torture. If I am right, the blessed need not worry that loved ones are in agony, and, as I will suggest shortly, they may even be allowed to hope that God's love will eventually

12. For a critical assessment of Talbott's biblical argument, see Larry Lacy, "Talbott on Paul as a Universalist," *Christian Scholar's Review* 21 (June 1992): 395-407. For some acute criticism of Talbott's two 1990 articles, see William L. Craig, "Talbott's Universalism," *Religious Studies* 27 (September 1991): 297-308.

13. Talbott, "The Doctrine of Everlasting Punishment," p. 23.

14. Talbott, "The Doctrine of Everlasting Punishment," p. 38; and "Providence, Freedom, and Human Destiny," p. 236.

15. Talbott, "Providence, Evil, and Human Destiny," p. 237.

16. Talbott, "Providence, Evil, and Human Destiny," p. 236.

achieve a reconciliation. But there is still the question of how, say, a wife could experience joy and happiness in heaven while her beloved husband was in hell. And that is the question I am unable to answer satisfactorily. It seems to me perfectly possible that the blessed in heaven will have no consciousness of hell or memory of those who are there. In other words, the experience of the beatific vision will be so overwhelming and all-encompassing that such memories will fade. Furthermore, it would seem unjust for God to allow the wrong choices of the damned (i.e., their rejection of God) to ruin the joy of the blessed, who have chosen to love God.[17] But how God brings it about that the blessed experience the joy of the presence of God despite the absence of others, I do not know.

V

What about the fate of those who die in ignorance of Christ? The main point to note here is that the Bible does not speak in any connected or clear way on this question. Christians must take seriously those exclusivistic sayings of Jesus and the New Testament writers (e.g., John 14:6; 8:23-24; Acts 4:12) that create this problem for us. As an orthodox Christian, then, I affirm that salvation is to be found only in Christ. If any person at any time in this life or the next is ever reconciled to God, it is because of the saving work of Jesus Christ. His life, death, and resurrection made it possible. If I am somehow to be reconciled to God, if our imaginary friend Oohku is somehow to be reconciled to God, it is only through Christ that it happens.[18]

Some Christians have taken to heart the Bible's exclusivistic sayings and have concluded that people like Oohku must be lost, that their eternal destiny is hell. But this is to confuse the claim that the Bible is authoritative on matters of faith and practice with the claim that the Bible authoritatively tells us everything that we might want to know about Christian faith and practice. It doesn't. I believe the Bible tells us enough so that we can read it, be convicted of sin, and come to God through Christ. But it does not answer all the questions that we might want to ask, and it certainly does

17. As suggested by C. S. Lewis in *The Great Divorce* (New York: Macmillan, 1957), pp. 120-24.

18. Thus I oppose the views of those contemporary Christian theologians who see Christianity as merely one of many equally valid and valuable avenues of salvation.

not say or imply that those who die in ignorance of Christ are lost. The Bible simply does not in any direct or thorough way address itself to the precise issue of the fate of people like Oohku. The Bible tells us what we *need* to know, not all that we might *want* to know.

What, then, must the separationist say about the fate of those who die in ignorance of Christ? Some have wrongly reasoned from the Bible's vague and unformulated hints on the matter to formulate a dogmatic position. For example, some use Paul's argument about Israel in Romans 9 to justify the position that all who die in ignorance of Christ are condemned to hell. They argue that we have no right to question God's sovereign authority to make whatever decisions God wants to make. God made us, they say, and we have no more right to question God's decisions than clay has the right to question the potter about how the potter has shaped it (see Rom. 9:19-24). I am certainly willing to agree that God can make us in any way God pleases and that we have no authority over God to challenge such a decision. But this by itself does not answer the question of the fate of those who die in ignorance of Christ, nor is Paul's argument in Romans 9 even concerned with that problem. He was wrestling there with the theological implications of Israel's election as God's people, its apparent rejection of Jesus, and its future in God's plan. He was not considering the fate of people who die in ignorance of Christ.

I have also heard the following sort of argument in favor of the claim that it is just for God to send the ignorant to hell: "We are *all* sinners, and thus we *all* deserve hell. So *no one* is sent to hell who does not deserve hell. It is simply the case that God has graciously allowed or elected some sinners to receive the unmerited gift of salvation. Like everyone else, Oohku deserves to go to hell, so she has no reason to complain when she is sent there."

But my response to this argument is that the described scheme is still radically unjust. Surely it is unfair to those who were not chosen to receive God's grace. Suppose I discover that my two sons are both equally guilty of some wrong — say they both trampled some of my wife's prized roses in the backyard. And suppose I say to one of them: "You are guilty and your punishment is that you will be confined to your room." And suppose I say to the other one: "You are equally guilty, but as a gift of love, I'm going to let you go without punishment." Surely it is obvious on the face of it that I have been unfair.

Returning to Paul, he does say some things in Romans 1:19-21 and 2:12-16 that seem relevant to the problem of the ignorant. In an effort to show that all people — Jews and Gentiles alike — are guilty in

God's eyes and without excuse for their sinfulness, he argues that everyone naturally knows certain truths about God and that those who are born apart from the Old Testament law (i.e., the Gentiles) are judged by what they know of God's will. They know God's will in rudimentary form because what the law requires is "written on their hearts" (2:15). Some have taken this to mean that those who die in ignorance of Christ are judged by God not on the basis of whether they become Christians but on the basis of how well they behave in terms of what they naturally knew about God and God's righteous will. This notion seems consistent with the traditional Roman Catholic view of those who die in "invincible ignorance": if they keep the natural law, are ready to obey God, and lead an upright life, they can, by God's grace, receive eternal life (see Peter's words to Cornelius in Acts 10:35).

I do not wish to reject this solution altogether; perhaps it can be made to work.[19] But there are difficulties with it that cause me to search elsewhere for an adequate resolution of the problem. In the first place, this solution seems inconsistent with much that the New Testament teaches elsewhere. It is true that all people who on their own achieve lives of perfect obedience to the law of God are justified. But Paul is most emphatic on the point that no one in fact does this: "All have sinned and fall short of the glory of God" (Rom. 3:23). The New Testament also stresses the additional point that we cannot be justified by our own effort: salvation depends on God's grace through faith, not on what level of obedience we obtain apart from Christ (Eph. 2:8-9). In the second place, Peter's words in Acts 10:35 refer to Gentile Christians or at least to "God fearers" such as Cornelius, not to righteous pagans who fail to believe only because they have never heard of Christ.

Is there, then, any way for the problem of the ignorant to be solved in separationist terms?[20] Here are three assumptions that underlie the

19. For a skillful defense of the position, see Stuart Hackett, *The Reconstruction of the Christian Revelation Claim* (Grand Rapids: Baker Book House, 1988), pp. 242-46.

20. I wish to point out that there are other alternatives available to evangelical Christians than the one that I am proposing. Most are clearly explored by John Sanders in *No Other Name: An Investigation into the Destiny of the Unevangelized* (Grand Rapids: William B. Eerdmans, 1992). In addition to these, William Lane Craig has suggested a unique solution to the problem based on the concept of middle knowledge; see "No Other Name: A Middle Knowledge Perspective on the Exclusivity of Salvation through Christ," *Faith and Philosophy* 6 (April 1989): 172-88.

position I will take: (1) the Bible does not tell us everything we might want to know about God and the divine will, (2) all people who are reconciled to God are reconciled to God through Christ, and (3) it would be unjust for God to condemn people to hell merely because they are ignorant of Christ. These assumptions push me in the direction of a theological proposal to the effect that there are ways by which those who are ignorant of Christ can be reconciled to God through Christ. In other words, if redemption is to be found only in Christ, and if the atoning work of Christ was intended for all people, and if God is loving and just, then it seems sensible to suppose that it must be causally possible for all people, wherever or whenever they live or however ignorant of Christ they may be, to come to God through Christ. Christian salvation, then, is universally available.

But in precisely what way is it universally available? Here I will propose a conjecture — namely, postmortem evangelism. I would like to stress that this is a conjecture, not a dogma or a teaching or even a firm belief of mine. It is, however, a conjecture that finds at least some support in the nearly universal Christian consensus that allowance is made for the salvation of infants who die despite their ignorance of Christ. It is true that the two cases — dead infants and unevangelized pagans — are not exactly parallel. But the point of similarity is that members of both groups die in ignorance of Christ. And if it is possible for members of the first group to be saved, why not members of the second?

Does anything in the Bible support this conjecture? Well, perhaps. Here are three relevant passages:

> Therefore it is said, "When he ascended on high he led a host of captives, and he gave gifts to men." (In saying, "He ascended," what does it mean but that he had also descended into the lower parts of the earth? He who descended is also he who ascended far above the heavens, that he might fill all things.) (Eph. 4:8-10)

> For Christ also died for sins once for all, the righteous for the unrighteous, that he might bring us to God, being put to death in the flesh but made alive in the spirit; in which he went and preached to the spirits in prison, who formerly did not obey, when God's patience waited in the days of Noah, during the building of the ark, in which a few, that is, eight persons, were saved through water. (1 Pet. 3:18-20)

But they [the Gentiles] will give account to him who is ready to judge the living and the dead. For this is why the gospel was preached even to the dead, that though judged in the flesh like men, they might live in the spirit like God. (1 Pet. 4:5-6)

Christian tradition has sometimes interpreted these texts (see also Matt. 12:40; Acts 2:24-31; Rom. 10:6-8) to mean that after his crucifixion and before his resurrection appearances, Christ descended into hades in order to rescue the Old Testament or antediluvian righteous, who were unable to ascend into heaven until Christ had done his atoning work. This is doubtless the biblical basis for the assertion in the Apostles' Creed that Christ "descended into hell." The New Testament, then, can be taken to suggest the possibility of postmortem salvation. (Besides the texts cited, note Paul's cryptic but apparently approving comments about baptism for the dead in 1 Cor. 15:29.)

It seems to have been a common teaching of the church from the time of the Apostolic Fathers onward that Jesus spent time between his death and resurrection in hades. The abode of the dead (roughly equal to the Old Testament sheol), hades was by New Testament times considered to be divided into two sections, the abyss (or gehenna) for evil folk, and paradise for the righteous. Early Christian teachers generally held that Christ's descent into hades was for the purpose of redeeming the righteous people of the Old Testament. And despite the scores of interpretations of the difficult texts just cited that have been suggested in the history of Christian thought, this still seems to be a possible and plausible exegesis of 1 Peter 3:18-20; 4:5-6.

Beginning with Clement of Alexandria (A.D. ca. 150–ca. 213), many of the Church Fathers (e.g., Gregory of Nazianzus in his *Orations,* 45.23, and Cyril of Alexandria in his *Paschal Homily,* 7) argued that Jesus' descent into hades had the effect of rescuing righteous pagans as well — people who had lived eminently moral lives according to their lights but never had the opportunity to be exposed to Christian teaching. In hades, Christ (or, Clement suggests, perhaps the apostles) preached the gospel to them; some accepted it and so were rescued.

Clement was sensitive to the charge that apart from such an opportunity, God's judgment of ignorant pagans could be considered unjust. "Who in his senses can suppose the souls of the righteous and those of sinners in the same condemnation, charging Providence with injustice?" he asked (*The Stromata*, 6.6; subsequent references to Clement are also from this source). Speaking of those who died before the incarnation of

Jesus, he said, "It is not right that these should be condemned without trial, and that those alone who lived after the advent should have the advantage of the divine righteousness."

Clement claimed that the denizens of hades, both Jews and Gentiles, heard the preaching of the gospel and then either gladly accepted it or else owned that their punishment was just because of their unbelief. Clement suggested two reasons why some of them repented and believed. First, he said, God's punishments are not retributive but rather are "saving and disciplinary, leading to conversion." Second (an odd, Platonic argument that I am unwilling to endorse), he argued that the disembodied state of the citizens of hades may have increased their susceptibility to accepting the good news: "Souls, although darkened by passions, when released from their bodies, are able to perceive more clearly, because of their being no longer obstructed by the paltry flesh."

But most interestingly, Clement suggested that God's redemptive power can even now recall postmortem souls: "I think it is demonstrated that the God being good, and the Lord powerful, they save with a righteousness and equality which extend to all that turn to Him, whether here or elsewhere. For it is not here alone that the active power of God is beforehand, but *it is everywhere and is always at work*" (italics added).

But if the gospel was once preached to the dead, perhaps this practice continues. If so, perhaps the ignorant are preached to after death and receive then the chance they never had before to receive Christ and turn to God. Perhaps they live in the disembodied state that Paul seems to speak of in 2 Corinthians 5:8 ("we would rather be away from the body and at home with the Lord") and Philippians 1:23-24 ("I am hard pressed between the two [life and death]. My desire is to depart and be with Christ, for that is far better. But to remain in the flesh is more necessary on your account"). In John 5:28-29, Jesus is even reported to have said that the dead will hear the message of the Son of God, and that when they do they will be bodily resurrected — "those who have done good, to the resurrection of life, and those who have done evil, to the resurrection of judgment."[21]

As long as it is recognized that these are conjectures without systematic or clear biblical warrant, we might even suggest that Christ has the power to save human beings *wherever* they are, even in hell.[22] I recognize

---

21. For a good discussion of whether the New Testament texts that I have cited should be interpreted along the lines that I am suggesting, see Sanders, *No Other Name,* pp. 207-8.

22. C. S. Lewis seems also to suggest as much (in literary form) in *The Great Divorce.*

that some will resist this suggestion. It is one thing, they might say, to suggest that the ignorant after death receive a chance (their first) to respond positively to the gospel, but it is quite another to suggest that those who have been condemned receive *other* chances to respond positively. But a question must be asked here: Is it possible that there are persons who would respond positively to God's love after death even though they have not responded positively to it before death? I believe this is possible. In fact, one reason for this latest conjecture is the observation that some who hear the gospel hear it in such a way that they are psychologically unable to respond positively. Perhaps they heard the gospel for the first and only time from a fool or a bigot or a scoundrel. Or perhaps they were caused to be prejudiced against Christianity by skeptical parents or teachers or by the manifold sins of the church or Christians. Whatever the reason, I believe it would be unjust of God to condemn those who did indeed hear the good news but were unable to respond positively. This is why I suggest that even in hell, people can be rescued.[23]

Does this bring in universalism by the back door? Certainly not. I have little doubt that some will say No to God eternally (the Bible predicts this, in fact), nor do I see any need for a "second chance" for those who have freely and knowingly chosen in this life to live apart from God. Perhaps God never gives up on people, but some folk seem to have hardened their hearts to such a degree that they will never repent. For such people, hell as separation from communion with God exists forever, just as it exists for them now. But perhaps some who die in ignorance of Christ will hear the good news, repent, and be rescued. Perhaps even some citizens of hell will do so too. Again, the key word is *perhaps*. We have no ground to dogmatize here. I do not think we *know* the fate of those who die in ignorance of Christ. All I am sure of is that God's scheme for the salvation of human beings will turn out to have been just, perhaps in ways we cannot now understand.

VI

By way of conclusion, let me make a few comments about the biblical concept of the wrath of God. It is clear that this notion plays almost no role in contemporary Christian teaching or preaching. Christians today seem embarrassed by the notion of the wrath of God, and most theo-

---

23. See Rev. 21:25, where the city of God is described as follows: "Its gates shall never be shut by day — and there shall be no night there."

logians, clergy, and laypeople ignore it altogether. I view this embarrassment as misplaced and the consequent avoidance of the notion of the wrath of God as unfortunate.

As I hope I have made clear by this point, I have no desire for the church to return to the "fire and brimstone" preaching with which both Catholics and Protestants of bygone days were all too familiar. The main idea of such preaching, I suppose, was to frighten people into making a religious commitment or into obeying the laws and expectations of the church by painting lurid pictures of the horrors of hell. I do not recommend a return to that sort of evangelistic or moral strategy, nor do I recommend that we abandon talk of the love and mercy of God.

Nevertheless, I think we ignore the concept of the wrath of God at our cost. Indeed, I would argue for the radical proposition that *our only hope as human beings is the wrath of God.* (It is also true, of course, that our only hope is the grace of God, but that is another matter.) The wrath of God shows that we do not live — as so many today suppose that we do — in a random and morally neutral universe. Morality is a human invention, so such people say; right and wrong are relative to who you are or what your society says or what you sincerely believe. Thus any honestly chosen path is as good as any other.

God's wrath shows us that right and wrong are objectively real; they are to be discovered, not created. The wrath of God is our only hope because it teaches us the moral significance of our deeds and shows us how life is to be lived.

To return to universalism, the most egregious error of this doctrine seems to me to come to light when we ask about evangelism. So far as I can tell, universalists have no urgent reason to preach the Christian gospel and urge people to decide. Universalists may be ethical persons; on other accounts they may be upstanding and righteous Christians. But if they act on their belief, they will feel no urgent need to evangelize. But we Christians are commanded to evangelize (Matt. 28:19-20). We must accept no theology that would tend to lessen our zeal to convert people to Christ.[24] Thus Paul says,

24. Some will respond that postmortem evangelism might also be interpreted as deemphasizing the need to engage in evangelism here and now. This might be true (I do not think even then that it need be) if universal postmortem evangelism were anything more than the sensible and hopeful theological conjecture I take it to be. Again, we do not know the fate of those who die in ignorance.

For, "every one who calls upon the name of the Lord will be saved."
But how are men to call upon him in whom they have not believed?
And how are they to believe in him of whom they have never heard?
And how are they to hear without a preacher? (Rom. 10:13-14)

We Christians are never to draw human limits around God's mercy.
It is not for us to decide who will be reconciled to God and who won't.
Nor are we to say dogmatically that the ignorant must be condemned
to hell. There is much in theology that we do not know, and this is one
such area. We do not know the fate of those who die in ignorance of
Christ. We must base our beliefs and our actions on what is clearly taught
in Scripture, not on conjecture. And what we are clearly taught is that
"there is salvation in no one else, for there is no other name under
heaven given among men by which we must be saved" (Acts 4:12).

9

Resurrection and Apologetics

I

People who reject the resurrection of Jesus typically do so on the grounds that the very idea of a dead man living again is absurd. Despite the fact that I have been arguing on behalf of belief in the resurrection of Jesus, and will continue to do so in this chapter, there is a sense in which I agree with this sentiment. I believe Christians need to recover a sense of the shocking absurdity of the very idea of resurrection.

"Do not be afraid." This is the opening line of the angelic message to the women who visited the tomb and found it empty on Easter morning (Matt. 28:5). Interestingly, the women were told not to fear but were unable to obey: "They went out and fled from the tomb; for trembling and astonishment had come upon them; and they said nothing to any one, for they were afraid" (Mark 16:8). In contrast, Christians today do not seem to be astonished at the idea of resurrection (after nearly two thousand Easters, we seem to have gotten used to the idea), but we ought to be. We should be shocked at the very idea that God would enter history and bring about such a surprising and deeply counterintuitive result. Aren't we all convinced — and for good reason — that people who die stay dead?[1]

Clearly, anyone who wants to argue in favor of belief in the resurrection of Jesus — as I am doing — must make a powerful case. It

---

1. On this point, see Helmut Thielicke, "The Resurrection Kerygma," in *The Easter Message for Today: Three Essays,* by Leonhart Goppelt, Helmut Thielicke, and Hans-Rudolf Müller-Schwiefe (New York: Thomas Nelson, 1964), p. 102.

must be strong enough to overcome the bias that all rational people share against highly unusual and miraculous events, their commitment to give naturalistic explanations of phenomena whenever possible. Recall the distinction I made in Chapter 1 between naturalists and supernaturalists. Naturalists are people in whom this bias is so strong as to be almost insuperable. Those who do not believe in God or in the possibility of miracles will doubtless reject the resurrection of Jesus regardless of any arguments they might encounter. I do not presume that anything I might say in this book will convince them. I am interested in trying to make a powerful enough case for the resurrection of Jesus as to prove — to any sensible person — that belief in it is rational from a supernaturalist perspective. This book is an essay in soft apologetics.

II

As noted in Chapter 1, some Christian devotees of hard apologetics make a stronger claim — namely, that the resurrection of Jesus can be established in such a secure way that *all* rational people must accept it. But I do not believe that anyone has accomplished this ambitious aim. The nearly universally accepted facts (roughly, that Jesus was crucified and buried, that certain folk had experiences that they took to be encounters with the risen Jesus, and that their belief in the resurrection of Jesus radically changed them and formed the heart of the message of the church that they founded) are too skimpy for that. And if we *could* deduce the resurrection from these facts, then (as I will argue shortly) they would no longer be universally agreed on. Furthermore, people who deny the resurrection can use the discrepancies in the New Testament to argue that the resurrection accounts are conflicting, late, and unreliable.[2] As I have tried to show, belief in the resurrection of Jesus can be defended against these arguments, but even if such a defense is achieved, this does not necessarily show that the position of such critics is irrational.

My main complaint against the hard apologists' way of arguing for the resurrection is that it is based on an oversimplified response to the naturalist rejection of miracles. Let me illustrate the problem by means of a frequently used but in my opinion flawed apologetic strategy. Some defenders of the resurrection of Jesus argue roughly as follows:

2. As, e.g., Willi Marxsen does; see *The Resurrection of Jesus of Nazareth*, trans. Margaret Kohl (Philadelphia: Fortress Press, 1970), pp. 27, 55, 68, 75-76.

1. The naturalistic explanations of the events following the crucifixion of Jesus (hallucination, swoon, etc.) are all improbable per se and inconsistent with certain widely accepted facts.
2. Therefore, the claim that Jesus really was raised from the dead, which is consistent with those facts, is confirmed.

The problem with this argument is that it ignores the question of the degree of improbability of the claim that Jesus died and then lived again. As I have been arguing, even supernaturalists must grant that the prior probability of a resurrection is low indeed; to naturalists, the prior probability of a resurrection is so low as to overwhelm the above argument. As noted, a naturalist can rationally respond to it as follows: "The rationalistic explanations do seem weak, and I don't claim to know what in fact happened, but the one thing I do know is that it wasn't a resurrection."

Gary Habermas argues that if we are going to use proper inductive research methods, we must be open-minded to all possibilities, that it is unscientific to make an a priori decision, before investigating the evidence, to exclude certain sorts of possible explanations of events — specifically, miraculous ones.[3] Now in the end, of course, I as a supernaturalist accept this argument. But the typical presentation of it by hard apologists seems to me too facile. It ignores the fact that the rationality of naturalism is based on the strong commitment of *all* rational human beings to give naturalistic explanations (i.e., explanations that do not involve violations of natural laws) of the phenomena we observe.

Surely there are *some* possibilities to which we need not be open. For example, how about the possibility that President John F. Kennedy was actually killed by a spy from the planet Tralfamadore cleverly disguised as Oswald? Or how about the possibility that Napoleon Bonaparte is still alive (at the age of 223) and is hiding in Paraguay? Now (again as a supernaturalist) I agree that if after careful examination we find that by far the best explanation of a given phenomenon is one that involves a miracle, we ought to swallow our reluctance and accept that a miracle has occurred. But my point is that *to a naturalist* the idea that Jesus was raised from the dead is at least as ridiculous as the ridiculous possibilities mentioned above. The "we should be open-minded to all possibilities" argument in favor of miracles will not be convincing to such a person.

---

3. Habermas, "Knowing That Jesus' Resurrection Occurred: A Response to Davis," *Faith and Philosophy* 2 (July 1985): 295-302.

Furthermore, even if the argument from "accepted facts" were valid, it would not necessarily convince rational naturalists. Such persons, I suspect, would quickly begin denying some of the accepted facts. And I think this would be (or least could be, given the circumstances) a rational thing for them to do. (Similarly, if someone were clever enough to take certain of my beliefs and show me that together they entail the nonexistence of God, I imagine I would quickly begin asking myself which of these beliefs to give up. My commitment to the existence of God would doubtless be stronger than my commitment to at least some of the beliefs.)

Habermas accuses those naturalists who reject the resurrection despite the evidence in its favor of what he calls "*a priori* reasoning."[4] But what exactly is a priori reasoning? I think by this term he means deciding on a conclusion before examining the evidence or even holding firmly to a conclusion despite overwhelming evidence against it. He argues that rational people investigate the facts and then on the basis of those facts reach a conclusion. And surely Habermas is right that a priori reasoning, understood in this sense, is something to be avoided. We should base our conclusions on the evidence available to us and even, whenever necessary, revise our conclusions in the light of contrary evidence.

But do naturalists who reject the claim that Jesus was raised from the dead commit the fallacy of a priori reasoning? Well, it is possible that they do, and perhaps some in fact do, but this need not be the case. For one thing, these naturalists are guilty as charged only if the evidence for the resurrection of Jesus is very strong indeed — so strong, in fact, as to outweigh the commitment virtually all rational people have made to the notion that dead people do not get up and walk around again. It seems to me perfectly possible for a naturalist to examine the relevant evidence objectively and carefully (i.e., not just dismiss it a priori) and still decide that no miracle occurred. As noted above, such a person could say: "Yes, there is evidence for the resurrection, and no, I don't know precisely what happened after the crucifixion, but *whatever* happened, since dead people stay dead, it surely wasn't a resurrection." Such a person has not necessarily rejected or ignored the evidence — which is to say that such a person is not necessarily guilty of a priori reasoning.[5]

---

4. Habermas, "Knowing That Jesus' Resurrection Occurred," p. 298.

5. As Van Harvey puts it, "One can . . . recognize a faulty justification of an explanation and withhold assent to it without being able to construct the proper explanation" (*The Historian and the Believer* [Philadelphia: Westminster Press, 1966], pp. 68-69).

Now, I am not a worldview (or conceptual) relativist, so I think it is possible to demonstrate the superiority of one worldview to another. Perhaps someday someone will refute the worldview that I have been calling naturalism. I just do not think anyone has done so yet. Naturalism remains a rational position.

But how can I claim that naturalism is rational, Habermas asks,[6] when I admit (in Chapter 1) that it is circular? Here Habermas has misinterpreted me. I am speaking only of a limited kind of circularity in the neighborhood of our discussion, both for naturalists and for supernaturalists. We can show that Humean arguments against miracles and rational belief in miracles fail. The real question is whether any miracles *have* occurred. To settle that question, we must obviously look to the evidence in human experience for and against purported miracle claims. But there is no such thing as bare, uninterpreted evidence or experience, and so the way we evaluate the evidence we encounter will inevitably depend to a great extent on our worldview — that is, on whether we think miracles are possible or probable. This is why certain believers (e.g., Habermas) consider the evidence for the resurrection of Jesus overwhelming, while certain nonbelievers (e.g., Antony Flew) think it perfectly absurd to believe that a dead man lived again.

This is a sort of circularity, but it is not an instance of committing the fallacy of circular reasoning. It is not equivalent to arguing, for example, that p is true because q is true and that q is true because p is true (or even any more subtle version of the fallacy). It would clearly be irrational for a person to argue that we know that Bach is a better composer than Paul McCartney because cultured people prefer Bach to McCartney, and we know that such people are cultured people because they prefer Bach to McCartney. But not all instances of circularity are irrational (i.e., they are not all *viciously* circular). Some are simply unavoidable. For example, we know that a logical person is in part one whose thought is consistent with the laws of logic, and we know that the laws of logic are authoritative in part because they are reflected in the thought of those persons whom we take to be logical.

Of course, a rational naturalist who faces overwhelming disconfirmation of the naturalist worldview must give it up (just as a rational supernaturalist who faces overwhelming disconfirmation of the supernaturalist worldview must give it up). But until the time is ripe for that sort of paradigm shift, it is rational for such people to interpret their

6. Habermas, "Knowing That Jesus' Resurrection Occurred," p. 300.

experience in terms of their worldview. That is why I insist that naturalism (a position I do not hold) is a rational position: the evidence (even evidence for the resurrection of Jesus) is not strong enough rationally to require its rejection. I frankly regard the claim that it is as a bit of apologetic bravado.

But how can I criticize Hume's rejection of miracles, Habermas asks,[7] given my position that naturalists can rationally reject the resurrection? Am I not inconsistent if I begin by arguing against Hume, who in effect says that no amount of evidence in support of a given purported miracle will allow rational belief in that miracle, and then proceed to argue on behalf of naturalists that it can be rational to reject the resurrection of Jesus despite the evidence in its favor on the grounds that "dead people stay dead." No, this is not inconsistent. I say that naturalists can rationally reject the resurrection of Jesus on the basis of *the presently existing evidence*. Obviously, I wouldn't say that they can rationally reject it on the basis of *any possible configuration of evidence*. In fact, I believe that in the eschaton it will be perfectly obvious to all rational observers that Jesus was and is alive — that he really was raised from the dead. Naturalism, then, will no longer be a viable position.

Let us return to the distinction between two sorts of apologetic arguments. A soft apologetic argument attempts to demonstrate the rationality of accepting the Christian position. A hard apologetic argument attempts to demonstrate the irrationality of rejecting the Christian position. Typically the soft apologetic argument claims that an intellectually acceptable explanation of some phenomenon x is some claim y, while the hard apologetic argument claims that the *only* intellectually acceptable explanation of x is y. (The variable x often stands for something like "The world has certain properties" or "Certain events have occurred in history" or "I have had certain experiences"; y is often something like "God exists" or "The Christian God exists" or "God raised Jesus from the dead.") The deepest difference between the apologists like Habermas and me is now clear: they are advocates of hard apologetics and I am an advocate of soft apologetics.

Both the hard apologists and I are interested in persuading people who do not believe in the resurrection of Jesus that it did in fact happen. We are all arguing, in effect, for a sort of *conversion*. And it must be granted that *if they succeed*, hard apologetic arguments are better (though not infallible) vehicles for producing conversions than soft apologetic

7. Habermas, "Knowing That Jesus' Resurrection Occurred," p. 299.

arguments. My point, however, is that I am not aware of any successful hard apologetic argument. Is there any general or theoretical or a priori reason why hard apologetic arguments fail? I do not know. Perhaps God is too hidden and mysterious. Perhaps God wants to preserve our intellectual freedom. Perhaps people are too blinded by sin. Perhaps Christian apologists just aren't clever enough.

Soft apologetic arguments will probably produce few conversions. It is not impossible that they would, however. Perhaps some people will be converted merely by coming to see that the Christian position is rational, even if they do not also see that unbelief in it is irrational. But in general, people who advocate soft apologetics will look elsewhere than philosophy for the efficient production of conversions — to preaching or to prayer, for example. The main aim of such apologists, then, is not to produce converts; if something like a conversion occurs, it will be a kind of serendipitous accident. The aim of the apologist is to show those inside and outside the circle of faith, both fellow believers and objecting nonbelievers, that Christianity is intellectually tenable.

III

An excellent case study on the relationship of faith and doubt in the resurrection is the apostle Thomas (see John 20:19-29). The story is familiar. The risen Jesus appeared to the other disciples at a time when Thomas was not present. When they told him that Jesus was alive, "doubting Thomas" replied, "Unless I see in his hands the print of the nails, and place my finger in the mark of the nails, and place my hand in his side, I will not believe" (20:25). Eight days later, Jesus again appeared to the disciples, and this time Thomas was present. When invited by Jesus to do the very things he had earlier demanded, Thomas answered, "My Lord and my God!" To this Jesus replied, "Have you believed because you have seen me? Blessed are those who have not seen and yet believe" (20:29).

The church's traditional exegesis of this text makes Thomas into a kind of skeptical villain. But this exegesis has always seemed to me dubious. In my view, Thomas did the correct thing: he believed when he became convinced by the available evidence that belief was warranted. This, in fact, is just what the other disciples had done — they believed when the evidence available to them (Jesus' prior appearance to them) was convincing. Now, perhaps Thomas should have believed merely on the basis of the testimony of his colleagues. And it is surely true, as Jesus says, that those (like us today) who are not exposed to resurrection appearances of Jesus should believe anyway — and that if we do, we are blessed. I do not wish to quarrel with those aspects of the traditional interpretation. I do wish to object to the castigation of the apostle Thomas as a "doubter," as if he were unwarrantedly skeptical, overly stubborn, an epistemological stick-in-the-mud. Perhaps he was more like a hero of faith. He believed when (and not before) there was sufficient evidence to convince him. And that is what I think everyone should do, though of course different people in different situations will require different degrees and amounts of evidence. Requirements less stringent than that make faith into gullibility or credulity.[8]

Note that Thomas, good Jew that he was, was a supernaturalist. He believed in God, and since he is nowhere identified as a Sadducee, he doubtless believed that God could and occasionally did intervene in history. This certainly made him more open to belief (once convincing evidence was present) than he would have been had he been a naturalist. But now resurrection appearances of Jesus — like the one Thomas was finally privileged to observe — have ceased. And for good reason. Had the church rejected the Lukan position that the ascension of Jesus brought the resurrection appearances to a close, the church might have found itself contending, throughout its history, with purported appearances of the Lord containing purportedly authoritative new revelations. No longer being able to point to the visibly present Lord, apologists for the resurrection must now appeal to historical arguments. A bit later I will do that very thing. From the perspective of supernaturalism, I will try to argue that belief in the resurrection of Jesus is rational.

IV

Let me return to James A. Keller, some of whose arguments I discussed in Chapter 1. His general position on the resurrection of Jesus, as well as his criticisms of my position, are relevant to the concerns of this chapter. There is no doubt that the most profound differences between Keller and me on the resurrection of Jesus consist in our different attitudes toward and conclusions about the New Testament evidence.

---

8. For my own views on the epistemological nature of religious faith, see *Faith, Skepticism, and Evidence* (Lewisburg, Pa.: Bucknell University Press, 1978).

The crucial issue that separates us is the reliability of the biblical texts that testify to the resurrection of Jesus. Keller's position is cautious and even doubting. I do not share his basic skepticism about the New Testament, about what we can and cannot know or rationally believe about the events following the crucifixion of Jesus.

Keller asks two main questions: (1) Are the New Testament accounts of the resurrection of Jesus primitive (i.e., do they reflect the views of the eyewitnesses to the resurrection events at the time they first came to believe)? and (2) Are those accounts true? Keller thinks we simply have no basis for any firm answer to these questions. This, combined with his endorsement of my own view that we ought to have a bias *against* supernatural events that can be overcome only by very strong evidence indeed, leads Keller to doubt that the resurrection (as I understand it) occurred.

Let me illustrate what I call Keller's basic skepticism. Concerning the views of the eyewitnesses, he says, "We do not have a historically reliable account of what the very earliest believers in the resurrection understood it to involve" — this because the accounts in the Gospels are all secondhand, sketchy, and late. "It is at least not clear," he says, "that the Gospel writers give historically reliable accounts of what happened." What Keller thinks we can learn from the empty-tomb stories is startlingly meager; virtually all he will allow is that the stories "probably show something about the understanding of the resurrection held by those who told the stories." Concerning the historical trustworthiness of the early chapters of Acts, he cites with approval those New Testament scholars who doubt their reliability. And concerning the New Testament evidence for the resurrection as a whole, he says, "All that the historian of today can reliably conclude is that certain first-century Christians said that Jesus appeared to certain people."[9]

Now, merely citing Keller's views and calling them skeptical does not refute them. I only wish to make it clear that I do not share those views, nor do I think the evidence justifies them.[10] Let me formulate replies to three of Keller's specific arguments.

9. See Keller, "Contemporary Christian Doubts about the Resurrection," *Faith and Philosophy* 5 (January 1988): 46-50.

10. I tried to establish this especially in Chaps. 3 and 4; furthermore, as I have already noted, I hold to a "high" doctrine of biblical inspiration and authority and am accordingly prepared to believe what the Bible says on matters that are relevant to Christian faith and practice unless there is overwhelming reason not to do so.

1. Keller argues that what we need to find is the understanding of the resurrection events held by those who witnessed them *at the time they witnessed them* — not the opinions of later converts or even of those same people much later. To a certain extent, I can appreciate this point. And I surely grant that Keller is right when he says that in general we do not have eyewitness accounts of the resurrection appearances of Jesus (1 Cor. 15:8 is an exception) and that the Gospels were written years after the events they describe. But it does not follow from this that the resurrection accounts are unreliable. Sometimes we do not realize the full meaning of an event until long after we see it. As a teenager, I once saw a world record set at a track meet. It made little impression on me at the time; only much later did I realize its significance. Thus it is perfectly possible that the eyewitnesses did not understand the full significance of Jesus' resurrection at the time and that their mature and reliable grasp of what happened and what it meant is found in the New Testament.

Furthermore, Keller has neglected to mention the fact that virtually all New Testament scholars feel sure that there is primitive material in the Gospels (most would argue that there is primitive material in the resurrection accounts at the ends of the Gospels), which would substantiate the assertion that the mere fact that the Gospels were written years later does not by itself render them unreliable.[11] Although it is clear that the Gospel traditions grew and changed as time passed, it can be plausibly argued that at least most of the Gospels reached their final, canonical form during a time when eyewitnesses to the events they record were still alive and capable of exercising critical control over what was said. Ancient traditions, some of which may well be true, even allege that some of the Gospels were written under the influence of such people. Finally, as Keller knows, in 1 Corinthians 15 (written in the early 50s), we have testimony to the resurrection of Jesus that is no more than twenty to twenty-five years from the events themselves, and in this chapter, Paul stresses that he is relying on traditions that are much older

11. Even Rudolf Bultmann acknowledged this; see *The Theology of the New Testament*, vol. 1, trans. Kendrick Grobel (New York: Scribner's, 1955), p. 45. See also Joachim Jeremias, *The Eucharistic Words of Jesus*, trans. Norman Perrin (London: SCM Press, 1966), p. 306; George Eldon Ladd, *I Believe in the Resurrection of Jesus* (Grand Rapids: William B. Eerdmans, 1975), pp. 75-77; Raymond Brown, *The Virginal Conception and Bodily Resurrection of Jesus* (New York: Paulist Press, 1973), p. 18; and Gary Habermas and Antony Flew, *Did Jesus Rise from the Dead?* ed. Terry L. Miethe (San Francisco: Harper & Row, 1987), p. 180nn.4-7.

than that (see v. 3). For various grammatical reasons having to do with the language Paul uses here and historical reasons having to do with the life of Paul, many scholars feel that Paul may well be relying here on traditions that date from a year or two after the events.[12]

2. Like German New Testament scholar Willi Marxsen (on whom he relies heavily), Keller stresses that there were no eyewitnesses to the resurrection event itself and that the faith of the earliest believers in the resurrection of Jesus was an inference. "To say that Jesus was resurrected is to express the conclusion of an inference, either based solely on the claims that certain people saw the Risen Lord or based on these claims and also on the story of the empty tomb."[13]

Now, the claim that belief in the resurrection is based on an inference, even for those who saw the risen Lord, is obviously true. I am not sure how helpful to Keller the point is, however, for surely there are inferences involved in most of our beliefs, and that fact does not make them suspect. If some time later today I were to see and converse with my own father (who died after an automobile accident in 1974, and whose body I saw in the casket at the funeral), I would be (or at least could be, depending on other circumstances) well within my intellectual rights in inferring that a resurrection had occurred. Similarly, the earliest Christians believed that they saw and spoke with Jesus. Thus it is misleading when Keller says, "The early Christians spoke of Jesus' resurrection not because they had seen it occur, but because of other experiences which certain Christians had had (being appeared to by Jesus and possibly seeing his empty tomb)."[14] I agree that nobody saw the event itself occur, but some such "early Christians" — including Mary Magdalene, Peter, and Thomas — saw the risen Lord. *That* is why they said, "He is risen." They did not have to rely on the experiences of other Christians.[15]

---

12. See especially Fuller, *The Formation of the Resurrection Narratives* (Philadelphia: Fortress Press, 1980), pp. 9-49; and Martin Hengel, *Between Jesus and Paul* (London: SCM Press, 1983), pp. 30-64. The evidence is effectively marshaled by Gary Habermas in *Did Jesus Rise from the Dead?* pp. 23, 30-31nn.38-42, 66, 91-92.

13. Keller, "Contemporary Christian Doubts about the Resurrection," p. 46.

14. Keller, "Contemporary Christian Doubts about the Resurrection," p. 46.

15. Keller argues that Paul is the only person in the New Testament to whom the resurrected Jesus appeared "who is said to have been an unbeliever at the time of the appearance" ("Contemporary Christian Doubts about the Resurrection," p. 58n.14). But this is to employ a rather restrictive understanding of the term *unbeliever.* Certainly Thomas (John 20:24-28) and even Mary Magdalene (John 20:11-16) showed some initial skepticism — as, for that matter, did all of the disciples (Mark 16:11; Luke 24:11).

3. Keller argues that we today cannot recover what was meant by the term *resurrection* as used by the earliest Christians. Did they think the tomb was empty? Did they think that Jesus' resurrection body was a physical object? We do not know, says Keller. But this conclusion is too skeptical. There are two questions here. First, do the New Testament accounts present a concept of bodily resurrection in which the resurrected body had spatial location, reflected light, and could be seen and touched? The answer is obviously Yes. As I granted in Chapter 3, there are some puzzling aspects to the descriptions,[16] but the accounts nevertheless stress heavily the physical nature of Jesus' resurrection body. We are told several times, in unmistakable terms, that Jesus walked and ate and that his body could be seen and felt.[17] Second, is the concept of bodily resurrection primitive (i.e., was it held by the earliest believers)? Again I think the answer is Yes, though it is true that some biblical scholars disagree. They hold that the earliest views of resurrection were spiritual in nature (a view they claim is confirmed by Paul in 1 Cor. 15:50) and that the later accounts grew more physical, primarily in response to apologetic pressures. But I find these views unconvincing; having discussed the point in Chapter 3, let me mention here just two important considerations.

a. Paul claims in 1 Corinthians 15:6 that the resurrected Jesus "appeared to more than five hundred brethren at one time, most of whom are still alive, though some have fallen asleep." Since the very idea of a group hallucination or vision is at best deeply problematical,[18] Paul seems to be presupposing here some sort of physical presence of Jesus. He is also in effect appealing to eyewitnesses. "If you don't believe me, you can check with them" — so he appears to be saying. Keller claims we know too little about this appearance to draw any inferences from it, and he explains it by suggesting that since "by then" the story of the appearance to Peter was well known, eventually many other people gradually joined in the claim to have seen Jesus, "not wanting to seem to lack faith or insight."[19] But it

16. These include the claims that Jesus "vanished out of their sight" (Luke 24:31), that Jesus twice appeared in a room despite "the doors being shut" (John 20:19, 26), and that Jesus was "lifted up" into the clouds (Acts 1:9).

17. Besides the four empty-tomb stories, which imply bodily resurrection, see Matt. 28:9-10; Luke 24:13-35, 36-43; and John 20:11-18, 19-29; 21:1-15.

18. Brown calls the idea "synchronized ecstasy" (*The Virginal Conception and Bodily Resurrection of Jesus*, p. 91). In addition, he argues strongly that the New Testament idea of resurrection is bodily resurrection (see pp. 70, 73, 85-86).

19. Keller, "Contemporary Christian Doubts about the Resurrection," p. 57n.14.

is clear that this is a mere conjecture on Keller's part, and an implausible one at that. There is no evidence to support it.

b. Bodily resurrection was the understanding of resurrection commonly held by Jews of Jesus' day. Of course other survival-of-death theories were then current (e.g., Greek immortality doctrines), but apart from further elaboration or explanation, any first-century Jew would understand the term *resurrection* to mean bodily resurrection (which would imply the empty tomb). Keller disputes this claim; we simply cannot know, he says, what the earliest believers in the resurrection held.[20] But I think it important that nowhere in the New Testament (not even in 1 Cor. 15) or in any of its literary ancestors hypothesized by scholars do we find firm evidence of the frequently made modern claim that Jesus was raised in only a nonbodily or purely spiritual sense.

V

Let me now mention six powerful arguments that seem to me strongly to support the claim that belief in a real resurrection of Jesus is rational, some of which I have already mentioned in earlier chapters. Again, I do not suppose that these arguments will convince naturalists, but for supernaturalists (especially those with broadly Christian assumptions) they are, I believe, more than sufficient to establish that belief in the resurrection is rational.

1. Virtually all scholars who write about the resurrection of Jesus, whether they believe it happened (in some sense or other) or not, agree that (a) while early first-century Jews expected a messiah, the idea of a dying and rising messiah was new to them; (b) Jesus of Nazareth died and was buried; (c) the disciples of Jesus were consequently discouraged and dejected; (d) soon after the burial of Jesus, his tomb was claimed to be empty, and some of the disciples had experiences that they took to be encounters with the risen Jesus; (e) these experiences caused them to believe that Jesus had been raised from the dead; and (f) they started a movement that grew and thrived and that was based on the idea that Jesus had been raised from the dead. My point here is that no one who denies that Jesus was raised from the dead or who offers reductive theories of the resurrection has yet been able to account adequately for these widely accepted facts. Though many have tried, no one who rejects belief in the

20. Keller, "Contemporary Christian Doubts about the Resurrection," p. 50.

resurrection of Jesus has been able to tell a convincing story of what occurred in the days following his crucifixion. As noted previously, the nineteenth-century rationalistic explanations of such individuals as Reimarus and Strauss collapse of their own weight once spelled out, and skeptical twentieth-century accounts are all subject to compelling criticism — including the accounts of such critics as Hugh Schonfield and the accounts of believers who propose reductive theories of Jesus' resurrection like that of Willi Marxsen.[21] The only theories that seem able to account for the accepted facts are those that affirm that Jesus was genuinely raised.[22]

2. Despite the frequently noted discrepancies in the New Testament accounts of the resurrection of Jesus, at important points the biblical texts speak with one voice. All of them affirm that Jesus was dead, that he was buried in a tomb near Jerusalem supplied by a man named Joseph of Arimathea, that early on the day after the Sabbath certain women in the company of Jesus (among them Mary Magdalene) went to the tomb, that they found the tomb mysteriously empty, that they met an angel or angels, that the women were either told or else discovered that Jesus had been raised from the dead, and that Jesus subsequently appeared a number of times to certain of the women and certain of the disciples. There seem to be no resurrection texts that question any of these items. Furthermore, even the discrepancies themselves testify in a left-handed way to the accuracy of the essential story: if the resurrection of Jesus were a story invented by the later Christian church, or by certain members of it, no discrepancies would have been allowed. The biblical accounts do not bear the earmarks of a lie or conspiracy.

3. The deliberate-lie thesis does not square with the radical change that came over the disciples in the days and weeks after the crucifixion. Confused, fearful, discouraged, and disorganized immediately afterward, they soon became bold and courageous revolutionaries who started a religious movement that changed the world order. Their unanimous testimony was that this change was due to their belief in the resurrection of Jesus. Their behavior was not consistent with the behavior of people who have intentionally perpetrated a fraud; they seem to have been

21. For Schonfield's account, see *The Passover Plot* (New York: Bantam Books, 1966).

22. As Hugo Staudinger puts it, "The credibility of sources on the resurrection of Jesus is impressively confirmed, not least by the fact that, up to the present day, not one single person has succeeded in giving a convincing interpretation of the sources without accepting the resurrection as a historical event" (*The Trustworthiness of the Gospels*, trans. Robin T. Hammond [Edinburgh: Handsel Press, 1981], p. 92).

people of integrity rather than deceivers. Furthermore, the thesis that a few of the earliest believers perpetrated a fraud on the rest of them is implausible because there is not one bit of evidence to support it. No such secret ever "leaked out," nor is there any evidence of an inner-circle controversy among the early Christians concerning the truth of the claim that Jesus was raised from the dead.

As noted above, most and perhaps all of the New Testament accounts of the resurrection of Jesus were written during a time when eyewitnesses to the events described were still alive and could easily have refuted erroneous claims. The evidence decisively supports the conclusion that all the earliest Christians believed wholeheartedly in the resurrection of Jesus,[23] even at the cost (for many of them) of their lives. Now this argument by itself does not rule out the possibility that earliest belief in the resurrection was a sincere and strongly held belief in an illusion (which could conceivably account for the change in the disciples). But this possibility does not seem in any sense plausible given the cumulative weight of all six of the points being made here.

4. The story of the empty tomb has about it the ring of truth.[24] Let me briefly recall some points I made in Chapter 4. (a) The empty tomb is widely taught in the New Testament — in all four Gospels (note especially that it appears in Matthew's special source, i.e., in material Matthew did not get from Mark or Q) and is possibly alluded to in both 1 Corinthians 15:4 and Acts 2:27-29.[25] (b) No story invented by later Christians to bolster their claims about Jesus' resurrection would have revolved so crucially around the testimony of women, whose value as legal witness in the culture of the day was virtually negligible.[26] (c) Most

23. See Bultmann, "New Testament and Mythology," in *Kerygma and Myth,* ed. Hans Werner Bartsch (New York: Harper & Row, 1961), p. 42. Virtually every New Testament scholar accepts this point.

24. According to John Frederick Jansen, "Today there is a growing consensus in New Testament scholarship that the tradition of the empty grave is early tradition, not a late addition" (*The Resurrection of Jesus Christ in New Testament Theology* [Philadelphia: Westminster Press, 1980], pp. 41-42).

25. Gerald O'Collins argues that Paul's theory of the resurrection expressed in 1 Corinthians 15 requires an empty tomb (*What Are They Saying about the Resurrection?* [New York: Paulist Press, 1978], pp. 43-44), and the empty-tomb tradition seems strongly supported by Keller's third canon of rationality in historical investigation — "independent testimonies which agree are generally more credible than either one alone or than the two testimonies would be if one were dependent on the other" ("Contemporary Christian Doubts about the Resurrection," p. 41).

26. See O'Collins, *What Are They Saying about the Resurrection?* p. 43.

conclusively, it is impossible to imagine the earliest believers having any success whatsoever in their attempt to convince people that Jesus had been raised from the dead without ungainsayable evidence of an empty tomb. Otherwise, their enemies could have refuted their testimony by simply producing the body. Keller replies to this argument by casting doubt on the early chapters of the book of Acts,[27] but it should be noted that many able New Testament scholars find the chronology of those chapters reliable.[28] (d) Contrary to what Keller says, the earliest believers in the resurrection must have believed in an empty tomb, for, as noted above, that is how virtually any Jew in early first-century Palestine would have interpreted the idea of resurrection. Jewish notions of resurrection were highly physical notions, quite unlike Greek concepts of immortality or the twentieth-century idea of "spiritual resurrection."[29] (e) The story of the guard at the tomb in Matthew's Gospel is often attacked by critics as an apologetic legend told by the later church. It is easy to see, however, that even if this is true (and I do not accept that it is), the telling of the story is senseless unless everyone — Christian and non-Christian alike — agreed that the tomb was empty.

5. For several obvious reasons, the resurrection appearances of Jesus do not seem to be hallucinations. The disciples were not expecting or wishfully believing in a resurrection. The very idea of the resurrection of one individual before the end of the world was religiously novel.[30] On at least three occasions, the resurrected Jesus was not immediately recognized. Some who saw him doubted (see Matt. 28:17; Luke 24:36ff.;

---

27. Keller, "Contemporary Christian Doubts about the Resurrection," pp. 49-50.

28. See, e.g., Patrick Henry, *New Directions in New Testament Studies* (Philadelphia: Westminster Press, 1979), pp. 156, 168; and A. N. Sherwin-White, *Roman Society and Roman Law in the New Testament* (Oxford: Oxford University Press, 1963), p. 189. For the basic argument here, see Wolfhart Pannenberg, "Did Jesus Really Rise from the Dead?" *Dialog* 4 (1965): 18-35; and Brown, *The Virginal Conception and Bodily Resurrection of Jesus,* p. 126.

29. For examples of the emphasis on bodily resurrection in early Jewish literature, see The Apocalypse of Baruch 50:2; 2 Maccabees 14:46; and 1 Enoch 51:1-2; 62:13-16.

30. See Wolfhart Pannenberg, *Jesus — God and Man,* 2d ed., trans. Lewis L. Wilkins and Duane A. Priebe (Philadelphia: Westminster Press, 1968, 1977), pp. 88-106. See also Habermas, "Knowing That Jesus' Resurrection Occurred," pp. 84-88; and Gerald O'Collins, *Jesus Risen* (New York: Paulist Press, 1987), p. 108. O'Collins skillfully rebuts the idea that one person's hallucinatory experience (e.g., Peter's) might have caused a "chain reaction" among other believers.

John 20:24-25). Many different people saw the risen Jesus, in different places and in different circumstances. There were none of the usual causes of hallucination present — drugs, hysteria, or deprivation of food, water, or sleep. So the evidence would seem to suggest that the appearances of Jesus caused the Easter faith of the disciples rather than (as is sometimes charged) the other way around.

6. There is the problem of the "initial ignition" that got the Christian movement going. People who deny or doubt the real resurrection of Jesus are faced with the daunting task of explaining why or how the church came into existence at all, why its earliest pillars began proclaiming the resurrection — a proclamation that (so scholars agree) brought the church into existence. If Jesus was not genuinely raised from the dead, it seems there would have been no Christian movement at all. Or, at the very least, its preaching would have taken on an entirely different character — Jesus might have been honored with the status of a "martyr-prophet," for example. Or if that were impossible, given the humiliation involved in crucifixion,[31] Jesus might have been remembered in some other way.

The point is, however, that the disciples were prepared neither psychologically nor theologically for the idea of the resurrection of a crucified messiah, and the fact that they arrived at this idea so early and so confidently needs explanation. As O'Collins says, "Contemporary Judaism had no concept of a dying and rising Messiah, nor any notion of one person enjoying a final, glorious resurrection from the dead even though the end of the world had not yet occurred."[32] The Easter faith of the disciples was something new; it cannot be traced to Jewish or pagan sources. Nor does it seem explicable in terms of the impact that the life and teachings of Jesus had on his followers, since Jesus' death on the cross tended strongly to negate that impact (see Luke 24:21).[33]

The advantage of belief in a real resurrection of Jesus at this point is that it provides an explanation of the existence of that Easter faith — namely, that the disciples saw the risen Lord, became convinced that he was alive, and interpreted their experience in a theologically

31. See O'Collins, *Jesus Risen,* pp. 90-91.
32. O'Collins, *Jesus Risen,* pp. 110-11.
33. See Walter Künneth, *The Theology of the Resurrection,* trans. J. Leitch (London: SCM Press, 1965), pp. 50-63. See also Murray Harris, *Raised Immortal* (Grand Rapids: William B. Eerdmans, 1983), p. 64; and William L. Craig, *Assessing the New Testament Evidence for the Historicity of the Resurrection of Jesus* (Lewiston, N.Y.: Edwin Mellen Press, 1989), pp. 407-16.

novel way (though of course they were helped by a subsequent reexamination of crucial Old Testament texts). C. F. D. Moule makes the point compellingly:

> I still find it difficult, if not impossible, to believe that the disciples had, in the scriptures and in the life, teaching and death of Jesus and their own circumstances, all that was necessary to create Easter-belief. Granted that they were thrown into an ecstasy of astonishment by what Jesus was and did, something more than this is needed (so it seems to me) to lead to the conclusion that Jesus had been not merely a superlatively great prophet, nor simply a man of the Spirit, nor just Messiah (the latter is an almost impossible conclusion, anyway, after the Crucifixion, without something to suggest it), but that he was alive in a unique and hitherto unexampled way, and *therefore* Son of God in a far more than Messianic sense, and "Lord," and the climax and coping-stone of the whole edifice of God's plan of salvation.[34]

The challenge, then, for those who deny the real resurrection of Jesus is to explain in a convincing way what actually happened in the days and weeks after the crucifixion. The advantage of belief in a real resurrection of Jesus is that that event provides a plausible explanation of the Christian movement.

If I were a supernaturalist, and if I discovered these six items of evidence about the claim that Jesus was raised from the dead, I would be justified in believing that claim. Thus, unless these arguments are defective, belief in the real resurrection of Jesus is rational from a supernaturalist perspective. Of course, given the extreme intellectual absurdity of belief in a resurrection, I agree that the burden of proof in some sense must be on those who argue that a miracle has occurred. But the evidence in favor of the claim that Jesus was genuinely dead and later genuinely alive is sufficient to render the resurrection belief of Christians rational. This is especially true since those who deny that there was a genuine resurrection seem quite unable to explain what did happen. Further, they seem equally unable to explain why an obscure itinerant rabbi who died a criminal's scandalous death became so quickly (in the eyes of many) the Christ, the savior of the world, the Son of God.

34. Moule, in "The Resurrection: A Disagreement," *Theology* 75 (April 1972): 515.

VI

It turns out that the central question to be asked in addressing the resurrection of Jesus Christ is what kind of universe it is that we live in. More to the point, we must ask whether God exists, and, if so, what God is like. It might seem odd that I would advocate making a decision about a historical issue in large part on the basis of metaphysics or theology, but that is what we must do. Christians believe that God exists and that we can trust God's promise to raise us from the dead. "Do not marvel at this," says Jesus; "for the hour is coming when all who are in the tombs will hear his voice and come forth, those who have done good, to the resurrection of life, and those who have done evil, to the resurrection of judgment" (John 5:28-29). Furthermore, "he who eats my flesh and drinks my blood has eternal life, and I will raise him up at the last day" (John 6:54).

But *does* God exist, and can we rely on these promises? Which worldview is true, naturalism or supernaturalism? How could we possibly know? Those are the questions naturalists will want to ask at this point. I have not attempted to answer them in this book.[35] Nor have I tried to refute naturalism. My argument has been restricted to the more modest notion that belief in both the resurrection of Jesus and the general resurrection is rational from the perspective of the worldview that I have been calling supernaturalism. As I have already suggested, the difficulty of arguing convincingly that disbelief in the resurrection of Jesus is irrational can be illustrated in this way:

1. Miracles occur only if supernaturalism is true.
2. The best evidence for the truth of supernaturalism is the occurrence of miracles.
3. But whether one believes that miracles occur is in large part a function of whether one is a naturalist or a supernaturalist.

Or to put the point the other way:

1. If naturalism is true, no miracles occur.
2. The best evidence for the truth of naturalism is the non-occurrence of miracles.

35. I have, however, addressed the question of the attributes of God in *Logic and the Nature of God* (London: Macmillan, 1983).

3. But whether one believes that miracles occur is in large part a function of whether one is a naturalist or a supernaturalist.

I have argued in this book in favor of the notion that Jesus was raised from the dead and that we will be raised from the dead. I thus oppose those Christian thinkers who hold that apologetics is to be eschewed because evidence, arguments, and proof are inimical to faith. They act as if the word *apologetics* were pejorative, as if apologetics were something essentially base or even un-Christian. A view somewhat like this seems to be held by Reginald Fuller. Speaking of the resurrection experiences of Mary Magdalene and the other women, he says, "It cannot be too strongly emphasized that it is not the task of the preacher to try and establish the truth or credibility of these alleged experiences and leave it at that. Resurrection faith is not the historical faith that the women found the tomb empty and the disciples saw Jesus risen from the dead: it is faith in the risen Lord."[36]

I can certainly agree with Fuller that apologetics is not usually the job of the preacher and that the Christian proclamation of the resurrection does not cease once the credibility of the witnesses to the resurrection of Jesus has been established, but I believe that resurrection faith includes the "historical faith" Fuller refers to. Thus, I could not disagree more with his claim that "whether the women's story was based on fact, or was the result of mistake or illusion, is in the last resort a matter of theological indifference."[37]

In truth, faith *needs* apologetics. It needs it both to answer the negative arguments of critics of the resurrection and to construct positive arguments in favor of it. Apologetics will not create faith, but perhaps, for some, it will pave the way for it or make it possible. What is destructive of genuine Christian faith, in my opinion, is not apologetics but unfounded beliefs, unjustified commitments, unsound arguments, and irrational "leaps of faith." It is the aim of apologetics to prevent Christian faith from amounting to anything like that.

Suppose we have made a good case for the claim that Jesus was bodily raised. Have we then left no room for faith? Not at all. As I have already suggested, I am opposed to any notion of faith that is based excessively on epistemic risk or venture (a notion often associated with Kierkegaard by those who interpret him in an irrationalist direction).

36. Fuller, *The Formation of the Resurrection Narratives*, pp. 182-83.
37. Fuller, *The Formation of the Resurrection Narratives*, p. 179.

Nevertheless, even a successful apologetic enterprise (especially the kind of soft apologetics I am doing in this book) leaves room for faith. For a cogent apologetic argument buttresses religious claims only with a certain amount of evidence or degree of probability, while faith calls for whole-hearted commitment. The practical level of commitment that Christians believe God asks of us exceeds by far that which could be proved or rendered evident by even the most successful of apologists.

How then should Christians respond to the naturalist rejection of the resurrection of Jesus? The first step is to show that naturalism is not rationally obligatory. As I have argued, this can in part be demonstrated by showing that Hume-like arguments against belief in miracles are not convincing. The second step is to show that from the perspective of Christian supernaturalism, belief in the resurrection of Jesus is rational. The two steps merge at one crucial point: Christians must never allow that the only background knowledge against which we are to evaluate the claim that Jesus was raised from the dead is the current state of empirically based scientific knowledge. If they grant that, Christians will inevitably lose the argument, because hidden in the concept of "the current state of scientific knowledge" is a commitment to naturalism.

It should never be the purpose of Christian apologetics to demonstrate to all rational people that the resurrection of Jesus is probable. Indeed, our point should be that it was highly improbable (at least as far as prior probability is concerned) but that belief in it, all things considered, is rational nonetheless. There are good and convincing reasons to believe it.

It cannot be too strongly emphasized that the resurrection must be viewed in its religious context and not as an isolated wonder. A proven but isolated miracle would have little apologetic value (aside, perhaps, from raising serious questions about naturalism) and no religious meaning. A miracle is not just a highly improbable event that for some strange reason happens to occur, as with the sorts of events that quantum physics tells us are quite possible but extremely improbable. A miracle — such as the resurrection of Jesus — occurs because of a command of God and fits within a religious context. Apart from that context, both the question of whether the miracle occurred and the question of what it means if it did occur cannot sensibly be answered.

For example, suppose that at some point shortly after Jesus' death, there was a living person walking about who — for all that any sensible person could tell after asking the appropriate questions — seemed to be Jesus. Would this *by itself* prove that the divinely wrought miracle we call the resurrection of Jesus had occurred? No. There would be plenty of other hypotheses available to explain the presence of such a person. Only the eye of faith, I believe, can reach the correct conclusion. Perhaps, in the end, the resurrection of Jesus from the dead is credible only to those who experience the new life that he offers us. That is, the resurrection makes sense only within its redemptive setting in the Christian worldview.

Here is a thought experiment: suppose that we possessed powerful evidence that some otherwise unknown figure from, say, Macedonia in the third century B.C. died and then was raised from the dead. What sense would this make to us? Why should we pay any attention? Why should we care? (That, I think, is an almost exact parallel to the approach that many modern people take to the claim that Jesus — a figure whom they do not know or care about — was raised.) Christians care intensely about the topic of this book because they believe that the one who was raised from the dead was also the Son of God and the savior of the world. The resurrection of Jesus is not an isolated anomaly but a crucial act — perhaps *the* crucial act — in the drama through which God achieved our salvation. It is part of the long story of our separation from God, of our longing for forgiveness and meaning in life, and of God's actions to produce them. This story is told in Scripture, the book that for Christians narrates the events of salvation history and into which the resurrection of Jesus fits as the key event. The reality of the risen Christ, experienced in the lives of those who follow and believe, provides the basis for and context of their acceptance of the testimony of the women and the apostles.

But at some point the apologetic enterprise must come to an end. Belief can't be coerced. You can't convince everybody. Some people will never believe, no matter how much evidence is amassed. We learn this fact, even in relation to risings from the dead, in the New Testament itself. Herod the Tetrarch's character did not change even though he was told that Jesus was John the Baptist, or one of the prophets, raised from the dead (Luke 9:7-9). Many of the Pharisees and chief priests were apparently hardened against Jesus after he raised Lazarus from the dead (John 11:46-47). The five brothers in Jesus' parable of the rich man and Lazarus would not believe — so Jesus teaches — even if visitors from the dead like Abraham were to speak to them. Jesus concludes by having Abraham say to the rich man, "If they do not hear Moses and the prophets, neither will they be convinced if some one should rise from the dead" (Luke 16:31).

VII

James Keller closes an article in which he discusses my views of the resurrection with a kind of appeal on behalf of people who are Christians but who doubt that the resurrection (in the traditional sense that I have been defending) happened. I accept that appeal. I myself would not want reductive theories of the resurrection to be recommended to the church as acceptable interpretations. And the view that the resurrection was real but in some sense spiritual faces, in my view, severe exegetical difficulties. But there are surely Christians who hold views less traditional than mine that I disagree with strongly for both exegetical and theological reasons but do not wish to consider outside the pale.

Of course there are Christians of such a persuasion. Of course they are making, as Keller puts it, "an honest effort to come to terms with the Christian scriptures in the light of all that we can learn."[38] I know some such folk; some of them are friends and colleagues of mine. Despite (what I view as) their errors, they do propose a Christian view of the resurrection. I have no desire to deny that they are Christians, convict them of heresy, accuse them of "bad faith," deny them tenure, or anything of the kind. I do want to reserve the right to disagree with them and to say why, because I believe a notion of resurrection like the one I have been defending is the most faithful and defensible one for Christians of today.

38. Keller, "Contemporary Christian Doubts about the Resurrection," p. 55.

10

Resurrection and Meaning

I

Why is it important that Christians believe that Jesus was raised from the dead? What is the meaning of the resurrection? In our age of science, skepticism, and scoffing, why should Christians continue to believe that a dead man lived again?

Let me begin to answer these questions by relating an experience of mine. One Lenten season several years ago I taught a series of adult Christian education classes at a nearby church. The topic was the resurrection. One of the people who faithfully attended the classes was an assistant pastor of the church, a woman who I am sure would classify herself as theologically rather liberal. At one point in about the middle of the course, when it was becoming clear that I viewed the resurrection of Jesus as a genuine event that occurred in history rather than merely a symbol or a way of communicating a theological message, she asked, with considerable feeling, this question: "Haven't you been taking the wrong approach? What really matters is not whether certain claims about ancient history are true. Whether or not Jesus was really raised from the dead is far less important than the meaning of the Christian proclamation of the resurrection. What matters is that we live like Easter people here and now."

This is an approach to the resurrection of Jesus that seems common among theologically sophisticated people today.[1] Though I do not accept

1. For example, in dialogue with C. F. D. Moule, Don Cupitt said, "What matters is not whether Peter saw Jesus alive then, but whether I see him alive now" ("The Resurrection: A Disagreement," *Theology* 75 [April 1972]: 512). Similarly,

it, I want to take this approach seriously. There is, I believe, both something right and something wrong in it.

To explain what is wrong in it, I will repeat what I said at the time in response to the assistant pastor's question. Whether — to put it crudely — the fact of the resurrection is more important than its meaning is an issue on which I have no opinion. As I noted in the introduction to this book, it is not even clear to me what such a claim might mean. I do hold, however, that the meaning of the resurrection *depends on* the fact of the resurrection. That is, if Jesus was not really raised from the dead, then the resurrection of Jesus has no particularly interesting meaning. There are few implications for our attitudes and behavior here and now. (Perhaps there are some lessons about facing death bravely.) So — I said to the assistant pastor — it is legitimate and important for Christians to ask whether there is good reason to believe that Jesus was genuinely raised from the dead. Such a question does not constitute a wrong approach.[2] (It *would* be wrong, however, to consider the historical issue the only one worth considering.)

But surely there is something correct in the assistant pastor's question too. Even those Christians who affirm a genuine resurrection ought to ask this question: *What good does it do merely to believe that Jesus was genuinely raised from the dead?* If the belief makes no difference in one's life, what good is it? No doubt many people today have what Cardinal Newman would have called notional belief in the resurrection of Jesus. They could in all sincerity affirm that it really happened, without that affirmation making any difference in their lives. As a blasé student of mine once wrote in a paper, "I was first told that Jesus was raised; only later was I told he wasn't; so I guess I'll go on believing he was."

As I argued in Chapter 9, for many contemporary Western people, with our Christian heritage and cultural memory of important biblical

---

Hans Küng says, "All questions about the historicity of the empty tomb and the Easter experience cease to count beside the question of the significance of the resurrection message" (*On Being a Christian,* trans. Edward Quinn [New York: Pocket Books, 1976], p. 379).

2. Speaking of the accounts of Jesus in the Gospels, Hugo Staudinger says, "If they are really only tales which have just been made up by some individuals or other in order to make certain statements about God, then these tales, in spite of all the grandeur which is contained within them, nevertheless have no unique and inescapable significance as 'interpretaments.' They are then only to be classified in fact with myths and poems in which there is also talk of the working of a god. They can then quite legitimately be replaced by other tales" (*The Trustworthiness of the Gospels,* trans. Robin T. Hammond [Edinburgh: Handsel Press, 1981], p. 104).

stories, it appears to be no great or difficult thing to believe that Jesus was raised. We are, so to speak, used to the idea. We need somehow to recover the sense of surprise, awe, and wonder that the earliest Christians felt when they came face-to-face with the idea that a dead man lived again. For them to say the words, "I believe that Jesus is alive" was tantamount to saying, "I am committed to the cause of Jesus; I am a Christian." The affirmation itself made a difference in their lives because the making of it tacitly committed them to membership in a community that saw itself as founded by Christ.

What, then, does the resurrection mean? That is what I want to consider in this chapter. I will focus on three different resurrection texts in the New Testament. Influenced by them, I will argue that the doctrine has (among others) three crucial implications.[3] It says (1) that Jesus is Lord, (2) that God will win, and (3) that we too will rise. When Christians recite the words "on the third day he rose again from the dead," they are indeed making a statement about a real event in history. But they are also making these three theological affirmations.

II

How, then, does the resurrection say that Jesus is Lord? Let me begin my comments about this affirmation by pointing out an obvious fact. Our lives as human beings are typically lives of struggle, and we are in desperate need of spiritual guidance. The struggle is varied. (1) We struggle with our fellow human beings. Life is a brutal competition for scarce resources — for a mother's affection, for an A in class, for admission to college, for a promotion and a raise, for that next sale. Life is a rat race, a jungle, a zoo. This makes us competitive, jealous, even violent. (2) We struggle with the fact that life is radically unfair. Some people are rich. Others, through no fault of their own, die of starvation. Some live to be a hundred. Others, through no fault of their own, die painfully at seventeen. Some are born with wit, intelligence, and good looks. Others, through no fault of their own, are born plain or disfigured and with only modest gifts. (3) We struggle with guilt. Constantly we find ourselves unable to live up even to our own minimal standards of right

---

3. For an impressive discussion of the meaning of the resurrection that focuses on points other than these, see chap. 6 of Donald G. Dawe's book *Jesus: The Death and Resurrection of God* (Atlanta: John Knox Press, 1985).

and wrong, let alone our highest ideals, and so if we are at all attuned to the accusations of conscience, we are tortured by feelings of inadequacy and guilt. (4) Finally, we struggle with our own mortality. We know that one day we will die, and that fact makes us shiver. We long for immortality, to know life and breath and sunshine and loved ones forever, but death will cut us short.

Since life is such a struggle in which typically no quarter is asked or given, it is little wonder we so desperately need spiritual direction. Human beings are spiritually hungry creatures. We long to know the answers to the questions that life poses, the solutions to its riddles. I believe that is why the human species is such a deeply religious species. That is why there has been such a proliferation of gurus, messiahs, sages, and saviors in human history. Many people have claimed to be able to answer our religious questions or even to save us — the Buddha, Zoroaster, Pythagoras, Lao Tsu, Joseph Smith, Mary Baker Eddy, the Reverend Sun Myung Moon. And at first glance Jesus of Nazareth appears much like one of these people, a member of the set of religious founders.

We live in a world that is and always has been religiously pluralistic. One of the places in the ancient world where this fact was most profoundly recognized was the city of Athens. In Acts 17, we read about a visit Paul made to that city. The days of Athens's political power were long over, but it was still an influential center of learning. Students gathered there to study under the greatest thinkers of the day. Some of these thinkers — Stoic and Epicurean philosophers — caught wind of Paul's new teachings and brought him to Mars Hill to let him hold forth. At first they apparently saw Paul as a philosopher like themselves — a sophisticated thinker propounding speculative propositions and defending them in argument. This explains their shock when Paul started pointing out that his message had practical implications for their lives. They wanted merely to ask clever questions and debate endlessly; he wanted them to repent.

Paul began his speech by making reference to an altar he had chanced to see in Athens bearing the inscription "To an Unknown God." Despite his disgust with the proclivity of the Athenians for polytheism and idolatry, Paul said of this unknown God: "What therefore you worship as unknown, this I proclaim to you" (Acts 17:23). You are a very religious people, Paul was saying, but as you admit, you are ignorant of God; now I will tell you about God.

In a world in which messiahs and gurus proliferate, we who need spiritual guidance are forced to ask how we can tell whom to believe.

How can we decide who is the true messiah and who are the false messiahs? Like Paul in Athens, we want to avoid idolatry; we don't want to worship a false god. But how do we know who is God?

Notice that, like many messiahs and saviors, Jesus made extraordinary claims. The Gospels record him claiming to be able to forgive sins, for one thing. He also claimed to have power over disease and over evil spirits. He also claimed to be the Son of God — "I and the Father are one," he said (John 10:30); "he who has seen me has seen the Father" (John 14:9). He is said to have claimed to be the one true path by which one could be reconciled to God — "I am the way, and the truth, and the life; no one comes to the Father, but by me" (John 14:6). A terrible egotist, we might say. And perhaps he was. But if he was — if these claims were false — then worship of Jesus is idolatry.

Paul's critique of the idolatry he saw in Athens was pointed and incisive. "The God who made the world and everything in it, being Lord of heaven and earth, does not live in shrines made by man," he said, "nor is he served by human hands, as though he needed anything, since he himself gives to all men life and breath and everything" (Acts 17:24-25). Paul went on to say, "We ought not to think that the Deity is like gold, or silver, or stone, a representation by the art and imagination of man" (17:29). In other words, God is not the made but the maker. The Deity does not live in temples or sacred groves or statues, nor does God need our worship. On the contrary, Paul said, we need God. God has made us in such a way that we need and long for God — we grope after God in vain till God is revealed to us.

Thus far the Areopagites raised no objections. They were merely sitting back comfortably listening to the exposition of just another philosophy of life. So far no action or commitment had been called for. Doubtless the Athenian intellectuals found Paul's ideas interesting, even entertaining. Notice Luke's ironic comment about them: "All the Athenians and the foreigners who lived there spent their time in nothing except telling or hearing something new" (17:21). Possibly as Paul spoke they were mentally preparing clever rebuttals to his argument, but so far nothing had been said that distinguished Paul's view from the many speculative religious and philosophical theories the Areopagites loved to debate endlessly.[4]

---

4. This is how I interpret Luke's editorial comment just cited about the particular philosophers Paul encountered. It needs to be pointed out, however, that most ancient and hellenistic philosophies did have practical implications for life;

But then Paul decisively moved from theory to practice. He then showed that if what he said were true, the lives of his listeners would have to change:

> The times of ignorance God overlooked, but now he commands all men everywhere to repent, because he has fixed a day on which he will judge the world in righteousness by a man whom he has appointed, and of this he has given assurance to all men by raising him from the dead. (17:30-31)

In other words, Paul said, God now no longer allows us ignorantly to grope about in the religious sphere. God has decisively been revealed to us once and for all through a man, Jesus of Nazareth. People must now repent of their sins, because a day of judgment is coming and because in proof of God's purpose Jesus has been raised from the dead.

Suddenly the Athenian philosophers became acutely uncomfortable. They were now being pressed not for clever replies but for a decision. A man was raised from the dead, Paul said, and your lives must change. This is not like an annoying television commercial that we can click off — this is like being confronted by an insistent door-to-door salesman who forces us to decide right here and now whether we will buy the product.

In my opinion, Paul's tactic was correct. Christians today are constantly tempted to relegate their message to the level of a philosophy of life. We are tempted to view it as just one among the almost infinite number of competing theories and life-styles in the air today — Zen Buddhism, EST, Marxism, Hare Krishna, drugs, transcendental meditation. But when we do so, we fail as Christians. The message Paul was preaching on the Areopagus is not a speculative theory or an alternative life-style but a decisive word of God to us that calls for a decision. Jesus is not a guru but the Savior.

The resurrection of Jesus from the dead is the heart of Paul's message, the gospel he spoke to everyone who would listen, Jews and Greeks alike. To the Athenian philosophers he said: God has now decided to judge the world by Jesus of Nazareth, and God's guarantee of this is that he has been raised from the dead. To the Romans Paul wrote that

---

indeed, the concern for achieving happiness in life was considered of first importance. This includes both Stoicism and Epicureanism, hellenistic philosophies listed by Luke as represented on the Areopagus.

Jesus was "designated Son of God in power according to the Spirit of holiness by his resurrection from the dead" (Rom. 1:4). This is what separates Jesus from all the false messiahs, gurus, and prophets — he was raised from the dead. There are many false messiahs with commanding personalities. There are many gurus who are full of spiritual wisdom. There are many prophets who recommend noble life-styles. But they weren't raised from the dead. Only Jesus is Lord.

The resurrection of Jesus, then, is God's decisive proof that Jesus is not just a great religious teacher among all the great religious teachers in history. It is God's sign that Jesus is not a religious charlatan among all the religious charlatans in the world. The resurrection is God's way of pointing to Jesus and saying that *he* is the one in whom you are to believe. *He* is your Savior. *He* alone is Lord. The resurrection was a graphic way to repeat what God had said about Jesus at his baptism by John: "This is my beloved Son, with whom I am well pleased" (Matt. 3:17).

Notice this argument of Paul about the resurrection in 1 Corinthians 15: "If Christ has not been raised, then our preaching is in vain and your faith is in vain. . . . If Christ has not been raised your faith is futile and you are still in your sins" (vv. 14, 17). If Jesus had not been raised, there would be no Christianity today. Jesus would have been at most a great religious teacher and a tragic martyr. He might have ended up a widely recognized teacher of religion and ethics, like Socrates or Gandhi, but not a savior. If Jesus had not been raised, the claims he made — to be able to forgive sins, to be the Son of God, to be the one true path to God — would not be worth believing. God's raising him from the dead was God's vindication of the truth of his claims.

But I need to be clear on one point. I am not saying that Jesus is the only person in the history of the world to have been raised from the dead. The Bible tells us that Lazarus was raised, for example, as well as others such as the daughter of Jairus and the son of the widow of Nain. There are even stories of people being raised from the dead in other religions, and perhaps some of them are true. I am willing to believe that God performs miracles in more than just the Christian context. But these raisings were of an entirely different sort than that of Jesus. We should call them resuscitations rather than resurrections, because the people were restored to their former mode of life. Lazarus, for example, was not transformed when he was raised. He was restored to his old mode of life and went on living normally, only inevitably to die a second time at some later point. Jesus was not resuscitated but resurrected. He was changed. His body was transformed into what Paul calls a glorified body. He was raised never to die again, and he still lives today. The claim that Jesus alone is Lord, then, is not based on the claim that he alone was raised from the dead but that he alone was resurrected from the dead.

In his speech, Paul referred to the era before Christ was revealed as "the times of ignorance" (Acts 17:30). In those times, he said, people attempted to "seek God, in the hope that they might feel after him and find him" (v. 27). In those days, Paul was saying, the truth had not yet been fully revealed, and people lived in darkness; they had to grope about for God. But now, through his resurrection from the dead, Jesus has been revealed as Lord. He is the one who can solve the human problems I mentioned above — he can create peace between us and our fellow human beings, he can assure us that despite the unfairness of life God loves us and works for our benefit, he can solve the problem of guilt by forgiving us our sins, and he overcomes our fear of death because his resurrection is a guarantee of ours.

We do indeed live in a religiously pluralistic world. People disagree about religion more than they disagree about almost anything else. The very idea of all human beings agreeing on religion and worshiping the same God sounds like the most absurd kind of pipe dream. But the Christian affirmation is that Jesus alone is Lord. One day it will happen. In Philippians, Paul says that God has bestowed on Jesus a name that is above every name. Paul looks forward to the time when "at the name of Jesus every knee should bow, in heaven and on earth and under the earth, and every tongue confess that Jesus Christ is Lord" (2:10-11).

III

The second thing the resurrection means is that God will win. This is an odd claim on the surface of it, for at times it seems that God has lost the battle. Justice does not prevail. The forces of evil run rampant. The world is full of enemies of God — sin, violence, poverty, injustice, suffering, war, crime, death. Confronting these ugly realities, we sometimes cry out in despair. Where is God? Where is goodness? Where is justice?

I can certainly imagine the dejected disciples asking such questions after the crucifixion of Jesus. They had given up their careers and families because they believed in this man. They did not understand much of what he taught, but they loved him and believed he was the Messiah.

They saw his power over disease, his sway over crowds, his ability to outpoint his enemies in debate. They allowed themselves to hope that here was the one who was to redeem Israel. Here was the one who would chase away the Romans, restore Israel to independence, and bring about a revival of Judaism. But their hopes all crashed when Jesus was arrested and crucified. It was a bitter pill to swallow. Their hopes had been in vain. He turned out to have been a good man with some excellent ideas, but the bottom line was that he had failed. In their disappointment, the disciples would somehow have to pick up the pieces and put their lives together again.

So it must have seemed to Cleopas and his unnamed companion on the road to Emmaus. Luke says they were "talking with each other about all these things that had happened" (Luke 24:14). It was obviously an earnest, anguished conversation, the kind of debriefing people often engage in after some important project has gone badly wrong. Perhaps they were discussing the problem of evil — how could a good God allow an innocent man like Jesus to die an ignominious death? That topic always makes for intense conversation.

As they walked, Jesus himself joined them, but as Luke says, "their eyes were kept from recognizing him" (v. 16). They were amazed when the stranger seemed ignorant of the events that had been taking place in Jerusalem. So they told him about Jesus and about the hopes they had placed in him. Their despair is poignantly captured in their words: "But we had hoped that he was the one to redeem Israel" (v. 21). In other words, that had been their hope, but now it was dashed. Chalk up another mark in the loss column for God.

And then Jesus, whom they still did not recognize, said to them, "O foolish men, and slow of heart to believe all that the prophets have spoken!" (v. 25). Through Jesus' eyes we now see the problem: Cleopas and his companion had been looking at the whole matter wrongly. Their ideas of Jesus and his mission were awry and were preventing them from seeing the truth. What they needed was for somebody to explain things to them. They needed a new interpretation of the role of the Messiah and of the recent events in Jerusalem. They needed, as it were, new eyeglasses to clear up the blur. So, Luke says, beginning with Moses and all the prophets, Jesus "interpreted to them in all the scriptures the things concerning himself" (v. 27).

At times we, too, need a new interpretation of the events we see, and some of those occasions have to do with our perception that God is losing the battle. Jesus was saying to the two disciples, The evidence is there; all you need do is look at it correctly. The Scriptures should have taught you that the Messiah must suffer, and the women's story of the empty tomb should have made you realize that something strange and wonderful is afoot. Sometimes, in a mysterious way, God uses evil events to bring about victory. Sometimes, in a way that we find hard to understand, evil events are necessary for God to achieve victory. The truth — as we see illustrated with great clarity in this story — is that, despite the evil that we see in the world, God's victory is just around the corner. We, too, in the midst of suffering, occasionally need somebody to tell us that.

In fact, this was just what Jesus explained to them: "Was it not necessary that the Christ should suffer these things and enter into his glory?" (v. 26). This is the Christian message. Out of the tragedy of the cross, God brings about our redemption. The Messiah had to suffer and pay the penalty for our sins in order to reconcile us to God. Horrible as it was for an innocent man to be killed unjustly, the cross is but a prelude to resurrection.

God's final victory will not be achieved until the kingdom of God. And although we can see glimpses of God's victory in such events as the resurrection of Jesus, that victory is hidden for now from all but the most discerning eyes. Notice that Jesus' resurrection from the dead was not shouted from heaven in a booming voice; it was not revealed to Caesar or Pontius Pilate; it was not revealed to the Jewish leaders. It was revealed to some obscure women at the tomb and to two equally obscure disciples on the road to Emmaus. Someday God's victory over all God's enemies will be evident to everyone; for now, only the eyes of faith can see it.

The three travelers reached Emmaus. Cleopas and his companion begged Jesus to stay with them, arguing that the day was nearly over and it was time to rest and eat. When Jesus broke the bread and blessed it, possibly the two disciples recalled accounts from the twelve disciples of the passover supper they had had with Jesus days earlier in Jerusalem. As if a blindfold had been removed, they suddenly saw the truth: they had been in the presence of the resurrected Jesus. When he disappeared from their sight, they said to one another, "Did not our hearts burn within us while he talked to us on the road, while he opened to us the scriptures?" (v. 32).

The message of Easter is that, despite appearances, God will win. We are on the winning side. Despite the disciples' dashed hopes, Jesus was, after all, the one who was to redeem Israel. In the resurrection of Jesus from the dead, we see God's decisive victory not only over death but over all God's other enemies as well. In that one climactic event we see the certainty that someday, in the kingdom of God, there will be no more violence, war, jealousy, or death. No more displaced persons. No more kidnapings. No more murder. No more disease. No more holocausts. No more terrorism. No more nuclear weapons. These forces are still alive and at work in the world, but because of the victory that God won at Easter, their doom is certain. One day death will die (Rom. 6:9).

This is why the resurrection of Jesus from the dead is the best piece of news that the world has ever heard. It assures us that God will win in the end and that accordingly the world is not mad. Events do happen that we cannot explain. Irrational tragedies and horrible outrages do occur. But because God raised Jesus from the dead after the catastrophe of the cross, we can be sure that God will one day overcome all catastrophes.[5] As the great medieval mystic Julian of Norwich put it, "All shall be well, and all shall be well, and all manner of thing shall be well."[6]

The resurrection of Jesus from the dead means that all the enemies of God have been defeated and that God will win. But what, concretely speaking, does this mean to us here and now? How should the resurrection affect our lives today? It means that we are allowed to have hope and that the world turns out to be the kind of world in which trust in God is justified. The resurrection is proof that no matter how bad things get, we can trust in God. God loves us. God has our interests at heart. God works to achieve what is beneficial to us. And in the end, God will win.

"Was it not necessary that the Christ should suffer?" Jesus asked the Emmaus pilgrims. In response to the outrages that we see in the world, Christians can say two things. First, we do not know why such events occur. But, second, someday they will be overcome. In some strange and mysterious way, just as out of the defeat of the cross God wrought the victory of the resurrection, so God will bring the kingdom of God out of the worst tragedies of history.

The Emmaus story ended joyfully. Imagine the happiness that must have filled that room in Jerusalem when the two disciples arrived there from Emmaus. Everybody had good news for everybody else. The Jerusalem disciples told Cleopas and his companion that Jesus had appeared to Peter; "The Lord has risen indeed," they said (Luke 24:34). Cleopas

5. My own views on the problem of evil are found in *Encountering Evil: Live Options in Theodicy*, ed. Stephen T. Davis (Atlanta: John Knox Press, 1981).

6. Julian of Norwich, *The Revelations of Divine Love*, trans. James Walsh (London: Burns & Oates, 1961), p. 92.

and his companion told the Jerusalem disciples "what had happened on the road, and how he was known to them in the breaking of the bread" (v. 35). In that room they had a slight taste of what we will all know in the kingdom of God. All tears will be wiped away. All diseases healed. All crimes forgiven. All suffering redeemed. All questions answered. In that room, comparing stories as they undoubtedly were, they may have sensed the sublime truth that out of the apparent defeat of the cross, God had wrought the greatest victory in redemptive history. The cause of God had looked like a dark horse in this race, as it often does in this troubled world, but it had won.

IV

The third thing the resurrection means is that we, too, will rise. If we added together all the sermons that were preached in Christian churches last Easter Sunday, it would be a considerable number. The trouble is that some of them were phony. Some preachers talked about resurrection but not about death. The Christian concept of resurrection makes no sense apart from a stark admission of the reality of death. And so we need to talk a bit about death.

I would like you to imagine the following picture.[7] A funeral procession is entering a cemetery. Through large wrought-iron gates the first three cars pass, black hearses, the first carrying a casket, the second and third carrying relatives of the deceased. Following are scores of mourners in cars, headlights ablaze but impotent in the afternoon sun. Slowly the procession draws to a halt before a newly dug grave, surrounded with flowers, fresh earth piled to one side.

But who is it that is dead? It is you. You are in the casket. It is your funeral; these bereaved are your relatives, these mourners your friends. The last moment has come and gone for your life on earth. You are being returned to it, from whence you came.

They gather around the grave as the casket, with you inside, is carefully lifted to its place. A minister says some solemn words, intones an ancient prayer, offers a last benediction. Some are in tears; all are deeply moved. You are gone. You will be with them no longer. Slowly, tediously, the casket is lowered into the grave till it comes to rest. A shaft of reflected

---

7. This image is not original with me. I read or heard it many years ago, but now cannot remember where.

sunlight is all that disturbs the darkness in the grave. The funeral is finished. Some walk away, slowly. Some hesitantly draw near the grave, hoping to breathe a few last words of farewell — farewell to you.

It is clear that some religions and philosophies deny death. They either insist that death is really a good thing and ought not to be feared, or else they affirm that immortality is a natural property of ours, so that death is only a kind of rite of passage to another life. The Christian faith can do neither. Surviving death is not something that we naturally do, a property with which we are naturally endowed. If God does not miraculously intervene, death is the end; death means final annihilation. So Christianity can never deny death. "What man can live and never see death?" asks the Psalmist (Ps. 89:48). Christians affirm that death is real and that death is frightening.

All people fear death. The thought of no longer being, of literally not being, has always been frightening to us. It is almost impossible for people to picture their absence from the world. Intellectually we know that we will die, but existentially the thought "one day I will no longer exist" is terribly difficult to countenance. We are the centers of our own universes, and it is difficult for us to imagine the universe continuing without us. Human beings are the only animals who know that they must die, and thus the only animals who try to hide from themselves the fact that they must die.

Isn't this the reason that in our society we hide from the face of death, try not to think about it? Isn't this why death is not the subject of polite conversation? To use the word *death* even at funerals somehow strikes "cultured people" as morbid. We pay funeral directors well to make death appear a little more distant, a little less real. We flood the mortuary with bright, colorful flowers; we try to "cheer up" the bereaved — as if somehow they were not supposed to be sad; we embalm and dress the body to make it look as lifelike as possible; we turn to polite euphemisms such as "passed away," "called home," "went to be with the Lord," "fell asleep," "called to the great beyond."

But why is it, exactly, that we fear death? Let me suggest six reasons.

1. Death is inevitable. The Bible tells of people who lived for a very long time, but even Methuselah eventually had to face death. Some people have close brushes with death and live to boast about them; the Bible even tells of people such as Lazarus who died and were brought back to life, but in the great scheme of things, it was only a brief respite. There is no escape. As Camus said, there are no loopholes in the inevitable.

2. We fear death because it is mysterious. What happens to us on the other side? We do not know, for, as Wittgenstein notes, "Death is not an event in life: we do not live to experience death."[8] We all have a certain dread of the unknown — enrolling in a new school, being in a room where we don't know a soul, having to face the first day on a new job. But death is the greatest of all unknowns. There are many opinions but few or no certain truths about death and what (if anything) happens after death. No one has ever come back to tell us. It is like jumping into a black, bottomless pit on a dark night.

3. We fear death because we have to face it alone. Perhaps if we could all hold hands and leap together into the void, so to speak, death would not be so frightening. But we can't.

4. We fear death because in death we will be separated from our loved ones.

5. We fear death because in death our personal hopes and aims will not be realized. Death is the negation, the absolute end of all our goals and achievements.

6. We fear death because death raises the real and frightening possibility that we will be totally annihilated, that "death ends all." After your death, you will simply no longer be.

For many, death is the most awesome reality they must face. It is the culmination of our deepest dreadings. It is that from which we all try to hide but from which there is no hiding. Shakespeare's Julius Caesar says,

> Of all the wonders that I yet have heard,
> It seems to me most strange that men should fear,
> Seeing that death, a necessary end,
> Will come when it will come.
>
> (Act 2, sc. 2, ll. 34-37)

Of course death will come when it will come. But despite Caesar's noble words, for most of us this does not in the slightest take away our fear of it. In fact, it may make it worse. Death is the great enemy of humankind. And if Christ was not raised from the dead, it is an enemy that has never been defeated.

In John 20, we find Mary Magdalene in emotional turmoil. It had been bad enough that her Lord had been unjustly and painfully put to

---

8. Wittgenstein, *Tractatus Logico-Philosophicus* (London: Routledge & Kegan Paul, 1961), 6.4311.

death. At that, her whole world collapsed, for Mary was one of Jesus' most loyal followers. She owed him her life, because he had exorcised seven demons from her. A Galilean, she began following Jesus after her healing, accompanying him on his ministry to Galilee and even helping to support him financially (Mark 15:40-41; Luke 8:1-3). But now another cruel blow struck — she came to the tomb in which he had been buried and found the stone rolled away and the tomb empty. Fearing that enemies had stolen the body, she ran to tell Peter and the Beloved Disciple.

They ran to the tomb and found it as she had said. Badly frightened, the two men went back quickly to their homes, but Mary, having followed them back to the tomb, lingered. As if refusing to believe that he was gone, she again stooped over and glanced into the tomb. There she saw something strange and wonderful that the two men had not been privileged to see. There were two angels dressed in white, sitting where the body had been. "Woman, why are you weeping?" they asked. Still assuming foul play on the part of the authorities, she said, "Because they have taken away my Lord, and I do not know where they have laid him" (John 20:13).

She then turned around and saw Jesus standing beside her. But she did not recognize him. Was it because it was still dark? Or because she was half-blinded by her tears? Or because in his new glorified body he did not look the same? We do not know. At any rate, as if to underscore the point that this was no time for sadness, Jesus asked the same question the angels had asked her: "Woman, why are you weeping? Whom do you seek?" Still without a clue that it was Jesus, Mary addressed him as the only person she could think of who might have had business in the garden that early in the day — the gardener: "Sir, if you have carried him away, tell me where you have laid him, and I will take him away" (v. 15). In her tears and confusion, she did not explain how she proposed to carry him away all by herself, nor even who the "him" was that she was speaking of; she assumed the gardener would know.

Next comes one of the most tender and notable greetings in all of literature. Jesus called her by name. "Mary," he said. I can never read this passage without recalling something Jesus had said to his disciples a few chapters earlier in John's Gospel:

He who enters by the door is the shepherd of the sheep. To him the gatekeeper opens; the sheep hear his voice, and he calls his own sheep by name and leads them out. When he has brought out all his own, he goes before them, and the sheep follow him, for they know his voice. (10:2-4)

I think it significant that Jesus' resurrection was not first revealed to his disciples. Virtually all of them, after all, had deserted him when he was arrested. He appeared first to what may have been his most devoted follower, the one who perhaps owed him the most. Mary Magdalene had gone with him to Jerusalem and stood by him at the cross when the others fled (Mark 15:40-41; John 19:25). She was the one who discovered the empty tomb, and she was the first person on Easter morning to see him alive.

"Rabboni!" she shouted, an Aramaic word meaning "my teacher." In the first flush of joy she reached out to embrace him. And here we see a crucial lesson that we learn from Easter — that our relationships with each other and with God will continue beyond death. Death seems to be the great terminus of all human relationships — we are bereaved when loved ones die because we will not see them again — but death was not strong enough to keep Jesus from Mary Magdalene and from the others who loved him. Their loving relationship continued beyond death because God is stronger than death.

We live in a time when the theological world tends to deemphasize this aspect of resurrection. Not much is said these days about seeing your loved ones again after death. Perhaps it is because we know so little about heaven. Perhaps it is because the desire to be with our loved ones again seems to some like selfishness. But loving human relationships are some of the best things we human beings enjoy in this life. They are a large part of what it is to be truly human. So it is theologically significant that, just as the relationship between Jesus and Mary Magdalene was not terminated by death, neither will some of the loving relationships that we enjoy.

More importantly, resurrection means that our loving relationship with God will continue beyond death. Our union with God, made possible by Christ's atoning death on the cross, is something that death cannot defeat. "Today you will be with me in Paradise," said Jesus to the repentant thief on the cross. If in this life we know something of the love of God, of God's forgiveness of our sins, of God's comfort in time of trial, of God's guidance in difficult situations — how much more will we know the presence of God in the resurrection? For the deep truth here is not just that our relationships with God and with each other will continue beyond death; the deep truth is that they will be transformed.

We see a hint of this already in our text. Mary wanted to embrace Jesus, but he knew their relationship must now be on a different basis. "Do not cling to me," the words are sometimes translated. In other words, "Don't try to keep me here, much as you would like me to. I must ascend to my Father and create a new relationship between me and those who love me. Don't try to keep me from retaining the place with God that was mine before my incarnation on earth."

To see the basis for the claim that our relationships can survive death, we must look at the basis of the claim that *we* will survive death. And here we must look at Paul's thoughts in 1 Corinthians 15: "Christ has been raised from the dead, the first fruits of those who have fallen asleep. For as by a man came death, by a man has come also the resurrection of the dead. For as in Adam all die, so also in Christ shall all be made alive" (vv. 20-22). Notice especially Paul's puzzling words "by a man came death." The man he meant is Adam, of course. According to Paul, death is not natural. Far from being a natural phenomenon, the inevitable accompaniment of life, as we so often imagine, death is instead an alien intrusion. We die because of sin. Death entered the world when sin did. As God said to Adam in the garden, "Of the tree of the knowledge of good and evil you shall not eat, for in the day that you eat of it you shall die" (Gen. 2:17). It was not God's plan that we all die; it was the result of sin. When sin is wiped out, as it is in the kingdom of God, then death will die.

If death entered the world by the sin of a man, so death is defeated, Paul reasoned, by the righteous act of another man, Jesus of Nazareth. "For as in Adam all die, so also in Christ shall all be made alive." Thus Jesus' resurrection from the dead that first Easter morning is a promise or guarantee of our resurrection from the dead.

So there is only one bit of evidence for life after death that is convincing to Christians. It is not philosophical arguments for the immortality of the soul. It is not supposed spiritualist conversations at séances with loved ones who are (as they say) "on the other side." It is not medical testimony about out-of-body experiences or the interesting stories told by people who were near death and then resuscitated. It is that Jesus was dead for three days and lived again. This, I take it, is why Paul also said to the Corinthians, "If Christ has not been raised, then our preaching is in vain and your faith is in vain. . . . If Christ has not been raised, your faith is futile and you are still in your sins" (1 Cor.

15:14, 17). The only evidence for life after death that we Christians need or want is summed up in the angel's words to Mary and the other women in the synoptic Gospels: "He is not here; for he has risen."

When Christians start talking about the next life, the danger is that they will forget this one. Fixated on fine fantasies about how great it will be in the future kingdom of God, they do nothing but talk, pray, and sing hymns about it. Pie-in-the-sky religion is something we must avoid, because God has placed us in this world for a purpose. We have, as it were, a job to do. Would pie-in-the-sky religion have been a temptation for Mary Magdalene in the garden? Perhaps so. I suspect that she would have been deliriously happy simply to have stayed there with her Lord for the rest of the day. But Jesus would not allow it; he gave her a job to do. "Go to my brethren and say to them, I am ascending to my Father and your Father, to my God and your God" (John 20:17). Mary fulfilled her commission. She found the disciples and said, "I have seen the Lord" (v. 18).

God gives all Christians a commission. We are not to sit idly by, doing nothing but daydreaming about the glories to come. Far from a denial of this life, the Christian message of resurrection is an affirmation of life here and now. This world is important. It is a gift, and a mission field, that God has given us. Our job as Easter Christians is to tell people, as Mary did, that the Lord is risen. Our job is to work to defeat all the forces in the world that oppose God — sin, suffering, poverty, war, death. The task is urgent precisely because we as Christians believe that death is real. If death were only an illusion or a rite of passage, then this world would not matter so much. But death is real, and death is frightening, and God calls us to tell people that death has been conquered by Jesus.

I said earlier that part of the reason we fear death is that it is mysterious. The heaven and hell of Christian theology are also mysteries. The familiar attempts to describe them — harps, clouds, wings, pitchforks — are meaningless and silly. All we know is that there is One who loves us and who promises to be very near to us (or apart from us) for eternity. It is in this confidence that those who know Christ, like the thief on the cross, like the martyrs of the church, can face death almost as a friend. In the words of the Psalmist, it is in this confidence that we can walk through "the valley of the shadow of death" and "fear no evil" — because "thou art with me" (Ps. 23:4; see also Heb. 2:15).

Death, the most fearful of all our fears, is not the final word. Because of the resurrection of the one who said "I am the resurrection and the life," we too will live. Our relationship with God is stronger than death.

That is what we Christians celebrate at Easter. Death was not strong enough to hold Jesus. Death will not be strong enough to hold us. New life awaits us.

V

This book is an effort in what I have called soft apologetics. In it I have tried, if you will, to paint a picture that might be called "A Christian Philosophy of Resurrection." That picture is, of course, only a detail of a much larger picture — a mural, if you will — that might be called a Christian worldview. This worldview constitutes a comprehensive way of looking at human history, at human nature and destiny, at reality as such. It crucially involves the existence of God, the creation of human beings by God, the gracious activity of God in human history, the redemption of human beings through Jesus Christ, and the final victory of God over all God's enemies.

In this book, then, I have tried to paint a picture of one aspect of that mural. I have argued that a pair of Christian beliefs — that Jesus was raised from the dead and that we will be raised from the dead — are fully rational. That is to say, I have argued that these beliefs are defensible on historical, philosophical, and theological grounds. In this chapter I have also argued that they have important practical and theological ramifications for Christians.

I will leave it to readers of this book to decide whether the picture that I have painted is coherent and plausible. And I will leave it to Christian scholars more able and more ambitious than I am to progress to the stage of hard apologetics, to establish the more difficult point that rejecting Christian beliefs about resurrection is irrational.

Bibliography

Anderson, Ray. *Theology, Death, and Dying.* New York: Basil Blackwell, 1986.

Aquinas, Thomas. *Summa Contra Gentiles.* Book 4. Translated by Charles J. O'Neil. Notre Dame, Ind.: University of Notre Dame Press, 1975.

Athenagoras. *Embassy for Christians and the Resurrection of the Dead.* Translated by Joseph H. Crehan. London: Longmans, Green, 1956.

Augustine. *The City of God.* Translated by Gerald G. Walsh et al. Grand Rapids: William B. Eerdmans, 1956.

————. *The Enchiridion on Faith, Hope, and Love.* Edited by Henry Paolucci. Chicago: Henry Regnery, 1961.

Badham, Paul. *Christian Beliefs about Life after Death.* London: Macmillan, 1976.

Baker, Lynne Rudder. *Saving Belief.* Princeton: Princeton University Press, 1987.

Bartsch, Hans Werner, ed. *Kerygma and Myth.* New York: Harper & Row, 1961.

Basinger, David, and Randall Basinger. *Philosophy and Miracle: The Contemporary Debate.* Lewiston, N.Y.: Edwin Mellen Press, 1986.

Bater, R. R. "Toward a More Biblical View of the Resurrection." *Interpretation* 23 (January 1969).

Bode, E. L. *The First Easter Morning.* Rome: Biblical Institute, 1970.

Boliek, Lynn. *The Resurrection of the Flesh.* Grand Rapids: William B. Eerdmans, 1962.

Broad, C. D. "Hume's Theory of the Credibility of Miracles." In *Human Understanding.* Edited by A. Sesonske and N. Fleming. Belmont, Calif.: Wadsworth, 1965.

210

Brody, Baruch A. *Identity and Essence*. Princeton: Princeton University Press, 1980.

Brown, Raymond E. *A Risen Christ in Eastertime*. Collegeville, Minn.: Liturgical Press, 1991.

————. *The Virginal Conception and Bodily Resurrection of Jesus*. New York: Paulist Press, 1973.

Bultmann, Rudolf. *Existence and Faith*. Edited by Schubert Ogden. New York: Meridian Books, 1960.

————. *Jesus Christ and Mythology*. New York: Scribner's, 1958.

————. *The Theology of the New Testament*. Vol. 1. Translated by Kendrick Grobel. New York: Scribner's, 1955.

Carnley, Peter. *The Structure of Resurrection Belief*. Oxford: Clarendon Press, 1987.

Carruthers, Peter. *Introducing Persons*. Albany: State University of New York Press, 1986.

Clarkson, John F., et al. *The Church Teaches: Documents of the Church in English Translation*. St. Louis: B. Herder, 1955.

Cobb, John B., Jr., and James M. Robinson, eds. *New Frontiers in Theology*. Vol. 3. New York: Harper & Row, 1967.

Cooper, John W. *Body, Soul, and Life Everlasting*. Grand Rapids: William B. Eerdmans, 1989.

————. "The Identity of Resurrected Persons: Fatal Flaw of Monistic Anthropology." *Calvin Theological Journal* 23 (April 1988).

Craig, William L. *Assessing the New Testament Evidence for the Historicity of the Resurrection of Jesus*. Lewiston, N.Y.: Edwin Mellen Press, 1989.

————. "The Bodily Resurrection of Jesus." In *Gospel Perspectives*. Vol. 1. Edited by R. T. France and D. Wenham. Sheffield: JSOT Press, 1980.

————. "The Guard at the Tomb." *New Testament Studies* 30 (April 1984).

———— "The Historicity of the Empty Tomb of Jesus." *New Testament Studies* 31 (January 1985).

————. "No Other Name: A Middle Knowledge Perspective on the Exclusivity of Salvation through Christ." *Faith and Philosophy* 6 (April 1989).

————. "Talbott's Universalism." *Religious Studies* 27 (September 1991).

Cupitt, Don, and C. F. D. Moule. "The Resurrection: A Disagreement." *Theology* 80 (April 1972).

Davis, Stephen T., *The Debate about the Bible*. Philadelphia: Westminster Press, 1977.

————, ed. *Encountering Evil: Live Options in Theodicy*. Atlanta: John Knox Press, 1981.

————. "Evangelicals and the Religions of the World." *Reformed Journal* 21 (June 1981): 9-13.

————. *Faith, Skepticism, and Evidence.* Lewisburg, Pa.: Bucknell University Press, 1978.

————. *Logic and the Nature of God.* London: Macmillan, 1983.

Dawe, Donald G. *Jesus: The Death and Resurrection of God.* Atlanta: John Knox Press, 1985.

Dilley, Frank. "Resurrection and the 'Replica Objection.'" *Religious Studies* 19 (December 1983).

Flew, Antony. "Can a Man Witness His Own Funeral?" *Hibbert Journal* 54 (1956).

————. *God and Philosophy.* New York: Delta Books, 1966.

————. "Immortality." In *The Encyclopedia of Philosophy.* Edited by Paul Edwards. New York: Macmillan, 1967.

————. *The Logic of Mortality.* Oxford: Basil Blackwell, 1987.

————. *The Presumption of Atheism and Other Essays.* London: Elek/Pemberton, 1976.

Fuller, Daniel P. *The Unity of the Bible.* Grand Rapids: Zondervan, 1992.

Fuller, Reginald. *The Formation of the Resurrection Narratives.* Philadelphia: Fortress Press, 1971.

Geach, P. T. *God and the Soul.* London: Routledge & Kegan Paul, 1969.

————. *Providence and Evil.* Cambridge: Cambridge University Press, 1977.

Geisler, Norman L. *The Battle for the Resurrection.* Nashville: Thomas Nelson, 1989.

Grant, Michael. *Jesus: An Historian's Review of the Gospels.* New York: Scribner's, 1977.

Gundry, Robert H. *Soma in Biblical Theology: With Emphasis on Pauline Anthropology.* Cambridge: Cambridge University Press, 1976.

Habermas, Gary. "Knowing That Jesus' Resurrection Occurred: A Response to Davis." *Faith and Philosophy* 1 (April 1984).

————. *The Resurrection of Jesus: An Apologetic.* Grand Rapids: Baker Book House, 1980.

Habermas, Gary, and Antony Flew. *Did Jesus Rise from the Dead?* Edited by Terry L. Miethe. San Francisco: Harper & Row, 1987.

Hackett, Stuart. *The Reconstruction of the Christian Revelation Claim.* Grand Rapids: Baker Book House, 1988.

Harris, Murray. *From Grave to Glory: Resurrection in the New Testament.* Grand Rapids: Zondervan, 1990.

————. *Raised Immortal.* Grand Rapids: William B. Eerdmans, 1983.

Harvey, Van. *The Historian and the Believer.* Philadelphia: Westminster Press, 1966.

Hawthorne, Gerald F. *Philippians.* Waco, Tex.: Word Books, 1983.

Helm, Paul. "A Theory of Disembodied Survival and Re-Embodied Existence." *Religious Studies* 14 (March 1978).

Henaut, Barry W. "Empty Tomb or Empty Argument: A Failure of Nerve in Recent Studies of Mark 16?" *Studies in Religion* 15 (1986).

Henry, Patrick. *New Directions in New Testament Studies.* Philadelphia: Westminster Press, 1979.

Herbert, R. T. *Paradox and Identity in Theology.* Ithaca, N.Y.: Cornell University Press, 1979.

Hick, John. *Death and Eternal Life.* New York: Harper & Row, 1976.

————. *Evil and the God of Love.* London: Macmillan, 1966.

————. *Faith and Knowledge.* Ithaca, N.Y.: Cornell University Press, 1957.

Hodge, Charles. *Systematic Theology.* Vol. 1. New York: Scribner's, 1895.

Hume, David. *An Enquiry concerning Human Understanding.* 1758. Reprint. LaSalle, Ill.: Open Court Publishing, 1946.

Jansen, John Frederick. *The Resurrection of Jesus Christ in New Testament Theology.* Philadelphia: Westminster Press, 1980.

Jeremias, Joachim. *The Eucharistic Words of Jesus.* Translated by Norman Perrin. London: SCM Press, 1966.

Julian of Norwich. *The Revelations of Divine Love.* Translated by James Walsh. London: Burns & Oates, 1961.

Kaufman, Gordon. *Systematic Theory: A Historicist Perspective.* New York: Scribner's, 1968.

Keller, James. "Contemporary Christian Doubts about the Resurrection." *Faith and Philosophy* 5 (January 1988).

Krausz, Michael. "History and Its Objects." *The Monist* 74 (April 1991).

Küng, Hans. *On Being a Christian.* Translated by Edward Quinn. New York: Pocket Books, 1976.

Künneth, Walter. *The Theology of the Resurrection.* Translated by J. Leitch. London: SCM Press, 1965.

Lacy, Larry. "Talbott on Paul as a Universalist." *Christian Scholar's Review* 21 (June 1992).

Ladd, George E. *I Believe in the Resurrection of Jesus.* Grand Rapids: William B. Eerdmans, 1975.

Lampe, G. W. H., and D. M. MacKinnon. *The Resurrection: A Dialogue.* Philadelphia: Westminster Press, 1966.

Larmer, Robert A. H. *Water into Wine? An Investigation of the Concept of Miracle.* Kingston, Ont.: McGill-Queen's University Press, 1988.

Lewis, C. S. *The Great Divorce.* New York: Macmillan, 1957.

Lewis, David. *Philosophical Papers.* New York: Oxford University Press, 1983.

Locke, John. *An Essay concerning Human Understanding.* Vol. 1. Edited by A. Fraser. New York: Dover Publications, 1959.

Marxsen, Willi. *The Resurrection of Jesus of Nazareth.* Translated by Margaret Kohl. Philadelphia: Fortress Press, 1970.

Mavrodes, George. "The Life Everlasting and the Bodily Criterion of Identity." *Nous* 2 (March 1977).

McDowell, Josh. *The Resurrection Factor.* San Bernardino, Calif.: Here's Life Publishers, 1981.

Moffatt, James. *The First Epistle of Paul to the Corinthians.* Moffatt New Testament Commentary. New York: Harper, 1938.

Moule, C. F. D. "St. Paul and Dualism: The Pauline Concept of Resurrection." *New Testament Studies* 12 (January 1966).

Noonan, Harold. *Personal Identity.* New York: Routledge, 1989.

———. "Reply to Garrett." *Analysis* 46 (October 1986).

O'Collins, Gerald. *Interpreting the Resurrection.* New York: Paulist Press, 1988.

———. *Jesus Risen.* New York: Paulist Press, 1987.

———. *The Resurrection of Jesus Christ.* Valley Forge, Pa.: Judson Press, 1973.

———. *What Are They Saying about the Resurrection?* New York: Paulist Press, 1978.

Pannenberg, Wolfhart. "Did Jesus Really Rise from the Dead?" *Dialog* 4 (1965).

———. *Jesus — God and Man.* 2d ed. Translated by Lewis L. Wilkins and Duane A. Priebe. Philadelphia: Westminster Press, 1977.

Parfit, Derek. *Reasons and Persons.* Oxford: Oxford University Press, 1986.

Penelhum, Terence. *Survival and Disembodied Existence.* New York: Humanities Press, 1970.

Perkins, Pheme. *Resurrection.* Garden City, N.Y.: Doubleday, 1984.

Perrin, Norman. *The Promise of Bultmann.* Philadelphia: Westminster Press, 1969.

———. *The Resurrection according to Matthew, Mark and Luke.* Philadelphia: Westminster Press, 1977.

Perry, John. *A Dialogue on Personal Identity and Immortality.* Indianapolis: Hackett, 1978.

Phillips, D. Z. *Death and Immortality.* New York: St. Martin's Press, 1970.

Price, H. H. "Survival and the Idea of 'Another World.'" In *Language, Metaphysics, and Death.* Edited by John Donnelly. New York: Fordham University Press, 1978.

Purtill, Richard L. "The Intelligibility of Disembodied Survival." *Christian Scholar's Review* 5 (1975).

Quinn, Philip. "Personal Identity, Bodily Continuity and Resurrection." *International Journal for Philosophy of Religion* 9 (1978).

Ramsey, A. M. *The Resurrection of Christ*. London: Fontana Books, 1961.

Reichenbach, Bruce. *Is Man the Phoenix? A Study of Immortality*. Washington: University Press of America, 1983.

———. "Monism and the Possibility of Life after Death." *Religious Studies* 14 (March 1978).

———. "On Disembodied Resurrection Persons: A Reply," *Religious Studies* 18 (June 1982).

Reid, Thomas. *Essays on the Intellectual Powers of Man*. Cambridge: M.I.T. Press, 1969.

Richardson, Cyril, ed. *Early Christian Fathers*. Philadelphia: Westminster Press, 1953.

Robinson, J. A. T. *In the End, God*. London: James Clarke, 1950.

Rockmore, Tom. "Subjectivity and the Ontology of History." *The Monist* 74 (April 1991).

Root, Michael. "Miracles and the Uniformity of Nature." *American Philosophical Quarterly* 26 (October 1989).

Rorty, Amelie, ed. *The Identities of Persons*. Berkeley and Los Angeles: University of California Press, 1976.

Sanders, John. *No Other Name: An Investigation into the Destiny of the Unevangelized*. Grand Rapids: William B. Eerdmans, 1992.

Schonfield, Hugh. *The Passover Plot*. New York: Bantam Books, 1966.

Scuka, Robert F. "Resurrection: Critical Reflections on a Doctrine in Search of a Meaning." *Modern Theology* 6 (October 1989).

Sheehan, Thomas. *The First Coming*. New York: Vintage Books, 1986.

Sherwin-White, A. N. *Roman Society and Roman Law in the New Testament*. Oxford: Oxford University Press, 1963.

Sider, Ronald J. "The Pauline Conception of the Resurrection Body in I Corinthians XV,35-54." *New Testament Studies* 21 (April 1975).

Staudinger, Hugo. *The Trustworthiness of the Gospels*. Translated by Robin T. Hammond. Edinburgh: Handsel Press, 1981.

Stein, Robert H. "Was the Tomb Really Empty?" *Themelios* 5 (September 1979).

Stump, Eleonore. "Visits to the Sepulcher and Biblical Exegesis." *Faith and Philosophy* 6 (October 1989).

Swinburne, Richard. *The Concept of Miracle*. London: Macmillan, 1970.

———. *The Evolution of the Soul*. Oxford: Clarendon Press, 1986.

———. *The Existence of God*. Oxford: Clarendon Press, 1979.

———. *Faith and Reason*. Oxford: Oxford University Press, 1981.

Talbott, Thomas. "The Doctrine of Everlasting Punishment." *Faith and Philosophy* 7 (January 1990).

————. "The New Testament and Universal Reconciliation." *Christian Scholar's Review* 21 (June 1992).

————. "Providence, Freedom, and Human Destiny." *Religious Studies* 26 (June 1990).

Thielicke, Helmut. *Being Human . . . Becoming Human.* Garden City, N.Y.: Doubleday, 1984.

————. "The Resurrection Kerygma." In *The Easter Message for Today: Three Essays,* by Leonhart Goppelt, Helmut Thielicke, and Hans-Rudolf Müller-Schwiefe. New York: Thomas Nelson, 1964.

Torrance, Thomas. *Space, Time, and Resurrection.* Grand Rapids: William B. Eerdmans, 1976.

————. "Universalism or Election?" *Scottish Journal of Theology* 2 (September 1949).

Van Inwagen, Peter. "The Possibility of Resurrection." *International Journal for Philosophy of Religion* 9 (1978).

Von Campenhausen, Hans. *Tradition and Life in the Church.* Translated by A. V. Littledale. London: William Collins, 1968.

Wenham, John. *The Goodness of God.* Downers Grove, Ill.: InterVarsity Press, 1974.

Wiggins, David. *Sameness and Substance.* Cambridge: Harvard University Press, 1980.

Williams, Bernard. "Bodily Continuity and Personal Identity: A Reply." *Analysis* 21 (December 1960).

————. *Problems of the Self.* Cambridge: Cambridge University Press, 1973.

Wolfson, Harry A. "Immortality and Resurrection in the Philosophy of the Church Fathers." In *Immortality and Resurrection.* Edited by Krister Stendahl. New York: Macmillan, 1965.

Index

217

Acknowledgments

Portions of this book appeared in somewhat different form in a variety of publications. The author and publisher wish to thank the editors of these publications for permission to use the following material in the form in which it appears in this book:

"Is It Possible to Know That Jesus Was Raised from the Dead?" *Faith and Philosophy* 1 (April 1984): 147-59.

"Was Jesus Raised Bodily?" *Christian Scholar's Review* 14 (1985): 140-52.

"Naturalism and the Resurrection: A Reply to Habermas." *Faith and Philosophy* 2 (July 1985): 303-16.

"Is Personal Identity Retained in the Resurrection?" *Modern Theology* 2 (July 1986): 328-40.

"Traditional Christian Belief in the Resurrection of the Body." *New Scholasticism* 62 (Winter 1988): 72-97.

"Universalism, Hell, and the Fate of the Ignorant." *Modern Theology* 6 (January 1990): 173-86.

"Doubting the Resurrection: A Reply to James A. Keller." *Faith and Philosophy* 7 (January 1990): 99-111.

"Was the Tomb Empty?" In *Hermes and Athena: Biblical Exegesis and Philosophical Theology,* edited by Thomas P. Flint and Eleonore Stump (Notre Dame, Ind.: University of Notre Dame Press, 1993), pp. 77-100.